The
Reference
Shelf

Representative American Speeches 1997–1998

Editors

Calvin M. Logue
**Josiah Meigs Professor of Speech
University of Georgia**

and

Jean DeHart
**Assistant Professor of Communication Arts
Appalachian State University**

The Reference Shelf
Volume 70 • Number 6

The H.W. Wilson Company
New York • Dublin
1998

The Reference Shelf

The books in this series contain reprints of articles, excerpts from books, addresses on current issues, and studies of social trends in the United States and other countries. There are six separately bound numbers in each volume, all of which are usually published in the same calendar year. Numbers one through five are each devoted to a single subject, providing background information and discussion from various points of view and concluding with a subject index and comprehensive bibliography that lists books, pamphlets, and abstracts of additional articles on the subject. The final number of each volume is a collection of recent speeches, and it contains a cumulative speaker index. Books in the series may be purchased individually or on subscription.

Visit H.W. Wilson's Web site: www.hwwilson.com

Library of Congress has cataloged this serial title as follows:

Representative American speeches. 1937 / 38–
    New York, H. W. Wilson Co.
        v. 21 cm.—The Reference Shelf
Annual
Indexes:
      Author index: 1937/38–1959/60, with 1959/60;
      1960/61–1969/70, with 1969/70; 1970/71–1979/80,
      with 1979/80; 1980/81–1989/90, 1990.
      Editors: 1937/38–1958/59, A. C. Baird.—1959/60–1969/70, L. Thonssen.—1970/71–
      1979/80, W. W. Braden.—1980/81–1994/95, O. Peterson.—1995/96–, C. M. Logue
      and J. DeHart.
      ISSN 0197-6923 Representative American speeches.
      1. Speeches, addresses, etc., American. 2. Speeches, addresses, etc.
      I. Baird, Albert Craig, 1883–1979 ed II. Thonssen, Lester, 1904–
      III. Braden, Waldo Warder, 1911–1991 ed.
      IV. Peterson, Owen, 1924– ed. V. Logue, Calvin McLeod, 1935–
      and DeHart, Jean. eds. VI. Series.
PS668.B3   815.5082   38-27962
                                              MARC-S
Library of Congress [8503r85] rev4

Cover: Documentary filmmaker Ken Burns visits Monticello during the production of his film *Thomas Jefferson*. He discussed this film as well as *The Civil War* in his speech "Sharing the American Experience."
Photo: AP/Wide World Photos

Printed in the United States of America

Contents

Preface

In 1997–1998, citizens continued to question what kind of nation the United States is to become. How did we arrive at our present state of affairs? What values should we preserve? In what arenas and ways can we improve? In his speech at Harvard University, published in this volume, Ken Burns insists that we "listen" to "varied voices," not "just those of the old top-down version" of history. In this anthology, we attempt to provide a forum for both prominent and less known participants.

Section I addresses the importance of celebrating and maintaining the best of the nation's common heritage.

Section II examines the power, abuses, and duties of media in democracy.

Section III confronts contemporary issues of race, from perpetuating affirmative action to racism and equal opportunity and achievement. The final speech in this section charges that welfare reform has harmed poor women.

Section IV wrestles with the legacy of past wars as well as present-day challenges, including nuclear danger and the establishment of peace in Ireland.

In Section V, speakers memorialize individuals whose passings have affected them on a personal level, and in the case of Princess Diana, on a public level.

Section VI looks to the future, and includes speeches in support of continued commitment to women's advancement, the labor movement, and environmental protection.

The editors express appreciation to Michael Hubler and Joseph Bellon for researching information on speakers and speeches, and to Rita VanZant, Owen Peterson, John Campbell, and the staff of the H. W. Wilson Company for providing assistance.

Calvin M. Logue
Jean DeHart

I. American Heritage, Academic Freedom, and Citizenship

Sharing the American Experience [1]

Ken Burns

Documentary filmmaker, 1975– ; born Brooklyn, NY, July 29, 1953; B.A., Hampshire College, 1975; co-founder, president, Florentine Films, 1975– ; producer, director, writer, The Brooklyn Bridge *(1981);* The Shakers: Hands to Work, Hearts to God *(1985); producer, director,* Huey Long *(1985);* The Statue of Liberty *(1985);* Thomas Hart Benton *(1988);* The Congress *(1988); co-producer, director,* The Civil War *(1990); executive producer,* Lindbergh *(1990);* Empire of the Air *(1992);* Baseball *(1996); executive producer,* The West *(1996);* Thomas Jefferson *(1997);* Lewis and Clark: The Journey of the Corps of Discovery *(with Dayton Duncan) (1997);* Frank Lloyd Wright *(1998).*

Editors' introduction: In a speech sponsored by the Harvard University Graduate School of Education, Ken Burns addressed students, faculty, and members of the general public in the Askwith Lecture Hall on campus concerning the importance of preserving and listening to the varied voices of history. By ignoring their past, Burns cautioned, Americans create a "gap in who we are." A spellbinding orator who enthralls lecture audiences with his extraordinary vision of the United States and who we are as a people, Burns imbues both his speeches and his documentary histories with an immediacy that more conventional approaches lack, his subjects are uniquely American. Commenting on Burns's award-winning PBS series *The Civil War*, a reviewer for the *New York Times* wrote that Burns "takes his place as the most accomplished documentary filmmaker of his generation." A major series on the history of jazz is scheduled to air in the year 2000.

Ken Burns's speech: Listen. In 1909, a man named Charles Hercules Ebbets began secretly buying up adjacent parcels of land in the Flatbush section of Brooklyn, including the site of a garbage dump called Pigtown because of the pigs that once ate their fill there and the stench that still filled the air.

He hoped eventually to build a permanent home for the lackluster baseball team he had once worked for and now owned. The

---

1. Delivered at Harvard University on May 8, 1997. Reprinted with permission of Ken Burns.

team was called the Trolley Dodgers, or just the Dodgers, after the way their devoted fans negotiated Brooklyn's busy streets.

In 1912 construction began. By the time it was completed, Pigtown had been transformed into Ebbets Field, baseball's newest shrine, where some of the game's greatest drama would take place. In the years to come, Dodger fans would see more bad times than good but hardly care, listen to the Southern cadences of a pioneer broadcaster, and witness first hand baseball's finest moment, when a black man wearing the number 42 trotted out to first base.

In 1955, after more than four decades of frustration, Brooklyn would finally win a World Championship only to know just two years later the ultimate heartbreak as their team moved to a new city 3,000 miles away leaving an empty shell in Flatbush that eventually became an apartment building and an even emptier spot in the soul of every Brooklyn fan.

Good afternoon. As the story of the arc of Ebbets Field that opens our recent series attests, the story of baseball is the story of America. Behind the exquisite play, the thousands of anxious games won and lost, the myriad heroic and not-so-heroic careers rising and falling lies a startlingly revealing mirror of our country.

I am honored and delighted to have this opportunity to speak with you today, to celebrate the messages the past— our common heritage—continually directs our way. Let us *listen.* Too often as a culture we have ignored this joyful noise, becoming in the process blissfully ignorant of the power those past lives and stories and moments have over *this* moment, and indeed, our unknown future.

I am interested in that power of history, and I am interested in its many varied *voices.* Not just the voices of the old top down version of our past, which would try to convince us that American history is only the story of Great Men. And not just those pessimistic voices that have recently entered our studies, voices which seem to say that our history is merely a catalogue of crimes. I am interested in listening to the voices of a true, honest, complicated past that is unafraid of controversy and tragedy, but equally drawn to those voices, those stories and moments, that suggest an abiding faith in the human spirit and particularly the unique role this extraordinary country seems to have in the positive progress of mankind.

The philosopher Jacob Needleman, who appeared in a film we made more than a dozen years ago on the history of the religious sect called the Shakers, once said to me that, "America is the land of zero. We start from zero. We start from nothing. That's the ideal of America," he said. "We start only from our own reason, our own longing, our own search." The last 20 years of my own life has been in a way a search, too; to learn about the mysterious inner workings of this remarkable republic and those strange and complicated people who like to call themselves Americans.

Listen. When I was working more than ten years ago on my film about the Statue of Liberty, its history, and powerful symbolism, I had the great good fortune to meet and interview Vartan Gregorian, who was then the president and director of the New York Public Library, and who is now the president of Brown University. After an extremely interesting and passionate interview on the meaning behind the statue for an immigrant like him— from Tabriz, Iran—Vartan took me on a long and fascinating tour of the miles of stacks of the New York Public Library. Finally, after a long time, he stopped and gestured wildly. He said, "This, this is the DNA of our civilization." That library and, indeed, all true libraries, archives and historical societies are the DNA of our civilization storing what we value most in our country, leaving a memory of excellence and intention for generations to come. It occurs to me this afternoon as we behold the rich history of service of the Harvard community that we must certainly include this institution in that list of the DNA of our civilization, and it is with great pleasure that I come to you this afternoon to share my thoughts about history. Thank you for that.

Listen. When I think about the great game of baseball, I first think about language and words, something close to the heart of each of us here, I believe. I also think of men, great men, heroic men and, well, *unusual* men.

One such unusual man was Lawrence Peter Berra, an immigrant bricklayer's son from the Dago Hill section of St. Louis. He got his nickname Yogi from his friends who said he just *walked* like one. After flunking a high school test, Yogi was asked by his teachers, "Don't you know anything?" He replied, "I don't even suspect anything." He was clumsy when he joined the Yankees. He played like the bottom man on an unemployed acrobatic team—one critic said—and there were those who thought him too odd looking for New York's elite team. One coach even called him "the ape."

But Casey Stengel, the improbable Yankee manager, saw the greatness that was in him and brought back the great Bill Dickey to teach him the finer points of playing behind the plate and Berra quickly became one of the greatest catchers in baseball history. He once went 148 straight games and 950 chances without a single error. He played in an incredible and record 75 World Series games and hit 71 times during the course of them and was three times named the American League's Most Valuable Player.

Like Stengel, though, Berra became as well known for what he said off the field as for what he did on it. And this is where the words come in that I mentioned before:

"Ninety percent of hitting is mental," he once said. "The other half is physical."

All true libraries, archives and historical societies are the DNA of our civilization.

"You can observe a lot by watching."

"If fans don't want to come out to the park, nobody is going to stop them."

Particularly helpful to me during the long promotional tour for the series: "Why buy good luggage?" Yogi said. "You only use it when you travel."

"I usually take a two hour nap," he declared one day, "between 1:00 and 4:00 in the afternoon."

"When you get to the fork in the road, take it."

My personal favorite: "If you don't go to their funeral, they won't go to yours."

When the wife of the Mayor of New York City said he looked very cool in his new summer suit, Yogi said, "Thanks, you don't look so hot yourself."

When he was introduced to Robert Briscoe, the first Jewish mayor of Dublin, Ireland, Yogi sighed and said, "Ah, only in America."

He was once asked what he would do if he found a million dollars, and he said with a straight face, "If the guy was poor, I'd give it back to him."

And he also said, "It ain't over till it's over." I do not need to remind anyone who has watched last year's dramatic post-season play of the sublime truth of that seemingly simple statement.

You know, critics questioned whether he ever really said some of his most celebrated maxims, but of course Yogi had a ready answer for them, too. He said, "I didn't say half the things I've said."

For many of us, we are brought to our history in just this fashion, with story, memory, anecdote, feeling. These emotional connections become a kind of glue which makes the most complex of past events stick in our minds and particularly in our hearts, permanently a part of who each of us is now.

But for most of the life of this republic, the way we have formerly told our history *was* from the top down. This has been called the history of the State and it basically focuses only on presidents and wars and generals—our political narrative. It relies, like certain current utterly discredited economic theories, on an erroneous belief that this history trickles down and touches experiences common to us all. It rarely does. It does exhibit, or has exhibited, an understandable arrogance, and we have had to rely on family memory and community recollection for the really good stuff. Or at least the stuff that made all that political history somehow meaningful.

But as we have grown older as a country, as we have moved around more, lost touch with place more, those personal histories have dried up for most people and we as a people have begun to forget. History became a kind of castor oil of dry dates and facts and events with little meaning;

We have had to rely on family memory and community recollection for the really good stuff.

something we knew was good for us, but hardly good tasting. History became just another subject, not the great pageant of everything that has come before this moment.

About 20 or 30 years ago, we woke up partially to this problem and began to insist on relevance in our teaching of history and on a new social history that would focus on real people doing real and recognizable things. This would be history from the bottom up not top down, and people would respond. They did not. Relevance became an excuse for not even teaching history and the new social history became so bogged down in statistical demographics and micro perceptions that history began to sound like the reading of the telephone book. A new arrogance replaced the old—equally understandable, I suppose, but equally devastating to the national memory. Someone expressed this new tyranny quite well when they said that a history of Illinois could be written without ever once mentioning Abraham Lincoln. Something obviously had to change, and I'm pleased to report that in some ways it has.

We have, as an academic community, begun to speak of a synthesis of the old and the new histories, a way to combine the best of the top-down version—still inspiring, even with its great-men addiction (those great men did do great things)—with the bottom-up version; so inspiring, too, at times with the million heroic acts of women, minorities, labor, ordinary people. And we've begun to use new media and new forms of expression to tell our histories, breaking the stranglehold the academy has had on historical exchange for the last hundred years.

Remember, until we adopted the Germanic academic model at the end of the 19th century, our greatest historians like Francis Parkman and Henry Adams were essentially amateurs—popular writers concerned with speaking to larger audiences—not just a handful of colleagues and scholars-unconcerned with how one wrote, or more important, who was *listening*.

Listen. "Baseball," the poet Donald Hall told us in a filmed interview, "because of its continuity over the space of America and the time of America is a space where memory gathers." It was my intention to pursue the game and its memories and myths across the expanse of American history. We quickly developed an abiding conviction that the game of baseball offered a unique prism through which one could see refracted much more than a history of a simple sport.

This is the story of race, central to our larger narrative, crucial to baseball. When Jackie Robinson walked out on to a ball field in the spring of 1947, his glorious moment was the first real progress in civil rights since the Civil War, making this recent production of ours in a way a sequel, a literal sequel, to the Civil War series. That glorious moment occurred not at a lunch counter in North Carolina, not on a city bus in Montgomery, Alabama, not in a school in South Carolina or Topeka, not even in the institutions of our military, but on the diamonds of our so-called national pastime. At that moment, when that proud grandson of a slave made his way to first base at Ebbets Field, his miraculous and heroic example, turning his cheek against the thousands of racial slights, threats and abuse that he would face, would be watched with awe and gratitude by a young junior at Morehouse College in Atlanta, Georgia, named Martin Luther King. In a sense, American social history made a profound turn that April afternoon.

But Jackie Robinson's epic story is not the whole of it. For decades African Americans struggled to offset the prejudice in their country and in their national game by creating and managing and owning teams and leagues of separate but athletically equal talent. And when Jackie finally did arrive, when baseball became in truth what it had always claimed to be—the *national* pastime—the struggle did not stop, as it has not stopped in our country at large. Curt Flood and Henry Aaron were ironically forced to confront again and again the pernicious racism that persists in this favored land, founded as it was more than 200 years ago on the most noble principle yet advanced in humankind, that all men were created equal.

It is unfortunate that we usually relegate this fascinating history to the coldest and shortest month. Because this is *our* story as well. Not just *their* story.

You know I must admit that I have, in many ways, made the same film over and over again. Each production asks one deceptively simple question: who are we? That is to say, who are we Americans as a people? What does an investigation of the past tell us about who we were and what we have become? Each film offers an opportunity to pursue this question, and while never answering it fully, nevertheless deepens the question with each project.

Listen. At 4:30 a.m. on the 12th of April, 1861, General Pierre Gustave Toutant Beauregard directed his Confederate gunners to open fire on Fort Sumter, at that hour only a dark shape out in Charleston harbor. Thirty-four hours later a white flag over the fort ended the bombardment. The only casualty was a Confederate horse. It was a bloodless opening to the bloodiest war in American history.

No one could have predicted the magnitude of the explosion that rocked America following that opening shot. Until then America had been, as Bruce Catton wrote, "small enough to carry in the mind and in the heart, and a young man's fatherland was what he could see from his bedroom window." Yet most of what America was before the Civil War went into sparking that explosion and most of what it became resulted from it. Entirely unimaginable before it

Each production asks one deceptively simple question: who are we? That is to say, who are we Americans as a people?

began, the war was the most defining and shaping event in American history—so much so that it is now impossible to imagine what we would have been like without it.

Shortly after Appomattox, Walt Whitman, a Brooklyn journalist and sometime poet who worked in the appalling Union hospitals, warned posterity of what he had seen. "Future years," he wrote, "will never know the seething hell and the black infernal background, the countless minor scenes and interiors of the secession war; and it is best they should not. The real war," Whitman insisted, "will never get in the books."

The writers and historians of future years have not been scared off by Whitman's admonition. In the 130 years since the war's conclusion, more than 50,000 books have been published on the Civil War. Each year dozens of new titles appear, again offering to revisit the war, to reinterpret or rearrange those strange days and hard events—faint traces and distant signals now—looking still for the coherent, the conclusive explanation.

And yet Whitman's words retain their force. The "real war" stays there, outside all the books, beckoning to us. Why *did* Americans kill each other and how did it happen? Who *were* these people who fought and killed, marched and sang, wrote home, skedaddled, deserted, died, nursed and lamented, persevered and were defeated? What was it like to be in that war? What did it do to America and Americans? What happened to the movement that freed blacks from slavery? Why have succeeding generations obscured the war with bloodless, gallant myth, blurring the causes and its great ennobling outcome—the freeing of 4 million black people and their descendants from bondage? What did it mean that the Union won? What does it mean to be a Union? Why are we still so drawn to this tale of suffering, catastrophe, heroism and death? These were the questions we asked as we began our series.

The historical documentary filmmaker's vocation is not precisely the same as the historian's, although it shares many of the aims and much of the spirit of the latter. Historians delight in telling us what our history is and what it means. The documentarian, on the other hand, as often delights in recording and conveying the simple fact that we have had a history at all: that there was once a time when people looked like this, or sounded like that, or felt these ways about such things. The historical documentary is often more immediate and more emotional than history proper because of its continual joy in making the past present through visual and verbal documents.

It is our belief that, so far as possible, the documents of the past must be allowed to speak for themselves, to convey meanings and emotions and stories on their own. In the course of producing our films, we go to scores of museums and libraries, and film thousands of photographs, paintings, lithographs, broadsides, and newspapers of the period. From these thousands of sources, we culled . . . images, moments, *voices*—in our opinion the most eloquent, compelling, amusing, curious, ironic and beautiful voices our history has to offer.

But we Americans still tend to ignore our past. Perhaps we fear having one, and burn it behind us like rocket fuel, always looking forward. And that's a bad thing. The consequences are not just ignorance, or stupidity, or even repeating. It represents the deepest kind of inattention, and it becomes a tear or a gap in who we are.

I think that in each of my own films, and with each film more strongly and completely, I have been seized or possessed by an aspect of American history: something that spoke of the aspirations and struggles and motives of people, in the Brooklyn Bridge, in the Statue of Liberty or the Shakers, something that went to the heart of who we have been, to become what we are. And I think that with each film, each story I have struggled with, my sense has sharpened that a thread runs through all the *stories*, connects these *his*tories, one to the other.

That thread is the essential American one: the struggle for human freedom—whether of movement and design, of sheer achievement in the Brooklyn Bridge, or of political freedom in the Statue of Liberty, or of spiritual freedom, freedom of the hand and heart, in the experiment of the Shakers. And I know this is what drew me to the Civil War, for in that war the issue of human freedom came for this country, for our people, to the profoundest and most tragic crux. The historian Shelby Foote has called it the crossroads of our being, but somehow when we crossed over, we forgot where we had been. Slavery. I think of what James Symington, a former Congressman, said in an interview for our film. "Slavery," he said, "was merely the horrible statutory expression of a deeper rift between peoples based on race, and this rift is what we struggle still to erase from the hearts and minds of people."

That rift stands at the very center of American history; it is the great challenge to which all our deepest aspirations to freedom must rise. If we forget that, if we forget, for example, the great stain of slavery that stands at the heart of our history, we forget who we are, and we make the rift deeper and wider: and that's what forgetting is: making the human rift wider.

And we are forgetting it even now—*on campuses* and in suburbs and cities—forgetting that, after all, less than 140 years ago, 4 million Americans were owned by other Americans; that 630,000 Americans died over the issue, when our population was a mere 30 million. Two percent died.

If we forget . . . the great stain of slavery that stands at the heart of our history, we forget who we are, and we make the rift deeper and wider.

What I am trying to say is that there is a profound connection between remembering and freedom and human attachment. That's what history is to me. And forgetting is the opposite of all that: it is a kind of slavery, and the worst kind of human detachment.

And which is why we must remember, even when, precisely when, what memory has to tell us is appalling. It has seemed to me that the meaning of our freedom as Americans is the freedom of memory, which is also a kind of obligation. We must remember that our country was born under the sign that all men were created equal, but we must remember also that that proclamation did not include blacks or women or the poor. We must remember that Abraham Lincoln signed the Emancipation Proclamation, but we must also remember that Lincoln thought of re-colonizing black Americans to Panama or Africa as late as April of 1861 as the guns opened up at Fort Sumter. We must remember that the 13th and 14th amendments secured some kind of equality before the law for blacks. But we must also remember that equality as a human fact did not come at once, has still to come, and if we do not believe that, *we forget*.

Lincoln, of course, said it best. Early in 1861, at his first inauguration, when he still hoped to keep his country together, he implored Southerners not to go to war. "We must not be enemies," he said, "we must be friends." But then he went on, "The mystic chords of memory, stretching from every battle-field and patriot grave, to every living heart and hearthstone, all over this broad land, will yet swell the chorus of the Union, when again touched, as surely they *will* be, by the better angels of our nature." Isn't that it?

Listen. There is an interesting story that takes place in the 1810s. A clergyman stops at Ford's Tavern along a road in Western Virginia and he encounters a man he terms "a respectable stranger." And he engages in a conversation at some length with this stranger. First they talk about mechanical operations and he's certain that the man is an engineer of some sort. Then they move on to matters of agriculture and he thinks this is, in his words, "a large farmer." Finally they talk about religion and he's certain that the man is a clergyman like himself.

The hour gets late and they go to bed and the next morning he arises and speaks with the innkeeper and asks for the stranger he had seen the night before and he describes him and the innkeeper says, "Why, don't you know, that was Thomas Jefferson?"

"Thomas Jefferson" is the first film in a series of biographical portraits we are producing over the next five years. It was shown on PBS this past February. Each film, like earlier ones on the turbulent Southern demagogue Huey Long, the painter Thomas Hart Benton, and the men who made radio, focus on the extraordinary power individual lives have had on American history and culture. The English historian Thomas Carlisle said that history is biography, that the most rewarding and dramatic study of our common past lay in the lives of remarkable people.

Listen. He was a farmer, a violinist, a writer; a surveyor, an inventor, a lover of fine wines—and a restless architect who could never quite bring himself to finish his own house.

He was a reluctant politician with a voice so soft he could barely make himself heard from the podium, but he helped to found America's first political party.

He denounced the moral bankruptcy he saw in Europe, but delighted in the gilded salons of Paris.

He was a statesman who was twice elected president of the United States—but did not think his presidency worth listing among the achievements on his gravestone.

"All the self-divisions of conflicts within individuals become a series of mirrors in which the plight of the country is reflected."
–Thomas Jefferson

He was a life-long champion of small government who took it upon himself to more than double the size of his country.

He endured the loss of nearly everything he held dear, but somehow never lost his faith in the future.

He distilled a century of Enlightenment thinking into one remarkable sentence which began "we hold these truths to be self-evident, that all men are created equal." Yet he owned more than 200 human beings and never saw fit in his lifetime to free them.

Thomas Jefferson was a "shadow man," said John Adams, [who was] first his friend, then his enemy, and then his friend again. His character was "like the great rivers, whose bottoms we cannot see and make no noise."

He remained a puzzle even to those who thought they knew him best, embodied contradictions common to the country whose independence it fell to him to proclaim, in words whose precise meaning Americans have debated ever since.

Listen. Several years ago, while working on our filmed history of our Civil War, I came across a curious little book by Robert Penn Warren, our nation's first poet laureate, called *The Legacy of the Civil War*. It was not much more than a hundred pages, an essay really, and on those pages I stumbled across an interesting passage, a "voice" if you will, that led me ultimately to Thomas Jefferson:

> A civil war is, we may say, [Warren writes], the prototype of all war, for in the persons of fellow citizens who happen to be the enemy we meet again with the old ambivalence of love and hate and with all the old guilts, the blood brothers of our childhood. In a civil war—especially one such as this when the nation shares deep and significant convictions and is not a mere hand basket of factions huddled arbitrarily together by historical happen-so—all the self-divisions of conflicts within individuals become a series of mirrors in which the plight of

the country is reflected, and the self-divisions of the country a great mirror in which the individual may see imaged his own deep conflicts, not only the conflicts of political loyalties, but those more profoundly personal.

As I think about Warren's stunning quote, and reflect about the great mirror our Civil War truly is, and contemplate, too, the master of Monticello and his central role in our country's often conflicted psychology. I am struck by how much the life and mysteries of Thomas Jefferson have animated, have confounded and may ultimately reconcile *our* national life.

He is a kind of Rosetta Stone of the American experience, a massive, tectonic intelligence that has formed and rattled the fault lines of our history, our present moment and, if we are lucky, our future. The contradictions that attend the life and actions of Thomas Jefferson are played out and made manifest in the trial—the trials—of the unfolding pageant we call American history. As a filmmaker, I began to see our pursuit of Thomas Jefferson on film as a "prequel" to the Civil War series, an autopsy performed to try to grasp the pathology of a nation soon to be forever traumatized in its adolescence by the unresolved questions left by its founder in its infancy. In Jefferson, we had found one of the most interesting and enigmatic human beings I've ever tried to get to know. As the scholar Joseph Ellis commented in an interview for our film, "He is the greatest enigma among major figures in American history and I think we're attracted to him in part because of his mysterious character. If he were a monument, he would be the Sphinx. If he were a painting, he would be the Mona Lisa. If he were a character in a play, he would be Hamlet."

Throughout the production, we were struck time and again by how contemporary it all seemed, from the easy accessibility of his handwriting to the myriad events and issues in his life that echo our own. Indeed, just below the surface of this one man's life lies a modern story of militias poised for rebellion and revolution, a religious right whose sanctimonious litmus test for moral acceptability in candidates insured a most un-Christian presidential election, an ongoing argument over prayer—and God—in schools, the ever-present tension between big government and states rights, and the gnawing reality of racial suspicion and hatred. This is a story about nasty political campaigns and a prying, often meddlesome press. It is about balanced budgets and deficits, about poignant political hesitation and ruthless political ambition, about class and money and power, and inevitably about the meaning of freedom in America.

In looking back at our years of work on Mr. Jefferson, more than anything, we were impressed by those words of his: brilliant, reasoned, frustrating, unexpectedly moving. Garry Wills, in an interview for our film, said that "the thing to remember from Jefferson is the power of the word. That ideas matter. That words beautifully shaped, reshape lives.

That a person who has certain disadvantages and flaws and even crimes, like holding slaves, can transcend his imprisonment within reality by casting out words that take you into a new reality."

Wills would say *listen* to the familiar words anew: "We hold these truths to be self-evident, that all men are created equal, that they are endowed by their creator with certain inalienable rights, that among these are life, liberty and the pursuit of happiness."

Or the poetry in a letter to his granddaughter: "Nothing new has happened in our neighborhood; the houses and the trees stand where they did; the flowers come forth like the belles of the day, have their short reign of beauty and splendor, and retire, like them, to the more interesting office of reproducing their like. The Hyacinths and Tulips are on the stage, the Irises are giving place to the Belladonnas, as these will to the Tuberoses and so on; as your momma has done to you, my dear Anne, as you will do to the sisters of little John, and as I shall soon and cheerfully do to you all in wishing you a long, long goodnight."

But there is also this from *Notes on the State of Virginia*: "I advance it therefore as a suspicion only, that the blacks, whether originally a distinct race, or made distinct by time and circumstances, are inferior to the whites in the endowments both of body and mind. This unfortunate difference of color, and perhaps of faculty, is a powerful obstacle to the emancipation of these people."

So how do we mediate the self-divisions, as Robert Penn Warren would say, in Thomas Jefferson? We want so to decide. To nail him down. Is he good? Is he bad? Is he a Democrat? Is he a Republican? Is he mine? Is he yours? Did he? Or didn't he? (That is to say, did he—or didn't he—sleep with Sally Hemings?)

But he is both and we are both and he and we are in it together. The greatest service we can do Jefferson is to accept his self-divisions as a great mirror of our own possibilities and failings and to go forward.

As he said: "Every human being must be viewed according to what it is good for; for none of us, no, not one is perfect; and were we to love none who had imperfections, this world would be a desert for our love."

Toward the end of his long life, Thomas Jefferson began writing letters to his old friend John Adams. For many years they had not spoken, their friendship strained by the partisan politics that afflicted, as it has our own time, the early days of the Republic. But now in the sunset of their lives, these two old men, destined to die within hours of each other, 50 years to the day since the signing of the Declaration, began a beautiful and elegiac correspondence, the greatest correspondence between public figures in American history, where they discussed so movingly their invention, the United States of America. Now Jefferson wrote to Adams this wonderful passage: "And so we have gone on and so we shall go on, puzzled and prospering beyond example in the history of man. And I do believe we shall continue to grow, to multiply and prosper until we exhibit an association, powerful, wise and happy, beyond what has yet been seen [by men]. I like the dreams of the future better than the history of the past: so good night. I will dream on, always fancying that Mrs. Adams and yourself are by my side marking our progress." Puzzled and Prospering. *That* is it.

The second film in this series, due out this fall, is on the remarkable journey of Lewis and Clark, an expedition as important as the moon landing, an expedition filled, as all good history is, with paradox and irony. Other films will be on the controversial, unusually influential and utterly American architect Frank Lloyd Wright, who lived to the fullest in what we now call the American Century. This film is due out in 1998. Our film on the lives of two pioneering feminists, Elizabeth Cady Stanton and Susan B. Anthony, who more than anyone else helped change the lives of women in the country, will be shown in 1999. The fifth film, scheduled to be released in 2001, will be on Mark Twain, who came to epitomize American literature and letters by reflecting back at us not only a uniquely American humor and optimism, but a dark and self-reflective side that we have come to see as equally our own.

Or as Twain himself put it: "It is by the goodness of God that in our country we have those three unspeakably precious things: freedom of speech, freedom of conscience and the prudence never to practice either of them."

Gerald Early, the Director of the African and African-American Studies Department at Washington University in St. Louis, speaking in an interview for our Baseball series said: "I enjoy the game of baseball. It's a beautifully designed game—a beautiful game to watch. It makes me feel more American. It makes me feel connected to this culture. And I think there are only three things that Americans will be known for 2,000 years from now when they study this civilization: The Constitution, Jazz Music and Baseball. They are the three most beautifully designed things this country's ever produced."

Having grappled with many Constitutional issues in the Civil War series and other films, and having explored our National pastime and its exquisite lessons most recently in *BASEBALL*, we agree with Professor Early and are just now turning our attention to our next major series, a 12-hour history of Jazz, that will be completed in the year 2000—after a century of enjoying this unique American art form.

As I hope these musings make plain and palpable, indeed all of the voices I have brought up this afternoon, American history is a loud, raucous, moving, *exquisite* collection of

It is a kind of emotional archeology that we are attempting; listening to the echoes and ghosts of an almost inexpressibly wise past.

noises, that in the aggregate often combine to make the
sweetest kind of music I know, and I have tried to listen to
this "music" as much as I can in putting together the films I
have made. It is a kind of emotional archeology that we are
attempting; listening to the echoes and ghosts of an almost
inexpressibly wise past.

Five years ago, the world lost a towering historical and literary figure, the novelist Isaac B. Singer. For decades he
wrote, almost sang, about God and myth and punishment,
fate and sexuality and family, and history.

He wrote in Yiddish, a marvelous expressive language, sad
and happy all at the same time, sometimes maddeningly all
knowing and yet resigned to God's seemingly capricious
will. It is also a language without a country, a dying language in a world more often interested in the extermination
or isolation of its troubled, long suffering speakers. Singer,
first writing in this country in the pages of the *Jewish Daily
Forward*, almost single-handedly helped to keep Yiddish
alive. Now our own wonderfully mongrel American language
is punctuated with dozens of Yiddish words and phrases,
parables and wisdom. And so many of these words are perfect onomatopoeis of disgust, hubris and humor. If you've
ever met a schmuck, you know what I'm talking about.

Toward the end of his long and prolific life, he expressed
wonder at why so many of his books, written in this obscure
and, some said, useless language, would be so widely translated. Something like 56 countries all around the world.
Why, for example, he wondered, would the Japanese care
about his simple stories of life in the stetles of eastern
Europe a thousand years ago? "Unless," Singer paused,
"these stories spoke of the kinship of the soul"; that which
connects all of us together, that which we all share as part of
the life on this planet.

Kinship of the Soul.

I have had my own wonderful brush with the "kinship of
the soul" the last few years as I attempt to digest the reaction
and impact of our films, both serious and frivolous, on the
country. You know, we've been, as a real barometer of your
effect on the culture, the subject of dozens and dozens of
editorial cartoons. After the baseball series aired I rather
proudly showed off one of these cartoons to my daughters as
they got back from school. It showed two young children,
obviously ogling the signature on a baseball freshly auto-
graphed by a man with a Beatles hair-cut, and the balloon
over the kids says, "Ooooh, Ken Burns!" At that moment, my
oldest daughter said, "Yeah, but look at this new cartoon
someone just faxed to us." It showed a bleary-eyed couple
sitting on a couch as the television was going and a huge balloon over the television says, "Coming soon to PBS: 'O. J.'—
A 2,575-hour documentary . . . " And the man on the couch

turns to his wife and says, "Ken Burns has got to be stopped."

But nowhere is the profundity of response more pronounced than in the wonderful, touching expressive letters I have received. To my surprise and delight, the eloquence of the common man that we had worked so hard to put in our film came through in thousands of new letters from Americans who were supposed to be completely numbed by television and a post-modern age that had lulled them to blissful, ignorant sleep. Let me read you just one example, received not too long ago:

> "Dear Sir:
>
> Again, I am watching "The Civil War"—enthralled, inspired, heartbroken. So much to think about, so much to feel:
>
> The eloquence of ordinary people resounds. It humbles me.
>
> Such dignity in the archival faces of my people, who were enslaved but who never surrendered their souls to slavery.
>
> I hear the Southerners who not only kept my ancestors in bondage, but fought to the death to do so. And I hate them for that.
>
> Then the choir sings: "Do you . . . do you . . . want your freedom?" A good question, for we are not yet truly free, none of us.
>
> To achieve that, white America must abandon its racial conceits—and I must abandon my hate. They must change, and I must forgive, for us both to be free.
>
> Lincoln was right. "Malice toward none, charity for all."
>
> So at the end, I wonder. Does my white counterpart, hearing that choir, realize that that final question is meant for both of us?
>
> "Do you . . . do you . . . want your freedom?"
>
> I know what my answer is. I will wait for his."

Most of us here, whether we know it or not, are in the business of words, and we hope, with some reasonable expectation, that those words will last. But alas, especially today, those words often evaporate, their precision blunted by neglect; their insight diminished by the sheer volume of their ever-increasing brethren; their force diluted by ancient animosities that seem to set each group against the other.

The historian Arthur Schlesinger Jr. said that we suffer today from "too much *pluribus* and not enough *unum*." Few things survive in these cynical days to remind us of the union from which so many of our personal as well as collective blessings flow. And it is hard not to wonder in an age when the present moment consumes and overshadows all else—our bright past and our dim, unknown future—what finally does endure? What encodes and stores the genetic material of our civilization, passing down to the next generation—the best of us—what we hope will mutate into betterness for our children and our posterity?

History holds the answer. Nothing in our daily life offers more of the comfort of continuity, the generation connection of belonging to a vast and complicated American family, the powerful sense of home, the freedom from time's constraints, and the great gift of accumulated memory than does an active and heartfelt engagement with our shared past.

Procrustes and the Culture Wars[2]

Anne Fadiman

Editor, the American Scholar; *born New York, NY, 1953; B.A., Harvard University, 1975; National Magazine Award for reporting; John S. Knight Fellowship, Stanford University; National Book Critics Circle Award for general nonfiction; author,* The Spirit Catches You and You Fall Down: A Hmong Child, Her American Doctors, and the Collision of Two Cultures (*1997*) *and* Ex Libris: Confessions of a Common Reader (*1998*).

Editors' introduction: Anne Fadiman gave this "Phi Beta Kappa Oration," a longer version of a speech she had given earlier at Yale University, at literary exercises during commencement week at Harvard University. She spoke to a few hundred persons in the Sanders Theatre. The speech was carried by WHRB. In the address, Fadiman "welcomed the new Phi Beta Kappa members into the community of intelligent thinkers by beseeching them to maintain their intellectual independence rather than surrendering to pressures to follow a party line in the culture wars." The oration was published in *Harvard College News* and studied by freshmen in seminars examining the issue of diversity.

Anne Fadiman's speech: You probably remember Procrustes. I like to think of him as the Hannibal Lecter of ancient Attica. Procrustes used to lure in tired tourists who happened to be walking through his neighborhood, and then do unspeakable things to them. In the words of Diodorus of Sicily, who wrote about him in the first century B.C., "This man used to seize passing travelers and threw them upon a certain bed. When they were too big for it, he lopped off the overhanging parts of their bodies. When they were too small, he stretched them out by the feet." I think the Procrustean Bed is, alas, an all-too-apt metaphor for the Culture Wars, with one crucial difference. Sometimes Procrustes lopped off his victims, and sometimes he stretched them, but the Culture Wars only lop off. I have never seen cultural politics enlarge a work of art, only diminish it.

By the Culture Wars I mean that peculiar development of the last decade or so which takes culture—a multidimensional thing if there ever was one—and attempts to squish it down to a skinny little monodimensional line running from Left to Right. Both armies in the Culture Wars try to do this

Few things survive in these cynical days to remind us of the union from which so many of our personal as well as collective blessings flow.

---

2. Delivered in Cambridge, Massachusetts, on June 3, 1997, at noon. Reprinted with permission of Anne Fadiman and Yale University.

with nearly every aspect of culture, although today I'll be concentrating on literature. No matter how oddly shaped a book or a play or a poem is, no matter how idiosyncratic, how ambivalent, how anarchic, how complicated, how big, how messy, it's just got to fit that Procrustean Bed. So out comes the handsaw (which is what Procrustes is supposed to have used on his larger victims), and WHOP! With a few quick strokes, there it is. Cut down to size. And in the process, as a kind of casual side effect, murdered.

Today I am going to make a plea. I am going to ask you not to choose sides in the Culture Wars. Not the Right. Not the Left. If you have already chosen sides, please consider giving back your uniform and your rifle. I'm sure you have already chosen your political party, and you'll probably, though not certainly, stick with it for the rest of your life. That's fine. I've done the same. But national politics and cultural politics are different animals, and the two-party system works far better when you vote for President than when you read a book.

We come to college to learn nuance. We learn, for example, that if you change a single word in a poem, that poem will change its meaning or its mood, or may even get ruined entirely. Then we're asked to join an army in the Culture Wars, either on the Right or the Left, and in one blow all that nuance is gone. And that is because polarization is the enemy of nuance. Monoliths are the enemy of nuance. And as Procrustes can tell us, the concept "One Size Fits All," which he invented, is the enemy of nuance.

Here's how it works. Without giving it much thought, you toe the party line—once. You think you've signed your name just to the top page, but then you discover that there are a thousand pieces of carbon paper underneath, all transferring your signature with perfect fidelity to a thousand different documents. In other words, you suddenly find you've lost your right to judge things on a case-by-case basis.

This sort of thing is hard to resist. It's a hell of a lot easier to get your marching orders and never think again. Nonetheless, I implore you not to enlist in the Culture Wars. I'm not asking you to be a conscientious objector. On each issue, if you feel strongly, cover yourself with blood if necessary. But when the next battle comes along, go back to square one and make up your mind again. From scratch.

My remarks today are aimed mainly at those of you who will graduate this Thursday, especially the humanists—but you scientists are going to face similar pressures too. No one who teaches, writes, or researches is immune to the pressure to choose sides. Each of you will be asked to be Procrustes. But if you start hacking the toes off your culture, I warn you that you'll soon find you are hacking your own toes off as well.

There are dozens of issues currently being debated in the Culture Wars. I'm going to look at five of them, all concerning the literary canon, and tell you where I stand on each.

I'm not going to do that because I insist that you agree with me. You may hold the opposite opinions. I'm going to do it just to show you that a perfectly sane, or at least more or less sane, person can entertain some ostensibly liberal views, and some ostensibly conservative views, and some utterly ambivalent views—and that this is not the product of schizophrenia but merely of a deep-seated abhorrence of the Procrustean Bed.

Here's the first one. Should we read great books because of their literary value or because they are moral examples—that is, because they teach us how to live?

David Denby wrote a book last year called *Great Books*. It's about how he returned to Columbia's Western Civilization course at the age of 48. On the first day of class, his teacher told the students, "You're here for very selfish reasons. You're here to build a self." That's a pretty clear statement of the moral-example school.

Now here's Hannah Arendt: "The trouble with the educated philistine was not that he read the classics, but that he did so prompted by the ulterior motive of self-perfection, remaining quite unaware of the fact that Shakespeare or Plato might have to tell him more important things than how to educate himself." That's a pretty clear statement of the literary school.

Now my view is that forcing us to choose between these two is incredibly stupid. Surely great books should be read for both literary and moral reasons! Especially in college. The late teens and early twenties are the time when we are deeply engrossed in building ourselves. Is it wrong to enlist the help of Shakespeare and Plato in this difficult task? But if that's all we do, then we are missing the entire aesthetic experience of reading poetry and prose beautiful enough to break our hearts.

These days, it's mostly the people who consider themselves to be on the cultural Left who ally themselves with the self-builders, and it's the Right who accuse the self-builders of shallow narcissism. Which just goes to show how fickle and crazy the whole Right-to-Left spectrum is. For I might remind you that the self-building position used to be considered conservative. Matthew Arnold, one of the greatest of all literary traditionalists, wrote in 1879: "Poetry is at bottom a criticism of life; and the greatness of a poet lies in his powerful and beautiful application of ideas to life—to the question: How to live."

I believe we are lopping literature off at the ankles if we restrict ourselves to one or the other. But, having said that, I'll risk some brickbats from the conservatives who are here today, by saying that if you're foolish enough to choose just one, I hope you choose self-building. You'll miss a great deal, but I think you'll miss even more if your reading is a disembodied intellectual experience that has nothing to do with your own life.

I might add that people who've concentrated only on the self-building aspect haven't come out so badly. For example, Vice-Admiral James Stockdale, who was Ross Perot's running mate in 1992. Stockdale's favorite book was the *Enchiridion*, the teachings of the Stoic philosopher Epictetus. Now, judging from Stockdale's total incoherence in the vice-presidential debates, I think it's fair to say that he didn't learn much about literary style from Epictetus. However, he did learn a great deal about how to build a self.

What happens if a book's plot fails to meet moral standards that have changed with the times?

Stockdale first read the *Enchiridion* at the age of 38, when the Navy sent him to Stanford to study international relations, and a professor he met by chance in the library suggested that he take a philosophy course. Stockdale learned in that course that Frederick the Great always had a copy of the *Enchiridion* by his side on his military campaigns, so when he was sent to Vietnam, of course he took along *his* copy. In September of 1966, Stockdale's plane was hit by flak over North Vietnam, and as he was descending by parachute, knowing he was about to become a prisoner of war, he said to himself, "I'm leaving the world of technology and entering the world of Epictetus." I would venture a guess that this is the first time a parachutist has thought about first-century Greek philosophy on the way down—though if there are any skydiving classicists here today who can offer evidence to the contrary, I'd like to hear from you. Of course, Jim Stockdale didn't have a copy of the *Enchiridion* with him. But he didn't need to. By this time he had the book virtually memorized. He ended up spending eight years as a prisoner of war. Two of those years he was in leg irons. He kept himself going by thinking about Epictetus, in particular about the assertion that there is only one thing that truly belongs to an individual: his own will. And that will cannot be thwarted by anything external. It was in this way, through solitary confinement and torture, that Stockdale was able to preserve the self that Epictetus had built for him. I think this was a pretty good way to use literature.

The second question I'd like to look at is: Should the life of the writer affect our valuation of the work? In other words, if the writer was a stinker, do we boot the book out of the canon? Or, as the *New York Times Magazine* put it in a recent article about Herman Melville, "Forget the whale. The big question is: Did he beat his wife?"

According to some relatively new evidence, Melville may indeed have beaten his wife. And some people say that therefore the stock of *Moby Dick* and *Billy Budd* and *Typee* should plummet. Similar things have been said about T. S. Eliot. Last year a controversial book was published about

Eliot's anti-Semitism. Ezra Pound was also an anti-Semite, and Philip Larkin, we now know, was a more Democratic sort of bigot. He hated almost everybody.

So the question is: do these things matter?

This seems to me to be closely related to the question of whether we read great books for their literary merit or for the purpose of self-building. And I believe it provides a compelling argument for doing both. If you believe that the purpose of literature is primarily moral, you're going to run into trouble if you find out that the book you've been using as a guide to living was written by someone who beat his wife.

Not surprisingly, it's the self-builders who tend to place a great deal of emphasis on biography, and who vote to expel someone from the canon if he or she turns out to have been a skunk. But if you believe that great literature can be written by bad people, then your library can stay intact, no matter how much respect you lose for their authors as individuals, and no matter how sadly disillusioned you feel.

Some people, mostly those who consider themselves conservatives, feel that biography is irrelevant, and *only* the work counts. I disagree. For instance, if you know that Melville was a terrible husband, you may be able to make more sense of the sealed-off, sea-bound world of *Moby Dick*, where everybody was male, even the whale. And even if there are no themes in the work that resonate with the life, surely knowing as much as we can about writers and their milieus helps us see literature not as a distant abstraction that we study, but as a vital part of life.

What do you do when a work's language leaves you out?

This leads me to the next question, which is: What about the content? What happens if a book's plot fails to meet moral standards that have changed with the times?

Here's an example from the letters column of the *New York Times Book Review.* The writer, Sharon Ronholt of Stockton, California, is berating the male reviewer of Robert Fagles's new translation of the *Odyssey.* She writes, "Nowhere in his review does Mr. Jenkyns draw critical attention to the fact that Homer's world is that of a quintessential male fantasy and may not meet with universal approbation. Homer's hero commits adultery with various gorgeous, high-class women, and the construction of the plot (his desire to depart for 'home') legitimizes his callous abandonment of his ever-changing women lovers." Ms. Ronholt therefore concludes that it is naive and, as she terms it, "pre-theoretical," to accept the *Odyssey* as "a timeless Great Book."

Now, the writer of this letter has put her finger on the paradox that women, or indeed anyone interested in equality, will always feel when reading works from other times or cultures. Except that Ms. Ronholt doesn't see it as a paradox, a word that suggests ambivalence. She sees it unambiguously as grounds for demoting the *Odyssey.*

A book belongs to the reader as well as to the writer.
The greater the work, the wider the ownership.

I too am a feminist, but I love the *Odyssey*. How can that be? Whenever I read Homer, I see ample evidence that women were treated abominably in ancient Greece, and I am very thankful that I live now and not then. In fact, I would rather be chopped up by Procrustes than marry any of Homer's heroes. Fortunately, none of them is asking me. The invitation Homer is offering me is a far broader one, and that is to enter a world that had different mores from ours, but that in its own "pre-theoretical" way possessed nobility and beauty. If I had to step into a polling booth and vote on Homer's sexual politics, I'd pull the NO lever. Strenuously. Which is why I'm very glad that the *Odyssey* is not a referendum but a poem. It therefore retains the power to move me.

Another example that has been in the spotlight lately is *Huckleberry Finn*. If you're on the cultural Right these days, you're supposed to think it's a masterpiece—the book from which, as Ernest Hemingway said, all modern American literature has come. (Of course, if you were on the Right a century ago, you would have found the book shockingly progressive, which shows that in the realm of cultural politics the ground can shift more seismically than a tectonic plate.)

If you're on the cultural Left today, you're supposed to think that *Huckleberry Finn* should be expunged from the reading lists of America's high schools. The anti-Huck camp has been most eloquently represented by Jane Smiley, who happens to be one of my favorite writers, though I disagree with her here. Smiley has written that one of the disqualifying flaws in *Huckleberry Finn* is that Huck takes Jim down the Mississippi River instead of across it to Illinois, a free state. She sees this as a moral failure on Huck's part, and therefore on Mark Twain's part as well.

Well, she's right in a way. Jim would have been freed from slavery a whole lot sooner if he and Huck had gone east instead of south. There's only one small problem. There would have been no novel.

There would have been no river. No raft. No adventures. No vacillation. No self-examination. No humor. No growing friendship. No journey at all, either geographic or emotional. So I'm very grateful that Huck Finn and Mark Twain were too confused and ambivalent to stop their book on page 43.

My fourth question has raised plenty of hackles, including mine. What do you do when a work's language leaves you out? If the very words exclude you, let's say because they are addressed to men and you don't happen to be one, should you stick out your tongue and say, "Well, if that's the way you feel about it, I reject you too"?

To answer this question, I will take as my text another Phi Beta Kappa oration, in fact the greatest one of all time. It was called "The American Scholar," and it seems appropriate to mention it today, because this year's literary exercises mark its 160th anniversary.

The year was 1837. The speaker was Ralph Waldo Emerson. The audience included James Russell Lowell, Oliver Wendell Holmes, Edward Everett Hale, and plenty of famous people who had only two names. Emerson orated for an hour and a quarter. "Our day of dependence, our long apprenticeship to the learning of other lands, draws to a close," he said. "The millions that around us are rushing into llfe, cannot always be fed on the sere remains of foreign harvest." By this he meant that American intellectuals should emancipate themselves from the European tradition and establish one of their own.

Some members of the audience were not impressed. Edward Everett Hale went home and wrote in his diary that Emerson was "half-crazy" and that his speech was "not very good, and very transcendental." But Oliver Wendell Holmes, though not immediately, called "The American Scholar" "our intellectual declaration of independence." And when Thomas Carlyle was sent a copy, he wrote to Emerson, "I could have *wept* to read that speech, the clear high melody of it went tingling through my heart; I said to my wife, 'There, woman!' She read; and returned; and charges me to return for answer, 'that there had been nothing met with like it since Schiller went silent.' My brave Emerson!"

The day I found I had been chosen as the editor of *The American Scholar,* a magazine that takes its name from that very speech, I ran to my bookcase, took down a volume of my brave Emerson, and opened it to his Phi Beta Kappa Oration. I expected, like Carlyle, to hear a clear high melody tingling through my heart. Instead, I read the following sentence: "In the right state, [the scholar] is Man Thinking." And my heart sank.

What Emerson meant was that his ideal American Scholar was not an academic but a thinker, a student of life. What *I* wondered was, when he said "Man Thinking," did he really mean, "Man and Woman Thinking?" In other words, was "Man" one of those capacious linguistic tents that once had room in it for everybody? The way "horsemanship" was supposed to include "horsewomanship," or "mankind" was supposed to include womankind?

In a word, no.

Emerson was perfectly clear about it. He really meant "*Man* Thinking." We know this because later in his speech he specifically distinguished the scholar from "the protected classes of women and children." Every word in his oration was about men. It was 1837. Women were not invited.

So even though Emerson supported women's suffrage and hung out with Margaret Fuller and Harriet Martineau and didn't complain when his wife served leg of lamb 20 days in a row, am I nonetheless forced to write him off as a wicked

There seems little doubt that some great writers have been neglected because they belonged to the wrong gender or nationality or ethnic group.

misogynist and cast from my bookshelf the very speech that gave my magazine its name?

No.

If I leave the speech *on* my shelf, does that mean I am forever excluded from the Emersonian fellowship, forced to press my nose against the glass of American intellectual life, as if the Man Thinking Club were some beer-swilling fraternity that invited me on the premises only on Saturday night?

No.

One of the convenient things about literature is that, despite copyright laws—which in Emerson's case expired long ago—a book belongs to the reader as well as to the writer. The greater the work, the wider the ownership, which is why there are such things as criticism, revisionism, and Ph.D. dissertations. I therefore have few compunctions about dragging Emerson kicking and screaming into the 1990s, and recasting "Man Thinking" in *My* mind as "Curious People Thinking."

I will not ask the sage of Concord to rewrite his great oration. He will forever retain the right to speak his own words. But I will retain the right to crash the party. You come too.

My last question is about the bloodiest battleground in all the Culture Wars: Should the canon be expanded?

Clearly, if you believe that books provide moral lessons, and that the books we regard most highly should match the moral lessons of the age in which they're read, then the canon will change every year. This can create some problems. For why do we have a canon at all? I think it's because it provides not only a fund of great literature, but also a common frame of reference. In the past, people were drawn together by sharing this heritage. They could quote a line or mention the name of a character from the Bible, or Greek mythology, or Shakespeare, or certain touchstones of English and American poetry, and know that it had the same resonance for the listener that it did for the speaker. If the canon is in a constant state of flux, we lose that commonality. That is why I think required courses are useful—and why, for example, I mourn the recent decision by many English departments that their students need no longer take a course in Shakespeare, a statement that will doubtless brand me as a conservative. However, I think that freezing the canon is an equally bad idea, a statement that will doubtless brand me as a liberal.

Canons, like people, need fresh air, or they will suffocate. And many writers who are now solidly enshrined in the canon were once rude parvenus. Today's parvenu may be, and perhaps should be, the subject of tomorrow's final exam. Also, there seems little doubt that some great writers have been neglected because they belonged to the wrong gender or nationality or ethnic group. Which does not mean that we need affirmative action to bring them in. Merit will suffice nicely. Some people are dubious on this point, and to them I say, do you really think that George Eliot and Derek Walcott are going to need to sneak in by some sort of quota system? That their SAT scores aren't quite up to snuff? If you really believe that, I'd like to take a look at *your* SAT scores, which I would expect to be grievously deficient in the verbal portion.

As we ponder the question of whether the canon should be frozen or thawed, it's useful to remember that this is not the first Culture War. In 17th century France, Boileau and La Fontaine duked it out with Fontenelle and Perrault in the Quarrel of the Ancients and the Moderns, a bitter argument over which was superior, classical or modern literature. The ruckus spread across the Channel to England. Swift satirized the whole thing in *The Battle of the Books*, in which the great classical authors and the great modern authors wage a gory but delightfully incompetent war. Aristotle, for example, aims an arrow at Bacon but instead shoots Descartes in the eye. Nobody wins, of course, because nobody can and nobody should. Swift's armies both demand that the world's readers choose A or B, not A and B, or A, B, C, and Z. That binary view of culture was just as reductive then as it is now, when the battle between the ancients and moderns is still raging—except that Aristotle and Bacon now find themselves fighting on the same side and being commanded to take pot-shots at Virginia Woolf.

I live in New York City, so of course I spend a good deal of time at Columbia. On the limestone pediment of Butler Library are incised the following names: HOMER. HERO-DOTUS. SOPHOCLES. PLATO. ARISTOTLE. DEMOS-THENES. CICERO. VIRGIL. During the 1989 graduation exercises, a student stood on the roof of Butler Library and unfurled a banner that read: SAPPHO. MARIE de FRANCE. CHRISTINE de PIZAN. JUANA INES de la CRUZ. BRONTE. DICKINSON. WOOLF.

Do I wish these seven names could be permanently graven in stone, alongside Homer and Herodotus? Certainly, although it would be even better if they didn't have to be ghettoized in a separate, all-female club, in which their gen-der becomes their primary attribute rather than one of many. A coeducational rather than a sex-segregated canon seems to me the best way to suggest their size: that they're larger than their gender, larger than their era, larger than their subject matter. That's what greatness is. Let us never forget that these great writers were women, but let us not stop there.

Now, I get the feeling that some of you are squirming in your seats, trying to figure out, well, which *is* she? Is she on the Right or on the Left? Not being able to pigeonhole some-one is an uncomfortable feeling. It's like being aboard a ship that's pitching and rolling, with no railing to hold onto. I don't mean to make you seasick, but I have deliberately removed the railings today in order to force you not to pigeonhole. So I will provide no clues. I will merely tell you that the battlefield of the Culture Wars is a fiction: a theoretical—or as Sharon Ronholt would put it—a "post-theoretical" construct.

And therefore, I would like to end this talk by returning, in a pre-theoretical way, to our friend Procrustes. Or rather, to his nemesis, Theseus. It was Theseus who slew Procrustes on his own bed, though it isn't recorded whether he stretched the old reprobate or lopped him off. When I was reading various accounts of Procrustes last week, I also read about some of the other unpleasant characters that Theseus ran into just before he met Procrustes, while he was walking from the Peloponnesus to Athens. There were five of them, and it seemed to me that, perhaps with a little Procrustean stretching, they too represented the various hazards you are likely to encounter as *you* wend your way through the Culture Wars Obstacle Course.

The first one was Periphetes, the Club-Bearer, who had the uncivil habit of beating travelers to death with a giant bronze club. So Theseus, who was never known for his subtlety, grabbed the club himself and bashed Periphetes over the head with it. Theseus was apparently so pleased with this club that he stole it and carried it around with him for the rest of his life. This little encounter reminds me of how the Right berated the Left for politicizing culture, and then went and appropriated the weapon of politicization themselves, so they could bash the Left over the head with it. Please don't do that yourselves.

The second fellow that Theseus met was named Sinis the Pine-Bender. Sinis liked to bend two trees down to the ground, tie his victim to them, and then let go. The trees sprang back, and the victim was torn in two. Surely these two trees are none other than the political poles, each pantingly eager to bind you to its bosom, with the danger that you, too, will be rent in half. The best—indeed, the only—tool you have to keep yourself in one piece is your common sense.

Theseus tore Sinis in two with his own killer trees, and then, after persuading Sinis's daughter that he would not harm her, he seduced her, got her pregnant, and abandoned her. It's no wonder, then, that the next challenge Theseus encountered was an angry female—in fact, none other than the Wild Sow of Crommyon, a very large and ill-mannered female pig who was rampaging around the countryside, eating people. Now, who could the Wild Sow be but every male academic's nightmare of the enraged feminist who, he fears, will get tenure instead of him, and in departmental meetings will act like—well, like a sow in a china shop? I have to say that I've never actually met any feminists like this, but there's no doubt that they run rampant in people's imaginations, where they probably gobble up more fragile male egos than if they really existed. So what did Theseus do to the Wild Sow of Crommyon? Of course, he did what we all want to do to our secret fears: he killed her.

After she was out of way, he met a murderer named Sciron. Sciron liked to make his visitors wash his feet, and after they finished, he kicked them off a cliff into the ocean, where they were eaten by a giant turtle. Surely, Sciron is none other than the forces who want you to take books that have always been an intimate part of your life, such as *Huckleberry Finn*, and kick them out of the canon. I particularly like the part about the giant turtle. Because if Huck Finn were not only banished but actually digested, there would be no danger of his ever creeping back into the canon. And this would make Jane Smiley and her fellow Huck-critics very happy.

After Theseus got rid of Sciron, he met Cercyon the wrestler, whom of course he outwrestled. I like to think of Cercyon as your own conscience, with which you will often wrestle as you grapple with these slippery and vexing questions of culture and morality. I hope, however, that, unlike Theseus, you do not choke your conscience to death

Now, let us imagine that you, as a modern-day Theseus negotiating the thorny path of cultural politics, have somehow managed to resist all these dangers, perhaps with a bit more finesse and less violence than your predecessor. Athens is still far away, and you are absolutely exhausted. Now what do you think you would long for most in all the world?

A bed.

And that is just what Procrustes offers you. A soft bed I am sure, made up with the most expensive linens. With a European duvet. And goosedown pillows.

All I can say is: *Do not do it!*

Do not permit him to throw you on his bed.

Do not permit him to lop off your legs at the ankles.

Make your own bed. Then lie in it.

Opportunity and Academic Integrity[3]

Roger Wilkins

Clarence J. Robinson Professor of History and American Culture, George Mason University, 1988–; commentator, National Public Radio; chairman of the board, CRISIS *(journal of the NAACP); born Kansas City, MO, March 25, 1932; A.B., 1953, and J.D., 1956, University of Michigan; caseworker, Cuyahoga County, Cleveland, OH, 1957; private law practice, Delson, Levin & Gordon, New York, NY 1956–62; special assistant, Agency for International Development, State Department, 1962–64; assistant director, U.S. Community Relations Service, Department of Commerce, 1964–65; director, U.S. Community Relations Service, Department of Commerce, 1965–66; assistant attorney general of the United States, 1966–69; program officer and assistant to the president, Ford Foundation, 1969–71; editorial writer,* Washington Post, *1972–74; member, editorial board,* New York Times, *1974–79 (columnist 1977–79); associate editor,* Washington Star, *1980–81; author,* A Man's Life: An Autobiography *(1982); co-editor,* Quiet Riots: Race and Poverty in the United States *(1988); writer and narrator,* PBS Frontline *documentaries:* Keeping the Faith *(1987) and* Throwaway People *(1990); winner of 1972 Pulitzer Prize for coverage of Watergate, shared with Bob Woodward, Carl Bernstein, and Herbert Block; chairman of the board of trustees, African-American Institute; steering committee, Free South Africa Movement (1984–86); commissioner, Citizens' Commission on Civil Rights; Roger Baldwin Career Service Award, New York Civil Liberties Union; Roy Wilkins Career Civil Rights Contributions Award, Los Angeles NAACP.*

Editors' introduction: Roger Wilkins gave the Seventh Annual University Senate Davis, Markert, Nickerson Lecture on Academic and Intellectual Freedom to some 350 persons attending a University of Michigan Faculty Senate meeting in the graduate school auditorium. In the address, Wilkins fostered "greater urgency about active citizenship" and promoted "a strong push by faculty and administrators for diversity in higher education." The well-received lecture elicited a number of supportive letters.

Roger Wilkins's speech: Speaking here at Michigan is wonderful for me. It is, in a real sense, a coming home. I entered this university as a skinny, scared 17-year-old nearly 48 years

---

3. Delivered in Ann Arbor, Michigan, on March 17, 1997, at 4:00 p.m.
Copyright © 1997. Reprinted with permission of Roger Wilkins.

ago, wondering: "What's to become of me?" Now, after all this time, I know.

I began forging the answer to that question in the seven years I spent here. I love this place. It is where I began in earnest the task of attempting to develop a deep and settled comfort in being a black citizen in a country that insisted on claiming to be white.

My deep affection for this university stems in part from the hard lessons I learned as I began that journey. I experienced Michigan as a white institution and I had to adjust my spirit in ways that helped prepare me for the soul-jarring contradictions blacks encounter just living in their own country.

I will return in a moment to Michigan and the hard lessons it taught at mid-century and to the lessons I believe it must now work very hard to teach to help prepare this country for the *next* mid-century. First, however, I want to touch on citizenship.

A couple of years ago, I became certain that my sense of American-ness had settled deep inside me during an exchange with a student that occurred during a question period at the end of a debate I'd had with a black conservative at George Mason University, where I teach. I interrupted a personal attack the student was leveling at my debate opponent.

"But Professor," the student complained, "he offended me as an African in America."

After commenting on what was required of us as hosts, I then blurted out words I'd never consciously thought before: "I don't think we're 'Africans in America.' At least I'm not.

"What kind of African is born in Kansas City; lives and dies for the University of Michigan football team; loves Toni Morrison, William Faulkner and the Baltimore Orioles; reveres George Washington and Harriet Tubman; and who, when puzzled by the conundrum of Thomas Jefferson, collects his thoughts while listening to B. B. King?"

I am profoundly connected to the ideas, the history, the soil and the culture of this vast complex and confounding country and as an active and concerned citizen, I am deeply disturbed about its future. I have strong ideas about what institutions like this one must do about the problems I see looming in that future. In order to do that, I need first to talk about the institution I encountered here almost 50 years ago.

In those days, just after Jack Roosevelt Robinson integrated major league baseball, but before the Supreme Court decision in *Brown v. Topeka Board of Education*, the University of Michigan *followed* American culture. No black person had ever represented this university on the basketball court or on the baseball diamond. Though racial designations weren't required on housing forms, we were assigned rooms by race on the basis of the photographs we were required to submit. The student who became my roommate in the second semes-

We students of the 1950s were called the silent generation. We were silent largely because the times frightened most of us.

ter of my freshman year was a light-skinned African American with straight hair. The housing authorities did the right thing for the wrong reasons by placing him with a Hindu from New Delhi and a Muslim from Karachi. He was forced to mediate the partition of the subcontinent all over again. In the meantime, he learned enormous amounts about the post-colonial subcontinent and the people who lived there.

I remember encountering no black adults either on the faculty or on the administrative staffs of the university during my seven years here. I was assigned no book, play, essay or poem by a black author nor did I have a reading assignment over those seven years that suggested that blacks had done anything of value in the history of the world except for the decision in *Brown v. Topeka Board of Education*, which I studied in law school.

Many of the whites on campus went off to live in their segregated fraternities and sororities. Whatever mixing there was usually ended on the steps of Angell Hall. By necessity, we blacks constructed a segregated social world for ourselves here.

The lessons that both we and our white fellow-students learned from all this were, of course, quite awful ones. The bloated sense of self and the sense of entitlement to unearned privilege was driven deeply into the spirits of our white classmates by the campus culture. For us blacks the answers to the fundamental questions that young people ask themselves were these: Who am I? *A semi-person.* Where do I fit? *At the margins.* What is my role in America? *To be an eternal supplicant.*

Perhaps worst of all, we were encouraged by what we found here to hold onto the belief we had come with: That we had nothing to learn from one another across the racial divide. Whatever we had in our heads on that subject at 17 or 18 was sufficient for our adulthood and for our joint citizenship in this country. Unfortunately, despite significant advances too much of what happens in higher education today teaches, though perhaps less powerfully and pointedly, those same lessons.

There was at least one other set of lessons that the university taught me by following the culture of the time. We students of the 1950s were called the silent generation. We were silent largely because the times frightened most of us. When we did attempt to speak up, we were slapped down. It was a dark time. The ugliest scar was inflicted during my first year here. In February 1950, Sen. Joseph McCarthy of Wisconsin delivered the speech at Wheeling, West Virginia, alleging that he knew of a large number of Communists in the State Department and thus gave his name to an ugly period that had already begun.

In my junior year, I was a new member of the student government—the only black—and the Chair of its Human Relations Committee. The Student Legislature adopted a resolution, proposed by our committee, which called on the Regents and the university administration to resist subpoenas to be issued by the House Un-American Activities Committee directed at Michigan faculty members. Because the House Committee proposed to probe faculty political beliefs and associations, we believed that the hearing constituted a serious violation of academic freedom. Our resolution was brushed aside by university administrators who said that since this hearing was to occur in Detroit, it was no concern of students, whose interests should not go beyond the campus.

Subsequently, the student government took one more foray into an area of politics that adults found difficult to treat honestly. We believed that fraternities and sororities that had national charters containing racially exclusive clauses were particularly obnoxious at an educational institution. Thus, the Student Legislature enacted a resolution that would have required Greek letter groups to eliminate such charter provisions over a reasonable transition period or face expulsion from the campus.

This action too was brushed aside by the administration. This time we were told that property rights precluded any action on our concern. This statement was buttressed by a citation of *Corpus Juris Secundum*. A couple of years later when I got to law school I learned that *Corpus Juris Secundum* was a legal encyclopedia which no one taking an argument seriously would have used as an authoritative statement of Michigan law.

As you might imagine, the idea of dissent in support of principle began to appeal to me as I pondered these actions by people who were supposed to be educating me as a person and as a citizen. I began to internalize active citizenship as a powerful personal value. I surely developed the idea that it was required to probe beneath the conventional wisdom dispensed by society in general or by interested bureaucracies in particular if one were to be in charge of her or his own moral bearings. Lone dissenters of conscience were imprinted on my spirit as the heroes of the time.

For that part of my education, I am deeply indebted to Chandler Davis, Clement Markert and Mark Nickerson whose acts of conscience earned them seared careers, but who simultaneously held up guiding torches for me in that decade of darkness.

Those men lit my way toward others carrying torches along the road. I have in mind here J. Waites Waring, the white Federal Judge in Charleston, South Carolina, who endured shunning by his local community as he followed what he understood to be the Constitutional requirement to admit blacks to full citizenship. They led me to Andrei Sakharov whose courageous dissent against the Soviet dictatorship

The United States is not immune to social pathologies that can destroy lives and rip at the very fabric of our democracy.

made him immortal. And they led me to believe that Martin Luther King Jr.'s finest hour was his dissent from our war policies in Vietnam—despite President Johnson's fury and dire warnings from virtually all of his civil rights colleagues.

My Michigan lessons were thus quite profound. They were that one could love something quite deeply while being aware of and impatient with ugly and glaring imperfections. They were that imperfections had to be addressed, not accepted passively. They were that individual belief in one's own principles and actions taken upon those beliefs could make a profound difference. They were that active citizenship is an obligation of people who value their freedom. And they were that institutions teach powerful lessons which matter down through the long decades of the lives they shape.

We should prob- ably remind ourselves that we are only glimpsing the foothills of the emerging world.

So, then, what are universities for? Are we simply here to help our students tuck into their souls the best of what's been thought and said as they fit themselves into the world as we have received it? Do we create new knowledge only to help these young people develop a better passive understanding of the world than earlier generations had? Is our function, in other words, to accept the world as it is and simply to equip our students with skills—to enjoy Shakespeare and to be computer literate, for example? Or is it to build some of that new knowledge on what we have come to know as human beings and to help equip our students with our understandings so that they may struggle more effectively with the problems that we believe are sure to come?

Should we not teach them about the dangers of national pathologies? No one could have lived through the last two-thirds of the 20th century without concluding that untended national pathologies can surely lead to the most disastrous national calamities. The pathologies that festered in Tsarist Russia led to the brutalities of Leninism-Stalinism. Pathologies festering beneath Weimar democracy led to murderous Hitlerism in Germany. And untended pathologies have ripped apart the country formerly known as Yugoslavia and the little Central African nation of Rwanda.

The dark American time of the 1950s taught that desplte our myths about how exceptional we are (and our persistent denials over the centuries of the pathology of racism), the United States is not immune to social pathologies that can destroy lives and rip at the very fabric of our democracy. This was understood as early as 1787. At the Constitutional Convention, in urging an end to the international slave trade, George Mason of Virginia told the notables assembled in Philadelphia:

". . . As nations can not be rewarded or punished in the next world they must in this. By an inevitable chain of causes and effects, providence punishes national sins by national calamities."

Another lesson of the 50's was that institutional and individual integrity and courage are rare commodities when a nation is in the grip of a fever. And yet, it is just such clarity and courage that are required to serve free institutions and free people during times of great peril. We professors are a privileged class in society. We have good lives and relative security. There is little excuse for us to fail to be brave or to fail to give back to a country that has treated us so generously.

You may think that my talk about pathologies is a bit overwrought as our nation glides through the decade after the collapse of European Communism while enjoying a prolonged period of economic growth. The trouble is that our ancient problems have not gone away and they threaten to get worse very soon.

Let me illustrate with a story from an issue of the *New Yorker* published just after the presidential election of 1992. A reporter watched the election returns in a working class bar on the West Side of Manhattan. The noisiest patron was a white man in a bomber jacket who was audibly distressed by the possibility that Bill Clinton might win. He began muttering about the role he thought Jesse Jackson might play in a Clinton administration. As the evening wore on and a Clinton victory became probable, the man became more agitated. Finally when Clinton's victory was confirmed the man threw his money on the bar and stormed out shouting: "I'm not going to be a minority in my own country."

I want you to remember that man's rage and fear as we peer into our future. Today the population of the globe is about 5.8 billion people, 75 percent of whom are poor. There are about 265 million Americans. Seventy-three percent of us are non-Hispanic white; 12 per cent are black; 10.6 percent are Hispanic; 3 percent are Asian Americans and less than 1 percent are Indians, Eskimos or Aleuts.

In the middle of the next century—when my daughter now in the eighth grade is about the age I am now—there will be 8.5 to 10 billion people in the world and 80 percent of them will be poor. The population of the United States will then be about 394 million, only 52.8 percent of whom will be "white." The 47.2 percent of the population that is "minority" will be distributed this way: 24.5 percent of the American population will be Hispanic; 13.5 percent will be black; 8.2 percent will be Asian American and 1 percent will be Native American, Eskimo or Aleut.

The world will be more closely connected and tightly wired. There will be more poor people in world's population than there are people on the planet today. As we now think of the world's poverty as the cause of enormous problems in immigration policy and the availability of drugs, we should probably remind ourselves that we are only glimpsing the foothills of the emerging world. America will be a much more crowded place with more competition for space and other pressures grinding away at our civility and our senses of personal and international security.

It will, of course, be much harder to think of America as a "white country" or as a new and improved version of Europe. It will be a true world country; a country whose citizens have families with origins on every conceivable spot on the globe.

I would now ask you to think about the man in the bomber jacket who was having an identity crisis in the bar. There are already distressing signs about what our demographic trend might mean for America. I think the Oklahoma City bombing and the national teach-in on militias and white identity groups it generated were deeply disturbing. There are true pathologies at work there. On the far other side of the cultural chasm in America, there is gangsta rap. It is a cultural phenomenon that I find profoundly distressing and I think the companies that profit from it are obscene. Someday scholars of music, poetry and sociology may tell us that this is a starkly beautiful and artistic representation of the spiritual life salvaged from the rubble of the American ghetto. But I find the murders of the gangsta rappers Tupak Shakur and Biggie Smalls to be representative of the economic and spiritual desolation that our country has dumped on our most vulnerable citizens. We, as a people, take our profits and our income where we can find [them] and then flee from the poverty and human wastage our social and economic dislocations cause.

Lost lives—whether on the streets of the inner city, in the rapidly growing number of prisons or in failed elementary schools—are held in contempt in this country. The contempt is shown by the brutal way society rations opportunity and by young black murderers, who are simply externalizing their own contempt for themselves. The murders and the murderers generate increasing amounts of fear of blacks in general and of the black poor in particular.

We thus already have the bookends of a dreadful American calamity. White identity groups are at one far side and black desperadoes who have absolutely nothing to lose are at the other. The only thing necessary for a full fledged pathology to begin raging is for the pressures of demographic trends to begin to fill up the middle.

My forebodings are not rooted in some ideological denial of the enormous progress in race that this nation has made in my lifetime or the enormous progress this university has made since my time here. America is a far better place today than it was when I was born in a segregated hospital in Missouri 65 years ago or when I began my formal education in a segregated one-room schoolhouse four years later. We are surely a fairer and more decent country than we were then and the education provided by this institution is far richer and more conscious of the realities of the society around it than the Michigan I attended. But that progress was achieved—to borrow a phrase—"with all deliberate speed."

I don't think we have the luxury of time anymore. The demographic shift we are experiencing suggests that over the next 50 years, the very identity of the nation will be up for grabs and that many people will be shaken to their roots. Being a human being is an uncertain, often painful and frightening business. People seek solace and security in the group identities which may cloak them with standing and some physical and psychic protection. From our earliest history, when it was already demonstrably not true, Europeans insisted that this was to be a white country.

In those days, the world was thinly populated with perhaps only around half to three-quarters of a billion people. From the 15th century on, the pace of intercontinental collisions of peoples quickened and human difference became a massive human problem. America's national pathologies began to take shape at Jamestown in 1607. Human difference was even more startling then than now and difference was taken to mean danger. The earliest English colonists grappled for ways to deal with people who were different from themselves and finally concluded that domination of the dangerous "other" would work best.

Domination required the creation of a culture which justified a good deal of violence and deviousness, and so *otherness* became forever dangerous and inferior whether in Native Americans, blacks, dark Latins or Asians. Such people were also pushed to the margins of a busy, thrusting and increasingly more powerful "white" country. Thus, whiteness provided privilege as well as protection. So the white American identity, originally potent because of primal fears, was pounded deeper into the soul of the nation by the cultural accretions that justified the subordination and marginalization of millions of human beings.

Much of the 20th century racial progress occurred on top of and around this seminal racial sludge that lies somewhere near the center of American culture. As the old caste structures have broken down and have lost their force in law and in the superficial structures of civility, the damage done to all of us by our culture has become more apparent as opportunities for people who are not white remain severely restricted. I will deal here only with the damage to whites and blacks, but I am sure that similar assessments could be made of Hispanic, Asian and Native Americans as well.

Some whites have become more fearful and have retreated into white identity movements of various kinds. Others have become sullenly resentful of any minority advances, which some of them view as personal assaults. Still others have organized highly effective movements to contest the gains blacks and others have made. Some, who believe themselves

The pathologies lurking just under the tissue of our national civility result from the way we all have been "miseducated."

to be racially decent, continue to behave and to exercise power in the old ways while denying—even to themselves—that they have "a racist bone" in their bodies. While we were once able to believe that "prejudice" was an individual thing, we have come to see during our 30-year attempt to live with civil rights laws that the virus of racism adapts to new circumstances replicates itself in new generations and affects profoundly how we think, live and make public policy. Laws did liberate millions of white Americans, but they did not root racism out of the culture.

Clearly blacks are damaged as well. In addition to the tangible injuries in the economic, educational, health and housing spheres, there is also the cultural battering of the soul. That takes many forms. For some of the poorest and least connected citizens, it takes the form of almost total demoralization and a collapse of the family structure accompanied by the horrendous collateral damage I have already mentioned. For others it means lowered self-esteem and a sort of constantly imploding rage. And for still others it means a serious confusion about personal identity.

So, I tell my white students that they need to be much more than a collection of fantasies about the magic of whiteness or about the inferiorities of blacks and others in order to be fully human. I tell my black students that they need to be much more than the sum of their injuries and their grievances in order to achieve their full humanity. But for now the injuries to all are there and they are real and they could surely provide the seeds for a new, intense manifestation of our national pathologies.

As politicians have sensed the powerful reactions to challenges to the white identity of the nation or to the individual identities of white human beings, many have chosen the course of least resistance and have pandered to those feelings. The results—whether on immigration and civil rights issues in California or the ugly and brutal welfare "reform" law—have suggested a national direction that does raise possibilities of massive national calamities as the pace of demographic change picks up speed. We are thus faced with the daunting question of whether we can find national leadership with the courage and principled fiber to see us through such dangerous times.

I can think of no more suitable institutions to take the lead than the nation's universities and colleges. Current academic responses to this danger are hopelessly out of date. Questions about affirmative action are being fought out and defeated in the courts and in the political arena on interpretations of the past. As you would expect, in my mind there is no doubt that minorities and women have enormous justice claims on this society, not just for past wrongs, but for current discrimination for which, in many cases, no adequate remedies other than affirmative action exist. Powerful and right as I believe these claims to be, they rest on past injustices rather than on the even more powerful claims the future makes upon us.

There is also the lumbering multifaceted debate about multiculturalism. This battle is littered with the bodies of "dead white males" and of their "victims. The struggle can be reduced to terms that make it seem pretty silly, but the dangers that grow out of virulent ethnocentrism are not at all funny. Many people just cannot see other people or other cultures. They see representations of their own fears and their own needs. They do not try to understand human behavior and motivation because it is more comforting to deal with myths and stereotypes than with the complexities ambiguities and gnarled histories that produce the boiling occurrences that we experience as contemporary life.

It therefore seems to me imperative that we change the debate in the society at large about how our business is to be conducted and why. We must also change the debate inside the academy about what we must teach and why. The essential question here is whether we are to follow the culture as universities did in the 50's when they permitted careers such as those of professors Davis, Markert and Nickerson to be damaged or whether we should try to *lead* the society because our mission is to educate people, most of them citizens, for a future that, thanks to the demographers, we can now see pretty clearly.

The essence of that mission in my view is to *maximize opportunity* and to make vigorous use of educational diversity in order to produce the extraordinarily able citizenry that will be required to guide America through the profound changes coming in the next few decades.

To chart such a course and to engage in such a dialogue will take courage because not everyone sees the same future or takes the same view of the educator's responsibility. Some disagreement with my view is clearly rooted in deep intellectual conviction that this is not the role of universities. Some might grow out of the traditional American optimism that we free and creative people, with the help of our free market, will work things out as we always have. Other opposition will surely be rooted in fear and the need for the crutch of white identity. Finally, there are people who are not about to give up their privileges, whether earned or not. Wherever the opposition comes from, it will be powerful and often bitter. Great courage and tenacity will be required to sustain the side of the argument I am suggesting.

One of the ways we might define our task is to recall the words of the pioneering black historian, Carter G. Woodson, who set out to correct what he called "the miseducation of the Negro." The pathologies lurking just under the tissue of our national civility result from the way we *all* have been "miseducated." It also results from the fact that millions of our fellow citizens are *undereducated* and are therefore easy prey for demagogues.

Not long ago, Michigan's Provost, Dr. Bernard Machen, made a statement about affirmative action that I would have applauded wholeheartedly a few years ago, but think is too narrow today. He said that the top value at Michigan "is a renewed commitment to diversity and informed affirmative action." Michigan's *University Record* went on to report that Machen said that "[While] there is a 'compelling case to be made about the need to prepare our students' for life in the 21st century, the key reason for the U-M 'is an intellectual one,' which he said is defined well by John Stuart Mill in *On Liberty*—'that it is of special benefit to the quality of thought and discourse for many opinions to be expressed.'"

As the *New Yorker* story about the man in the bomber jacket or my observations of blacks whose horizons are crimped by pain and bitterness demonstrate, there are vast and dangerous numbers of Americans who are not prepared either emotionally or intellectually for the changes we face in the 21st century. And many of these people will become parents who will pass their injuries on to their children thus perpetuating our cultural pathologies. So, I would reverse and enlarge Dr. Machen's vision.

> *Our job as citizens and scholars and teachers is to turn out citizens with the emotional and intellectual capacities to "keep" and improve upon our democracy.*

In short, we need to retell the story of human beings in ways that emphasize our membership in the same species and to retell the story of our country in ways that make it clear that however much white domination there has been, the creation of American culture and identity has always been a multi-racial enterprise; *that we have enormous amounts to learn from each other* and that our greatest achievements as a nation lie ahead of us as we struggle to become the first country on the planet where the entirety of the human species is present and fully respected in the polity.

In calling for such a national discourse and such a curriculum, I am not calling for "victim" studies or courses designed narrowly to raise the self-esteem of one group or another. I am seeking ways to include material in our curriculum that seeks to make students more comfortable with their full humanity (with all the existential peril that involves) and with all other kinds of human beings. In addition to revised intellectual content, this would include emotional education to help Americans get through the turbulence of the shifting nature of American identity.

It may help if I give an example of what I mean by emotional education. I learned powerful emotional lessons during the mid and late 1940s in a Grand Rapids high school in which I was, for much of my time there, the only black student in a population of about 1,100. In this time before the Civil Rights Movement, I learned valuable lessons about white people and about myself.

Even though the customs of the times did not constrain whites from expressing belief in their own superiority or their dislike of blacks, I still learned that whites were not supermen and that many of them were quite likeable. I found that some of them were smarter than I, and that lots of them weren't; that some of them were better athletes than I, but many weren't and that while there were plenty of racist bozos, there were a lot of really decent people as well.

In sum, I learned—deep down in my soul—that whites were human and so, indeed, was I. Those lessons undoubtedly accounted for the fact that I later had the confidence here at Michigan to run successfully first for the student government and then for the presidency of my class. Moreover, a number of my old high school friends say that knowing our family was the most powerful lesson they learned during their high school days and that the experience enriched them in wonderful ways.

That would suggest that we must begin to take what we *say* about the benefits of diversity in education seriously. Effective education for American citizenship cannot occur without a richly diverse student body. Every student should be regarded as a potential educational opportunity for every other student and students should be made to understand that concept from the very beginning of their educational experience. Students should be given every opportunity and should be encouraged at every turn to meet, mix and learn with people with different backgrounds from themselves. This effort should include living arrangements, educational exercises in the classroom and extra-curricular activities. To the greatest extent possible, we should make sure that students do not retreat easily into the comfortable, but narrowing, habit of spending all of their time with exactly the same kind of people they spent time with in high school—that is with people from homes, parents and family incomes exactly like their own.

But in order to accomplish that on the campus, we must intervene in the national debate on behalf of providing the broadest possible opportunity and explain clearly that our country's future depends upon it. We educators were citizens before we were intellectuals and somewhere, deep in our souls as American citizens, we all know that we owe a great deal to this country. I think we also know that the imperfections we have accommodated for so long are weakening our nation and sapping the vitality of our democracy. Finally, I think we know that however damaging to the country the silence of my student generation was, our silence or passivity as adult educators in the face of the current threats to our democracy will be infinitely worse.

As the story of Germany in the 20th century tells us, democracy is both precious and perishable. The Founding Fathers expected us to work hard at being citizens and at taking care of our democracy. It has been said that a woman encountered Benjamin Franklin on the street in Philadelphia just after the secret Constitutional Convention had ended.

"What have you made in there, Dr. Franklin?" she is supposed to have asked.

Franklin's reply: "A republic, madam, if you can keep it."

"If you can keep it." Our job as citizens and scholars and teachers is to turn out citizens with the emotional and intellectual capacities to "keep" and improve upon our democracy. The fact is, I learned to think that was my lifetime job when I was a student here back in the 50's. For that lesson above all others, I am deeply grateful to the University of Michigan.

II. Freedom and Responsibilities of the Press in a Democracy

Keeping Our Open Form of Government[1]

John V. R. Bull

Assistant to the editor, Philadelphia Inquirer, *1972– ; born Southampton, NY, 1939; B.A., Lafayette College, 1961; reporter/ city editor,* Easton (PA) Express, *1961–72; Founder, First Amendment Coalition of Pennsylvania, 1977, and president, 1990– ; president, Pennsylvania Society of Newspaper Editors, 1976–77 and 1988–89; president, Pennsylvania Associated Press Managing Editors Association, 1981–82; president, Greater Philadelphia Society of Professional Journalists, 1985–87; executive vice president, New Jersey Press Association, 1996–97; chairman, editor's liaison committee with Pennsylvania State University School of Communications, 1985– ; President, Organization of News Ombudsmen, 1998–99.*

Editors' introduction: John V. R. Bull gave this speech at a rarely held social event in the Four Seasons Hotel, sponsored by the Civil Litigation Section of the Pennsylvania State Bar Association. Some 90 civil litigation lawyers, persons actively involved in courtroom cases, attended. In his address, Bull employed specific examples to show "where free speech and an informed citizenry are in jeopardy." He sought to "build understanding in hopes that lawyers might not always press for confidential products liability settlements, closing courtrooms to the public, doing public business in secrecy." While most persons listened respectfully, one lawyer "tried three times to slug" Bull, objecting to virtually everything he said in the speech.

John V. R. Bull's speech: Looking over the room of distinguished lawyers reminds me of Mark Twain's definition of The Perfect Audience: Intelligent, Inquisitive and Drunk.

Whether you're drunk or sober, I am delighted to speak with you. Since both our professions are on the public firing line more than either of us would like, we need to talk with each other more and understand each other better.

I have no doubt that some of you feel the press asks too many questions and seeks too much information, but we should not be

---

1. Delivered in Philadelphia, Pennsylvania, on March 27, 1997, at 7:00 p.m. Reprinted with permission of John V. R. Bull.

antagonists or opponents in some testosterone power play. At heart, we both are public servants.

And since we are in a virtual dead heat in public popularity polls, sharing the same level of community trust and admiration, we may have to hang together lest we hang separately. And from my perspective, an awful lot of people out there would just love to hang us both!

As you probably know, the Pennsylvania Bar Association and the Pennsylvania Newspaper Publishers Association have done a wonderful thing by forming a joint Bar/Press Committee to explore ways in which we can come to common understandings and avoid confrontations that help neither of our disciplines. Similar committees are being formed in many other states.

So since it seems we may be stuck with each other, I'd like to share some thoughts on issues in which the legal community and the press are often at loggerheads.

Mostly, these involve issues of secrecy, privacy and access to information—problem areas I approach not only as a newspaperman but as a concerned citizen.

This country was founded on the unique idea that its citizens should be educated and informed about how their government operates—or DOESN'T function.

I need not remind you that this country was founded on the unique idea that its citizens should be educated and informed about how their government operates—or DOESN'T function—so they can make intelligent decisions about public policy.

Never mind that "intelligent decisions about public policy" may be an oxymoron, the theory stands as our national ideal.

But both as a newsman and a citizen, I fear that if current trends continue, we will be lucky indeed to keep our open form of government—our democracy—intact much into the next century, for exaggerated fears for personal safety—evidenced through our all-consuming concern for privacy—and the irresistible passion for judicial and governmental secrecy threaten the very foundations of our society.

Frankly, far too many courts seem more interested in cloaking themselves in secrecy, too many governmental agencies on all levels—federal, state and local, particularly school boards—want to operate behind closed doors.

The picture is not *all* black: There are *some* court decisions, *some* administrative directives, even a few legislative actions that go against the trend, but my sense is that the forces of darkness and secrecy are in the ascendancy.

It seems that almost every day we see a new attempt to close our courtrooms to the public, to confirm secret court actions—particularly discovery items, settlements in product liability cases and other suits—in effect, hiding the workings of our legal system from the public.

I hope I'm not overstating the case, but I worry that we may be inching ever-closer to the English Star Chamber proceedings of the Middle Ages.

The same bad impulses are true of many governmental agencies which seem to divulge public records grudgingly—if at all. In too many instances, agencies and governing bodies refuse to give out even the most rudimentary information about their activities, forcing newspapers and broadcasters to sue on behalf of the public for even the most minor information.

At a January meeting of First Amendment lawyers representing Pennsylvania newspapers, one lawyer offered a sad rule-of-thumb, i.e., public officials only release information they are comfortable with. If they don't like it, they just ignore the law and make us fight for every scrap.

Access and privacy outrages abound. I'll mention a few:

Item. In Bucks County, a judge ruled that the Sunshine Law's Public Comment provision does not apply to school boards, meaning that parents can be muzzled from speaking at a public school board meeting. Corrective legislation to overturn that ruling failed.

Item. Members of the Spring-Ford Area School Board in Montgomery County gave themselves new fax machines—*in their homes, at taxpayer expense*—to communicate with each other. Obviously, that means in private.

Item. In New Jersey, the Legislature adopted a bill allowing counties and municipalities to publish ordinances and budgets by title and summary only. No details. No spending amounts. No information.

Item. Here in Philadelphia, District Court Judge Raymond Broderick restrained photographers from *Inside Edition* (which I acknowledge is no paragon of professional virtue) from taking long-distance photographs and using a boom microphone—from a boat in the Intracoastal Waterway—to invade the privacy of U. S. Healthcare officers.

This may be the first time the Intracoastal Waterway has been held to be private property!

Item. Last year Congress passed a law closing off public access to Motor Vehicle records unless individual states pass legislation to Op-Out. Will property tax records be the next category to be closed to the public?

An even bigger threat to public access comes from municipalities contracting out their databases to third parties that buy the governmental information—which at state and local levels can be copyrighted—then repackage it and sell it to the public. At worst, public access to public information may be limited. At best, the public would pay twice for it.

Item. As a consequence of the first O. J. Simpson trial, the issue of cameras in the courtroom is dead—probably for another generation. Even judges who formerly favored cameras have backed away.

The problem as I see it is that the current trend goes against our traditions of openness. Louis Boccardi, president of the Associated Press, observed recently that "public access

Louis Boccardi, president of the Associated Press, observed recently that "public access to independent information is a bulwark against excesses of power."

to independent information is a bulwark against excesses of power." He's absolutely right.

And Peter Brown was quoted in *American Lawyer* as saying: "Too many lawyers have forgotten that the main purpose of the law profession is to serve the public interest." It's very sad if he's right.

Referring to judicial secrecy, a lawyer friend said it succinctly: "All this does is create terrible suspicion and lack of confidence in the legal system. And that's all we have. Without public confidence, the system won't work."

That being said, I am the first to recognize that public perception of the "news media"—a term that usually applies more to television than newspapers, although newspapers are certainly included—plays a major role in how much access the press is given.

There have been several horrible cases in the past year that prompt extreme concern. In some cases, we in the "media" have not exactly covered ourselves with glory, but in others we are getting blamed for the actions of other people or institutions.

These cases which I'll mention briefly are having a major Chilling Effect on press reporting in general—and investigative reporting in particular.

Some examples:

- The Richard Jewell case in Atlanta in which NBC and CNN settled a threatened libel suit *even before* a claim was filed in the Olympics park bombing. Jewell's lawyers *have* sued the *Atlanta Journal-Constitution.*

The paper claims it got its information from FBI and local police sources, so I don't know whether it went too far in identifying Jewell as a suspect or whether it correctly asserted that Jewell fit the FBI's "profile" of the bomber.

But from this distance, it does seem that the paper joined in a disgusting media "frenzy"—fueled in part by an FBI press conference and by quotes from Piedmont College officials where Jewell formerly worked.

Nonetheless, it seems that the press is being held to account for reporting the views of law enforcement officials. Do we really think that that kind of coverage is out-of-bounds, particularly in the context of the public outrage—and fear—surrounding the bombing?

- Even more troubling is the $5.5 million award against ABC for fraud and trespass in the Food Lion supermarket case.

I'm not about to defend ABC's smarmy methods, apparently driven by the network's need for film—something newspapers don't need, I remind you.

But that's a far cry from awarding $5.5 million which was, in effect, a penalty for what Jane Kirtley, editor of *The News*

Media and the Law, called "newsgathering that offends someone's standard of taste."

Moreover, if its report of selling bad meat was accurate, ABC was punished for telling the truth—a circumstance that stands logic and libel laws on their head.

There's also a serious danger that the verdict will invite similar lawsuits designed to intimidate and dissuade legitimate investigation into corporate operations and practices. The Chilling Effect is very, very real.

While it certainly is legitimate to debate whether ABC's conduct crossed an ethical line, a court is not an ethics tribunal and the courtroom is not the place for such a discussion.

"If the laws of trespass and fraud can be used against journalists without the leavening influence of the First Amendment," Kirtley correctly observes, "all investigative reporting is at risk."

Stuart Taylor Jr., a legal columnist for *The American Lawyer* magazine, agrees that there was nothing "so malicious or oppressive about ABC's conduct as to warrant a punitive award."

"ABC did not kill or batter anyone," Taylor wrote. "It did not defraud anyone of money or property. It did not break and enter. It did not invade the privacy of anyone's home or eavesdrop on private conversations or publish intimate details of anyone's life. It was not found to have defamed anyone or to have broadcast anything inaccurate or unfair."

- *The Dallas Morning News*'s publication of Timothy McVeigh's alleged confession in the Oklahoma bombing case also is troubling, but the situation is too murky to yet make a judgment as to the newspaper's ethical decision.

Sometimes there is good reason to withhold information, but that should not be done lightly.

McVeigh's lawyer is telling one story after another; I even watched a rather far-fetched late night television discussion Sunday on whether the "confession" was made-up and deliberately leaked by McVeigh's lawyer to taint the jury pool.

But the issue really isn't whether the *Morning News* had the right to print information from documents that might have been stolen, for since the 1971 Pentagon Papers case, a newspaper's right to print such documents has not been in serious question.

The more debatable issues are whether the story will jeopardize McVeigh's ability to get a fair trial—the classic clash of First and Sixth Amendments—and the responsibility of newspapers to society.

While no one at this point knows the source of the "confession" document, it seems clear that *any* confession by McVeigh would be of great public interest, certainly to the families of the hundreds of victims.

Sometimes there is good reason to withhold information, but that should not be done lightly. While newspapers have been known to hold back—usually only briefly—that danger is that that could imperil the paper's credibility with readers who might wonder what *other* information is being withheld—and for whose benefit.

Regardless, I don't accept for one minute the contention that publication means that McVeigh cannot get a fair trial. As you know far better than I, there are ample remedies in the law to ensure a fair and impartial trial—even if the alleged "confession" turns out to be true.

The lamentation we are now hearing about a tainted jury pool is baloney. If Patty Hearst, John Erlichman, Bob Haldeman, John Mitchell and O. J. Simpson could get a fair trial, so can Timothy McVeigh.

Locally, we had two very troubling criminal cases last year.

- The disappearance and suspected murder of Anne Marie Fahey of Wilmington in which the FBI—showing a callous disregard for individual rights—named a Delaware lawyer as the sole suspect in Anne Marie's death. Bad enough he's a lawyer, but even now he has been charged with exactly Nothing.

- The murder of Amy Willard in which law enforcement officers publicly identified a young Main Line man as their suspect—and then never charged him.

In both cases, law enforcement vastly overstepped the bounds of fairness. And we in the press feel used. Unfortunately, it is virtually impossible to ignore—to NOT report—what police are saying at press conferences: The public outcry would be enormous—and entirely justified.

- In the JonBenet Ramsey case, law authorities are doing the right thing: They simply are not talking publicly. More law enforcement agencies should follow that course.

There's one other subject of vital importance I'd like to quickly touch upon before closing and that is the proliferation of mind-boggling libel judgments and their chilling effect on gathering and reporting the news.

Just last week, a jury ordered Dow Jones to pay $222.7 million—the largest libel judgment in U. S. history—to a Houston bond firm that claimed it was forced out of business by a story in the *Wall Street Journal*.

That award dwarfed a $58 million judgment imposed on the A. H. Belo Corp., owner of the *Dallas Morning News*.

Even without these two massive judgments, the average libel award last year was $2.8 million—more than double the previous year.

And even though nearly half of all libel awards are reversed, the cost of fighting these lawsuits is virtually prohibitive to all but the wealthiest—or most dedicated—newspaper or broadcaster. And even then, the press lost 10 out of 14 trials last year.

All of this means that the ability of the press to gather and report the news is under attack as never before. It means that the public's access to information that might protect the general welfare or educate citizens is in jeopardy.

We as citizens need to consider whether we really do believe in freedom of speech and press. There are many days when I think we really don't.

The Bottom Line is that there is a price to pay for democracy—for free speech and press—and that is that we have to be willing to tolerate speech that is offensive, stupid, insulting, even just plain wrong. The Supreme Court called it "robust debate."

Remember that when our Founding Fathers wrote the Bill of Rights, they didn't do it in a vacuum, but in a wild, freewheeling atmosphere of pamphleteering and slanderous attacks on individuals on all sides.

And yet, they preferred that cacophony of voices, those frenzied assaults on personal dignity and honor to the alternative—the deafening silence of controlled thought and speech.

There ARE places, you know, where that silence is institutionalized. They are called dictatorships.

Television and Democracy[2]

Newton N. Minow

Partner, Sidley & Austin, Chicago, IL, 1965– ; Annenberg Professor of Communications, Law and Policy, Northwestern University, 1987– ; born Milwaukee, WI, January 17, 1926; B.S., 1949, and J.D., 1950, Northwestern University; U.S. Army, China-Burma-India theater, 1944–46; associate, Mayer, Mayer, Austrian & Platt (later Mayer, Brown & Platt), 1950–51 and 1953–55; law clerk to Chief Justice Fred M. Vinson, U. S. Supreme Court, 1951–52; administrative assistant to Governor Adlai E. Stevenson, Illinois, 1952–53; partner, Stevenson, Rifkind & Wirtz, 1955–61; chairman, Federal Communications Commission, 1961–63; executive vice president, general counsel and director, Encyclopaedia Britannica, Inc., 1963–65; John Henry Wigmore Award, Northwestern University School of Law, 1950; George Foster Peabody Broadcasting Award, 1962; Ralph Lowell Public Broadcasting Award, 1982; elected fellow, American Academy of Arts & Sciences, 1989; Abraham Lincoln Centre Humanitarian Service Award, 1990; author, Equal Time: The Private Broadcaster and the Public Interest *(1964); co-author,* Presidential Television *(1973); co-author,* For Great Debates *(1987); author,* How Vast the Wasteland Now *(1991); co-author,* Abandoned in the Wasteland: Children, Television and the First Amendment *(1995)*

Editors' introduction: Newton N. Minow spoke to 750 successful Chicago business and civic leaders in the Palmer House Hotel at a regular meeting of the Economic Club. His purpose was to call attention to how television has "create[d] for us . . . a dictatorship of the dollar." Minow was "satisfied with the response of the audience in the room," but not pleased "that the issues were not picked up in national debate."

Newton N. Minow's speech: Campaign spending is as old as the republic. When George Washington ran for the Virginia House of Burgesses in 1757, his total campaign expenditures, in the form of "good cheer," came to "28 gallons of rum, 50 gallons of rum punch, 34 gallons of wine, 36 gallons of beer, and two gallons of cider royal."

Today, the era of good cheer is gone. For four decades now, campaign expenditures have been driven relentlessly upward by one thing: television. In 1960, in what would be the first

2. Delivered in Chicago, Illinois, on April 16, 1997, at 8:00 p.m. Reprinted with permission of Newton N. Minow.

presidential campaign to make wide use of television, Democrats and Republicans together spent $14.2 million on radio and television commercials. In 1996, candidates for federal office spent more than 128 times that amount on television and radio commercials, an estimated $1.8 billion.

After the presidential campaign scandals of 1972, Congress tried in 1974 to end the suitcases of cash which sloshed around campaigns in return for favors. But as we now know—and continue to learn—the 1974 campaign reform law has failed to solve the problem.

In the 1996 federal elections, the campaign finance laws were bent beyond recognition. We learned about the availability of the Lincoln bedroom to major contributors; the President's meeting with a convicted stock swindler, a Chinese arms merchant, and others of dubious background and intention; the Vice President's raising campaign cash at a Buddhist temple; and the Republicans soliciting "season ticket holders," donors of 250,000 who hoped for special treatment for their special interests, including access to important government officials. Add don't forget Congressional censure of Newt Gingrich for mixing campaign cash with his television program. The only bi-partisan agreement in Washington these days is on one proposition: "Show me the money!"

Strict limits on campaign contributions imposed by the 1974 Act were washed away this year in a flood of "soft money," donations not limited by law because of the foolish fiction that such money was not used to support or oppose particular candidates. Together, the two parties collected $88 million in soft money in 1992; last year they multiplied this by three—to $263.5 million.

Interest groups ranging from the AFL-CIO to the U.S. Chamber of Commerce bathed in another form of soft money, which they used to broadcast so-called "issue" commercials. Theoretically, at least, issue commercials are not supposed to advance or oppose anyone's candidacy, and so are exempt from the 1974 law's requirement of full disclosure of who contributes money and how that money gets spent.

How did this happen? Dick Morris claims the credit for himself. After the 1994 Republican Congressional victory, Morris developed the Democrats' 1995 and 1996 campaign strategy: take control of the airwaves early, before the Republicans could pick their candidate—and never let up. To pursue this strategy, the Democratic National Committee and the Clinton-Gore campaign spent an estimated $1 million to $2 million per week.

On October 13, 1995, President Clinton signed the Federal Elections Commission vow that in return for public financing, he would spend no more than $37 million in privately raised funds during the upcoming primary season. That

Thomas Jefferson, James Madison, and Benjamin Franklin would be horrified to learn how we have abused the democratic process they bequeathed to us.

same morning, a White House coffee for large donors to the Democratic National Committee began what would soon become a habit. The money raised from that event and others like it eventually allowed the DNC to spend an additional $44 million for television ads. Because so many of those commercials were issue ads, federal contribution caps did not apply. Donors to the cause, including corporations and labor unions, both of which are barred by law from giving money directly to a candidate, spent freely, without accountability.

The Republicans did even more. By election day, the Republican National Committee had raised more money than the DNC. The Party solicited record contributions from telecommunications, tobacco and pharmaceutical companies, enough to pay for $18 million in television advertising between May 1996 and the GOP convention in August. They, too, pursued the "issue advertisement" strategy. One of the RNC's more controversial issue advertisements was a 60-second spot with 56 seconds of biographical material about Senator Dole and 4 seconds of issues. The RNC insisted this was not a plug for Dole and so was within the federal election guidelines.

Not only did Democrats and Republicans take advantage of the law, so did countless organizations with a cause and the ability to finance it. Millions of dollars in cash swept through House and Senate elections in the states, turning campaigns into ideological contests with little or no relevance to local voters. Some candidates for Congress discovered ads for the first time on radio and television—as many as 300 a day in their districts, either attacking or favoring them—but had no idea where the ads had come from, or who had paid for them.

Former Israeli Prime Minister Shimon Peres once said that "television has a good side and a bad side. The good side," Peres said, "is that television makes dictatorship impossible. The bad side is that it makes democracy unbearable."

Tonight, I suggest we amend Mr. Peres' observation, in two respects. First, television does not necessarily make democracy unbearable. At its best, television makes democracy stronger by opening the workings of government to the public. In our own country, whether television's cameras are on the floor of Congress, in a courtroom in Los Angeles, or at a Presidential Debate, they provide unique opportunities for the public to see and to understand how their government works—and, just as importantly, where it fails.

At its worst, however, television can become a tool of dictatorship. In any country that suffers a coup, the nation's television and radio broadcast facilities are the very first institutions to come under siege. Rulers and rebels alike know that whoever controls the airwaves controls the country.

In our country, we have allowed television, the greatest instrument of communication in history, to create for us a different kind of dictatorship—a dictatorship of the dollar. In the 1996 elections, total expenditures on all federal races came to approximately $2.1 billion, of which $1.8 billion was spent to buy broadcast TV time! Thus, almost $9 out of $10 went to buy time on radio and television. Fund-raising, not governing, became the principal business of our elected officials. Our best public officials are leaving public service, sick and tired of the current system. Al Hunt in *The Wall Street Journal* quotes a model of integrity, Democratic Congressman Lee Hamilton (Chairman of the House Foreign Affairs Committee) when he announced this year that he would not run for re-election. "My colleagues talk about money constantly. The conversation today among members of Congress is so frequently on the topic of money: money, money, money, and the money chase. Gosh, I don't think I ever heard it when I first came here."

The rest of the world looks with horror at our national campaigns. They are too long, they are too negative, they constantly make personal attacks on the opposition, they are exercises in deception, they turn the voters off and away from the voting booth. In 1996, fewer than half the nation's registered voters even bothered to go to the polls, the second lowest turnout since 1824.

By allowing unlimited political advertising on television and radio, the United States stands almost alone in the world. Only three countries do not require some form of free broadcast time for candidates in national election campaigns. They are Malaysia, Taiwan, and the United States. Thomas Jefferson, James Madison, and Benjamin Franklin would be horrified to learn how we have abused the democratic process they bequeathed to us. Television authorities in Great Britain, France, the Netherlands, and Japan ban political advertising from the airwaves entirely. In England, the law prohibits advertisements by any person or organization that is "wholly or mainly of a . . . political nature" or "directed towards any political end." Instead, British law provides free television time to political parties to air their own programs on important public issues.

Most of the world's democratic nations which do allow candidates to buy advertising time—such as Australia, Canada, Germany, and Sweden—also provide free time to candidates and their parties. Unlike our own country, these democracies do not believe the only way to provide political broadcast time is to sell it.

As you know, there are many proposals in Congress and elsewhere to "reform" campaign finance. Most proposals focus on the supply side of the problem: on who gives the money, how much they can give, and for what purpose. There are proposals to limit contributions, to prohibit "soft

"Money in politics is like water running downhill; it will always find its way . . ."
—**Jonathan Alter, Newsweek**

money", to prohibit contributions from labor unions and corporations, to raise the limit on individual contributions, to curb spending on behalf of candidates by independent organizations, to prohibit PACS, to encourage candidates voluntarily to limit spending, to speed up disclosure of contributors and their contributions, to use public money to pay for campaigns, and to amend the Constitution of the United States. Former Senator Howard Baker suggests that if you can't vote for a candidate, you can't contribute to the candidate.

There are a lot of good ideas—and some bad ideas—being discussed and debated. I do not favor limiting individual contributions, but I do favor immediate public disclosure of contributions, even before checks are cashed. I favor ending "soft money," PACs, contributions from unions and corporations, and ending phony outside expenditures unless they are truly independent and not developed in concert with candidates and their campaigns. But dealing only with the supply side of the equation will not work so long as demand exists. I agree with a young journalist from Chicago, *Newsweek's* Jonathan Alter, who writes, "money in politics is like water running downhill; it will always find its way . . ."

So, this evening, my focus is exclusively on the demand side of the equation—which has received little attention in the current debates. And I will focus—ruthlessly focus—on one specific public policy decision that our country will soon make on the relationship of television and political campaigns.

Let us focus on four words: "public interest" and "digital television". You've been hearing a lot about digital television lately—but not much about the public interest.

Last year, Congress passed and the President signed the 1996 Telecommunications Act. Under the new law, broadcasters are eligible to receive new digital television channels. Congress directed that, unlike other telecommunications service providers, broadcasters do not have to pay for their new channels. They get them free. Digital transmission will allow broadcasters to offer multiple channels instead of one, and if they wish, to use those extra channels for services such as data transmission, paging services, or pay-per-view movies. Estimates of the value of these new digital channels range from $30 billion to $70 billion.

Why should broadcasters receive this spectrum, these digital channels, free? This was the question former Senate Majority Leader Bob Dole put to his colleagues on the Senate floor last year before the law was passed. Senator Dole said: "Spectrum is just as much a national resource as our nationts forests. That means it belongs to every American equally. No more, no less. If someone wants to use our resources, then we should be fairly compensated."

Should broadcasters have specific public-service obligations in return for their use of a big slice of the publicly owned spectrum—property now known to be worth many billions of dollars?

Last month, former Senator Dole wrote in the *New York Times*: "We don't give away trees to newspaper publishers. Why should we give away more airwaves to broadcasters?" Senator Dole wants broadcasters to pay for spectrum, just like everybody else. Why should we give away a national resource that could be worth as much as $70 billion?

Senator John McCain, Republican Chairman of the Senate Commerce Committee, said the spectrum is "the most valuable asset that I know of in America today. Perhaps in the world today."

Congress, however, rejected that advice, and decided to give the spectrum away for free. The Federal Communications Commission began to award digital spectrum assignments to broadcasters on April 3rd. However, under the law, including recent emphasis in the 1996 Telecommunications Act, the FCC made it plain that those receiving digital channels are obligated to serve the public interest. So the question before us is this: What should be the public interest obligations of digital broadcasters?

On March 11, President Clinton announced that he will soon appoint a Presidential Commission to advise him, the Congress, and the Federal Communications Commission on this question. Should broadcasters have specific public-service obligations in return for their use of a big slice of the publicly owned spectrum—property now known to be worth many billions of dollars?

I have been deeply involved in these issues for many years. In 1969, I served as chairman of a bi-partisan Commission for the Twentieth Century Fund on Campaign Costs in the Electronic Era. Over the decades, I have testified in Congress many times on these issues, and written extensively on them.

Based on that experience, I suggest the time has come to do some thinking outside the box, outside conventional approaches, and outside the Beltway.

We can begin by examining the British system of using broadcasting in political campaigns in the public interest. The British system is simple and direct. Political parties are granted, by law, free time on radio and television in the three or four week period before the election. The parties have complete freedom to make their cases; smaller parties receive time on an equitable basis. This year, for the first time, there will also be debates between the leaders of the political parties. There is no sale or purchase of broadcast time—no money is involved. The campaign is mercifully short, and the voters are well informed. Indeed, because the campaign programs are simulcast on all channels, there is ample political discussion for the voters.

We should connect the dots: digital television and public interest. We should condition the awarding of digital broad-

As Justice Stevens emphasized, as long as the law does not regulate the content of speech rather than the structure of the market, the law is consistent with the First Amendment.

cast licenses on a broadcaster's commitment to provide free time and not sell time.

People who understand television well—and make their living from it—like this idea. Don Hewitt (producer of *60 Minutes* on CBS) and Reuven Frank (former President of NBC News) advocate an end to buying and selling political commercials. Barry Diller (formerly of ABC and Fox Television) favors specified free time for candidates during campaigns as part of campaign reform.

There are, of course, many other important policy questions about free time. I have addressed Presidential elections only, not Congressional elections, not primaries, not state and local elections. This is to focus our analysis on the basic principle: No citizen has a constitutional right to buy or sell our natural resources—land, minerals, water, trees, or broadcast spectrum--without Congressional approval. Just as Congress has the authority to clean up our natural environment, it has the authority under our Constitution to clean up the current political broadcasting mess we have inflicted on our republic. Once that principle is established, we can analyze and debate many other vital questions about how to apply that fundamental concept fairly to our political process.

What about the First Amendment? The First Amendment is the highest value and treasure in our life. As Judge Learned Hand said so well, "We have staked upon it our all."

First, there is the issue of whether Congress can constitutionally require broadcasters to give free time contemplated by this approach. In resolving that issue, let us listen again to Senator McCain—a courageous man who suffered four years of torture as a war prisoner in Vietnam—four years to reflect on democracy and freedom. Here's Senator McCain:

"Let me go back to the First Amendment thing. What the broadcasters fail to see, in my view, is that they agree to act in the public interest when they use an asset that is owned by the American public. That's what makes them different from a newspaper or a magazine. I have never been one who believes in government intervention, but I also believe that when you agree to act in the public interest—and no one forced them to do that—you are then obligated to carry out some of those obligations . . . If I want to start a newspaper, I buy a printing press and [get] a bunch of people and we start selling newspapers on the street. If I want to start a television station, I've got to get a broadcasting license. And that broadcasting license entails my use of something that's owned by the American public. So I reject the thesis that the broadcasters have no obligation. And if they believe that there is no obligation, then they shouldn't sign the statement that says they agree to act in the public interest. Don't sign it, OK?"

Senator McCain has accurately described the public trustee concept for broadcasting, found to be constitutional by the

Politicians sell access to something we own: the government. Broadcasters sell access to something we own: the public airwaves. Both do so, they tell us, in our name.

Supreme Court repeatedly, in 1943, 1969, 1993, and again on March 31 this year. Indeed, the issue here is not free time, but the *voters'* time. Professor Cass Sunstein, the distinguished and respected First Amendment scholar at the University of Chicago Law School, writes: "Requiring free air time for candidates, given constitutional history and aspirations, is fully consistent with the basic goals of the First Amendment. The free speech principle is, above all, about democratic self-government."

Then there is the second issue. Could Congress at the same time lawfully say to the candidates, "You have been given a generous, free opportunity to reach the electorate over the most powerful medium, broadcasting, to say, without interference, whatever you want. As a condition of accepting that offer, you will not buy further time on this medium. For experience has shown that with such purchases comes the drive to raise great sums of money, with all its abuses and detriments to sound governance."

I believe Congress could do these things, and that they would be constitutional because, in the current language of the Supreme Court, such a law would be "content neutral." As Justice Stevens emphasized, as long as the law does not regulate the content of speech rather than the structure of the market, the law is consistent with the First Amendment. I believe Congress could go even further and constitutionally prohibit broadcasters from selling time for political purposes. Congress has already passed the Equal Time law and a law guaranteeing candidates the right to buy time at the broadcasters' lowest rate. Both have been held constitutional by the courts. Banning cigarette commercials on television has been held constitutional in light of the danger to health and broadcasters' public interest obligations. Congress should debate whether our current system of buying and selling broadcast time is a grave danger to our national health. I would happily see these reforms tested at the Supreme Court.

Three years from now, we will have entered a new millennium and a new presidential campaign season. By then, we will also be into the era of new digital television. Almost 50 years ago, E. B. White saw a flickering, experimental television demonstration and wrote, "We shall stand or fall by television—of that I am sure . . . I believe television is going to be the test of the modern world, and that in this new opportunity to see beyond the range of our vision, we shall discover either a new and unbearable disturbance to the general peace, or a saving radiance in the sky."

Instead of a saving radiance in the sky, we now have a colossal irony. Politicians sell access to something *we* own: the government. Broadcasters sell access to something *we* own: the public airwaves. Both do so, they tell us, in our name. By creating this system of selling and buying access, we have a campaign system that makes good people do bad things and bad people do worse things, a system that we do not want, that corrupts and trivializes public discourse, and that we have the power and the duty—a last chance—to change.

Will we change? I leave you with a story President Kennedy told a week before he was killed. The story was about French Marshal Louis Lyautey, who walked one morning through his garden with his gardener. He stopped at a certain point and asked the gardener to plant a tree there the next morning. The gardener said, "But the tree will not bloom for one hundred years!" The Marshal looked at the gardener and replied, "In that case, you had better plant it this afternoon."

The Sins of the Press[3]

Anthony Lewis

Editorial columnist, New York Times, *1969– ; born New York, NY, March 27, 1927; B.A., Harvard University, 1948; deskman, Sunday department,* New York Times, *1948–52; reporter,* Washington Daily News, *1952–55; as reporter, Washington, D.C., bureau of* New York Times, *1955–64, covered Supreme Court, Justice Department, and government's handling of civil rights movement; Nieman Fellow, Harvard Law School, 1956–57; chief of* New York Times *London bureau, 1964–72; based in Boston from 1973; author,* Gideon's Trumpet *(1964);* Portrait of a Decade: The Second American Revolution *(1964);* Make No Law: The Sullivan Case and the First Amendment *(1991); Pulitzer Prize for national reporting, 1955, 1963; lecturer on law at Harvard University, 1974–89; James Madison Visiting Professor at Columbia University, 1983–.*

Editors' introduction: Anthony Lewis gave this Sibley Lecture in the chapel at the University of Georgia, Athens, to students, faculty, and local citizens. Sponsored by the University of Georgia Law School, the Sibley Lecture Series brings outstanding legal scholars to the campus. In his address, Lewis explored "how wisely" the press has "used the power given by freedom."

There you have the classic justification for silencing expression: that a speech or publication has a dangerous tendency—that it may threaten the existing order.

Anthony Lewis's speech: Professor Larson, ladies and gentlemen, it is an honor to be giving the Sibley Lecture, and a pleasure to be back at the University of Georgia. I was first here in a very different time—a different world, really. It was 1961, and I was covering the Justice Department in Washington for *The New York Times*. Robert Kennedy was attorney general. On May 6 he came to the University of Georgia to make a Law Day speech at the Law School. His subject was civil rights: a subject that aroused emotions and violent conflict difficult to imagine now. Seven years after the Supreme Court's decision in *Brown v. Board of Education*, the Deep South's political leaders were committed to resisting its implementation. Not one public school in the region had been desegregated, and the process had barely begun in public universities. This university had admitted its first two black students four months before; one of them, Charlayne Hunter, was in the audience for Robert Kennedy as a journalist. The attorney general spoke forcefully about the need for

---

3. Delivered at the University of Georgia, Athens, on March 11, 1998, at 3:30 p.m. Reprinted with permission of Anthony Lewis.

equal rights for white and black Americans. The state's politicians stayed away, but I reported that the audience responded to the speech with enthusiastic applause.

This country has come a long way in race relations since 1961, especially the South. It is important to remember that, even as we are aware of the discrimination and disadvantage that remain.

But my subject today is the press. Its faults—its sins, if you will—are very much in people's minds right now because of the way newspapers and magazines and broadcasters and strange new non-journalists on the Internet have covered the story of President Clinton's alleged affair with Monica Lewinsky. The lurid coverage has been seen by some of us in the business as a depressing fall from the highest tradition of the press in this country, one that goes back to the First Amendment, added to the Constitution in 1791.

James Madison, the principal author of the First Amendment, said it was necessary to protect the press's freedom because it played a different role in this country from others. In the United States, he said, "the people, not the government, possess the absolute sovereignty." That was "altogether different" from Britain, and it followed that the press must have "a different degree of freedom" in order to inform the sovereign people about the government they had chosen. The American press, Madison said, must be free to "canvass the merits and measures of public men."

That seems unarguable to us now. We expect the press to challenge those who hold power. We are used to "a cantankerous press, an obstinate press, A ubiquitous press"—the words used by Judge Murray Gurfein when in 1971 he rejected the Nixon Administration's attempt to stop *The New York Times* from publishing the Pentagon Papers, the secret history of the Vietnam War.

But we should not fool ourselves into believing that Madison's view of freedom of the press has prevailed throughout American history. That is not true: not at all. It has taken a long struggle, in law and in public opinion, to establish the Madisonian position. Indeed, the very words I quoted from Madison were used by him to attack a measure designed to silence the press—designed and vigorously used to that end. It was the Sedition Act of 1798, which made it a crime to publish false criticism of the President or the Government. The President at the time was John Adams, a Federalist; and the Federalist Party controlled Congress. The statute did not forbid criticism of the Vice President: Thomas Jefferson, who led the opposition that eventually became the Democratic Party. In short, the Sedition Act was a highly political piece of legislation. Its main purpose was to suppress pro-Jefferson newspapers in the run-up to the election of the year 1800, when Jefferson was to run against Adams.

Editors and publishers of the leading Jeffersonian papers were in fact prosecuted under the Sedition Act. They were convicted, on grounds that would strike anyone today as simply amazing. Charles Holt, publisher of the New London, Connecticut, *Bee*, was convicted of sedition for describing the army proposed by President Adams as a "standing army" instead of what Adams had called it, "provisional." For that seditious libel of the President, Holt was sentenced to three months in prison and a fine of $200, a substantial sum in those days. Thomas Cooper, editor of a Pennsylvania paper, the *Sunbury and Northumberland Gazette*, was convicted for having said of President Adams: "Even those who doubted his capacity thought well of his intentions." Justice Samuel Chase of the Supreme Court, who presided at the trial as a circuit judge, called Cooper's words "the boldest attempt I have known to poison the minds of the people . . . This publication is evidently intended to mislead the ignorant and inflame their minds against the President and influence their votes in the next election." Cooper was sentenced to six months in prison and a fine of $400.

The constitutionality of the Sedition Act was never tested in the Supreme Court before it expired, on Inauguration Day 1801. Jefferson, who had defeated Adams, said he regarded the law as a constitutional "nullity," and he pardoned all those who had been convicted under it. But James Madison's view of the press's great function as a corrective mechanism in a democracy had not yet taken hold, in law *or* public opinion.

The danger faced by an editor with strong beliefs was demonstrated in the 1830s. Elijah Parish Lovejoy was a minister who published a religious newspaper in St. Louis and used it to call for the abolition of slavery. A mob wrecked his press, so he moved across the Mississippi to Alton, in the free state of Illinois. But Alton was no more tolerant of an anti-slavery newspaper. Three times a mob threw Lovejoy's press into the river. He bought a fourth press and paid for his determination with his life. This time the mob destroyed the press and killed Lovejoy.

Intolerance for anti-slavery views was not limited to that part of the country. Three weeks after Lovejoy's murder a leading Boston minister, William Ellery Channing, planned to hold a protest meeting in Faneuil Hall, the building where Sam Adams and other American patriots had spoken against British tyranny before the Revolution. But the city authorities refused permission for the meeting, saying that it would be "inexpedient" for Faneuil Hall to be used by "any party who have taken a side upon a highly exciting and warmly contested question." So much for Sam Adams and the other revolutionaries! The Massachusetts Attorney General, James Austin, went so far as to defend the mob suppression of Lovejoy's paper. "Satisfy a people that their lives are in dan-

Some may regard that phrase—the conscience of journalism—as an oxymoron.

ger by the instrumentality of the press," he said, "and the people will act."

There you have the classic justification for silencing expression: that a speech or publication has a dangerous tendency—that it may threaten the existing order. Exactly that argument is used around the world nowadays to suppress critics of the regime. Governments from Croatia to Mexico have prosecuted editors and reporters for publishing articles that made officials look bad.

A century after Elijah Lovejoy's martyrdom, a newspaper was suppressed by judges in Minnesota for publishing nasty attacks on political leaders. *The Saturday Press*, a weekly, accused officials of having ties to gangsters. It was no doubt a scurrilous paper; its editor, Jay M. Near, was a virulent anti-Semite. But the United States Supreme Court held that could not, constitutionally, justify shutting *The Saturday Press* down. It was a prior restraint disfavored by the First Amendment, the Court said, adding in an echo of Madison that a vigilant press was needed to look out for wrongdoing in government. And now a footnote. Many years later Fred Friendly, the great television documentary producer who died just the other day, wrote a book on the case of *Near v. Minnesota*. He was talking about it in the dining room of the Ford Foundation and was overheard by Irving Shapiro, then chairman of the DuPont Company. Shapiro came over and said, "I knew Jay Near." His father ran a dry cleaning store in Minneapolis. Gangsters demanded he pay protection money; when he refused, they threw acid on the clothes. The established Minneapolis newspapers did not report the story. But Jay Near came around to the store, spoke with the Shapiros—father and son—and published a story that led to the prosecution and conviction of the gangsters. So even a scurvy newspaper may perform the Madisonian function.

But it was not until our own time that Madison's understanding was wholly embraced by our constitutional law. It happened in a case that arose out of the civil rights struggle in the South. On March 29, 1960, supporters of Dr. Martin Luther King Jr. placed a full-page advertisement in *The New York Times* under the headline "Heed Their Rising Voices." The ad described brutal tactics used by segregationist officials against the civil rights movement. It named no names. But a city commissioner of Montgomery, Alabama, L. B. Sullivan, sued *The Times* for libel, claiming that statements in the ad about police brutality in Montgomery had injured his reputation because the police were under his jurisdiction. (Justice Hugo L. Black of the Supreme Court, who came from Alabama, said later that if anyone in Commissioner Sullivan's community had seen the advertisement, his reputation there was probably enhanced.)

The libel suit was tried by an all-white jury and a judge, Walter B. Jones, who was a great fan of the Confederacy; on

Reliance on unidentified sources is in general a dangerous practice, one that I think should be reserved for the most exigent occasions.

the anniversary of its founding, he dressed the jurors in his courtroom in Confederate military uniforms. The jury awarded Commissioner Sullivan all the damages he had sought: $500,000, at that point the largest libel judgment in Alabama history. Other officials, including the Governor of Alabama, also sued over the advertisement. In the next case that went to trial, the plaintiff was also awarded all he had claimed. *The Times* was facing damages totaling $2,500,000, enough to put the paper out of business in those days. And others began suing *The Times*, broadcasters and magazines over *news* reports on the civil rights movement. Officials who wanted to maintain the status quo thought they had found a weapon to keep the interfering national press out of the South. And it was a powerful weapon. Most Americans did not know the indignities and cruelties inflicted on blacks. Dr. King's whole strategy was to awake them to the realities by his protests, and thus to build pressure for change. Shut off press coverage, and you would have broken the strategy. But it did not work.

In 1964, in the case of *New York Times vs. Sullivan*, the Supreme Court set aside Commissioner Sullivan's judgment. It held that a public official may not win damages for a supposedly damaging publication about him unless it was deliberately or recklessly false. Justice Brennan, quoting Madison's attack on the Sedition Act of 1798, said "the central meaning of the First Amendment" was the right to criticize officials.

It was a great victory for Madison, embodying as it did his vision of the press as the instrument that would tell the citizens of a republic what their governors were doing. And the Madisonian system, freed from legal threats, worked exactly as it was supposed to. The American public saw the realities of state-enforced racism, did not like them and pressed for change. Congress passed civil rights laws that transformed political life in the South.

The Sullivan case established the meaning of First Amendment freedom as we understand it today. Americans can criticize the holders of power harshly without fear of the criminal law. Just about everyone understands that, except perhaps Kenneth Starr. The universality of the understanding was demonstrated by the negative public reaction when Mr. Starr brought a White House assistant, Sidney Blumenthal, before a grand jury to be questioned about whether he had spread mistaken criticism of Mr. Starr's office.

The press in particular has benefited from the broad freedom defined by *New York Times v. Sullivan*. We in the business are much less likely now to rely on the press-release version of events. We look deeper, challenge official truths. We seek out corruption.

The question is how wisely we have used the power given by freedom. Have we played the role that Madison envis-

"News organizations that had the least facts and the weakest sourcing tended to pretend that they knew the most."—Tom Rosensfeil, Committee of Concerned Journalists

aged, as guardians of democracy? Or have we become gossip-mongers, driven by a desire for larger audiences?

Even before Monica Lewinsky became a household name, the questions had been nagging at the conscience of journalism. Some may regard that phrase—the conscience of journalism—as an oxymoron. But many journalists have plainly been troubled by our performance as a profession. There has been an extraordinary amount of self-examination by the press. The American Society of Newspaper Editors set up a study to try to find out why we have lost credibility, as surveys show. A Committee of Concerned Journalists was formed to look into what has gone wrong. James Fallows, a respected correspondent who is now editor of *U.S. News and World Report*, published a book entitled *Breaking the News: How the Media Undermine American Democracy.* All that before Monica Lewinsky.

You can report any fantastic rumor and just add 'if true.'

But the great White House sex scandal, or perhaps not so great, has produced the most intense criticism of press behavior in memory. And again, much of it comes from within the profession. The March issue of the *American Journalism Review* has a report on the press's handling of the Clinton-Lewinsky story, under the headline "Standards Are the First Casualty." The subhead says: "Once again coverage of a mega-story was dominated by rumor, innuendo, undersourced stories and snap judgments." I think that is an example of something rather rare in journalism: understatement.

When the story broke, on January 21, there was a rush to judgment. Reports on television, in newspapers and in magazines had the fateful tone of the press at its most pompous. President Clinton faced a charge of perjury, we were told. Impeachment loomed. On CNN, Wolf Blitzer said high White House advisers were discussing resignation. On the ABC television Sunday show, "This Week," the panelists opined that the scandal would overwhelm the Administration "in days, not weeks." Sam Donaldson said: "Okay, we're all sort of agreed that if the facts don't bear him out, spinning won't help and he's going to leave. So what does President Gore do?"

Or here is an example from *Time Magazine* last month. "In the gaudy mansion of his mind there are many rooms with heavy doors, workrooms and playrooms, rooms stuffed with trophies, rooms to stash scandals and regrets. He walks lightly amid the ironies of his talents and behavior, just by consigning them to different cubbies of his brain." That baroque passage was noted by Richard Harwood, a *Washington Post* columnist. It sounded as though it came from a John Updike novel, he said, but it was actually the lead of a piece in *Time* on President Clinton dealing at the same time with the Lewinsky story and Saddam Hussein. Harwood said readers 9 might wonder how reporters got inside the President's head with their notebooks. But actually, he said, the writers "can fantasize and produce whatever gaudy prose seems suitable to the occasion."

One of the worst features of the coverage from day one has been the extravagant use of unnamed sources. Reliance on unidentified sources is in general a dangerous practice, one that I think should be reserved for the most exigent occasions. But it has been growing, and in the Clinton-Lewinsky story it has gone out of control. We the readers have been given not just supposedly the first-hand observations of an unnamed person but a chain of two or three anonymities. For example, the *Washington Post* reported that Ms. Lewinsky, when she was about to give a deposition in the Paula Jones case, telephoned President Clinton to ask him how to proceed. The *Post* story went on: "One source paraphrased the President's response, as conveyed by Lewinsky: 'You must deny this.'" Ms. Lewinsky supposedly conveyed that response to Linda Tripp.

So what does the *Washington Post* actually rely on? An anonymous source paraphrasing Ms. Lewinsky characterizing the President's words to a purported friend who is secretly taping the call. You can hardly imagine a less reliable report of what the President said. Yet the *Post* put his supposed response in quotation marks: "You must deny this." It thus attributed to him, through that chain of unconfirmed sources, what would be a criminal offense.

As journalism, that is a disgrace. In fairness to the *Washington Post*, I should tell you that the example was pointed out by the *Post's* ombudsman, Geneva Overholser, in her column. She has written strong pieces about the overuse of anonymous sources by the *Post*.

Early on in the Lewinsky story, on ABC News, Peter Jennings and his colleagues were discussing the Linda Tripp tapes of Monica Lewinsky, which the ABC reporters had not heard. One said, "*A source* tells ABC that Lewinsky's charges include . . . ." There again you have the remotest account of what Ms. Lewinsky said on the telephone to Linda Tripp. When unnamed sources are used in stories about a matter as sensitive as this one, the press should at a minimum indicate the possible bias of a source: whether, for example, it was someone in the Independent Counsel's office. But that has hardly been done. One story in the *Wall Street Journal* spoke successively of "individuals with knowledge of the investigation," "an attorney close to the investigation" and "one individual with knowledge of the negotiations." My guess is that all of those were euphemisms for sources in Kenneth Starr's office.

The Committee of Concerned Journalists, which I mentioned earlier, did a study of the White House scandal coverage in its first week. The study included the leading television news and comment broadcasts, five newspapers and the news magazines. It found that only about a quarter

The press has always been competitive, a dog-eat-dog business.

of the statements made in the news reports were attributed to named sources. The rest came from anonymous sources, from repetition of what other press outlets had said or from analysis or mere speculation, without any source at all. "Given the limited number of reporters who actually had listened to the tapes (made by Linda Tripp of her conversations with Monica Lewinsky) or interviewed Linda Tripp," the report of the study said, "most news organizations did not have any confirmation of the major allegation that drove this story—that Lewinsky had talked about having an affair with Clinton and the possibility of lying about it." The report concluded: "The picture that emerges is of a news culture that is increasingly involved with disseminating information rather than gathering it." The vice-chairman of the committee, Tom Rosensteil, added this comment: "News organizations that had the least facts and the weakest sourcing tended to pretend that they knew the most. They engaged in the most conjecture, speculation and opinion."

As an example, here is the lead of a newspaper story at the end of the first week: "Monica Lewinsky believed that President Clinton 'cheated' on her with four other women—three of whom worked at the White House—it was alleged yesterday. Ms. Lewinsky is said to have named her rivals and told her friend Linda Tripp during a taped conversation that they could cope with the jealousy better than she . . . The fresh details of the President's alleged affair added to the turmoil in the White House . . ." None of the statements in that supposed news story has a source of any kind. Instead we have that lovely passive "it was alleged and "is said to have" and the unattributed turmoil in the White House. Well, ladies and gentlemen, I threw in that example just to show you that the sins are not confined to the American press. That story appeared on page 1 of *The Times of London*, a once serious newspaper that has been tabloidized under the ownership of Rupert Murdoch.

Some reporting has not simply lacked credible sources; it has been false. The *Dallas Morning News* reported that a Secret Service agent was ready to testify that he saw the President and Ms. Lewinsky in a compromising situation. That zinger of a story raced around the press; the *New York Daily News* slapped on page 1 the headline "Caught in the Act." Then the *Dallas News* retracted its story, explaining that the source had come back to it and said the information was "inaccurate." The *Wall Street Journal*, which you might think does not have to sink to the tabloid level, reported that a White House steward had said he saw the President and Ms. Lewinsky alone together—and he disposed of tissues with "lipstick and other stains." Five days later, after television had run with that lurid tale, the *Journal* withdrew it and apologized. Larry King, on his television show, said the *New York Times* was going to report the next morning on a telephone call from President Clinton to Ms. Lewinsky: "more than just a how-are-you call," King said. Later in the program he made what he called a "clarification." "We may have jumped the gun," King said. "We have no information on what the *New York Times* will be reporting tomorrow." No such story has appeared, to date, in the *Times.*

ABC News correspondent Jackie Judd had a sensational item early in the game—two days after the story broke. She said that, according to "a source with direct knowledge," Monica Lewinsky said she had "saved, apparently as a kind of souvenir, a navy blue dress with the President's semen stain on it. If true, this could provide physical evidence of what really happened."

Don't you love that 'if true'? It is such a useful journalistic device. You can report any fantastic rumor and just add 'if true.'

The story about the supposed dress made the rounds. The *New York Post*, Rupert Murdoch's American voice, decided that it was a "black cocktail dress." But Ms. Lewinsky's lawyer then told us that there was no such dress. And the press seems to have abandoned that piece of gossip.

As I indicated earlier, members of the press have become concerned at their performance. Alarmed would not be too strong a word. Walter Isaacson, the managing editor of *Time Magazine,* said: "It does feel, when you look at this whole scenario, we must have lost our minds." Geneva Overholser, the *Washington Post* ombudsman, commented on a *Post* story about Ms. Lewinsky's mother, Marcia Lewis. The story "couldn't say where she was born or went to college," Ms. Overholser noted, "but it had plenty of juicy stuff from divorce records." It said, "This mother is built for speed." Ms. Overholser commented: "Yuk." Bill Moyers said the scandal had "sent what remains of our craft crashing through the floor. . . . What's wrong with being slow and right instead of being fast and wrong?"

Now we have to ask ourselves why these things have happened. Why did the editors in charge—some of whom are now crying mea culpa—allow them to happen? There are many possible reasons. I shall suggest a few, in no particular order.

One reason is competition. The press has always been competitive, a dog-eat-dog business. In the post-war years it seemed to become less so because so many newspapers went out of business. Most cities in the United States now have only a single newspaper ownership. But in fact newspapers have to compete with many other sources of news now. Television is one, although it seldom produces much by way of scoops or thoughtful probing. Radio has become more important with the growth of National Public Radio News. And now we have the Internet, with its limitless quantity of unprofessional assertions. A self-proclaimed reporter with no

The executive vice president of CBS News, Jon Klein, put it: "We make shows for a mass audience. Right there, you begin to make a bargain with the devil."

claim to credibility, Matt Drudge, was the originator of some of the far-out rumors in the Clinton-Lewinsky story. How does an editor who wants to be serious maintain care and reliability when he has to compete, around the clock, with many others who do not care? James Naughton, a wise former editor, put the problem in a sentence: "The digital age does not respect contemplation." He added: "The deliberative news process is being sucked into a constant swirl of charge and countercharge . . . spin and counterspin."

Related to the effects of the frantic race to be first with every tidbit is another kind of competition: to attract more readers and viewers. Television has been corrupted by a kind of Gresham's Law; as bad money drives out good, so we have cheap, vulgar programs driving out any attempt to inform viewers about their country and the world. That was the phenomenon that drove Fred Friendly out of the presidency of CBS News. He resigned when the head of the network canceled coverage of a crucial Senate hearing on the Vietnam War and instead put on a rerun—a fifth rerun—of "I Love Lucy." Very little on network television today aims higher than infotainment, because that is where the audience and the money are thought to lie. Some newspapers have fallen into the same trap. That is especially so in Britain, where the process of tabloidization has gone far. But a leading British columnist, Joe Rogaly, was not talking only about the British press when he said the obsession with President Clinton's sex life was "the product of a persistent dumbing-down of the media." The press critic of the *Los Angeles Times*, David Shaw, said that "the (allegedly) responsible media"—he put the word allegedly in parentheses—have become "much more willing in recent years to abandon the standards that have long separated them from publications that specialize in stories about two-headed fat ladies from Mars who gave birth to Elvis's love child after discovering a cure for cancer." Howard Kurtz of the *Washington Post* said: "Each new media frenzy, whether it's O. J. or Marv Albert, lowers the bar a bit for what kind of journalistic excesses or sloppiness are deemed acceptable."

Sex has a lot to do with the mania over the Clinton-Lewinsky story, though the press likes to pretend otherwise. That has been so since reporters found out about Senator Gary Hart's voyage on the good ship Monkey Business; editors insisted that they went after the Senator's extracurricular activities not because sex was involved but because it was vital to explore the character of a man who wanted to be President. Ever since, says David Shaw of the *Los Angeles Times*, "our powers of rationalization have been at a seemingly permanent fever pitch." The fact is that our readers were interested in the Clinton-Lewinsky story not for the profound reasons that we floated from the first day: the fate of the Presidency and all that. They were interested in sex: sex in the oval office. Polls show that a majority of Americans think the President had an affair with Ms. Lewinsky, but an even larger majority think that is not a reason for him to leave office.

One more reason for the rush to judgment and haphazard reporting of the Clinton-Lewinsky story has to be mentioned. Washington reporters on the whole do not like Bill Clinton. They think he has deceived them, slipping away too often when they believe they have him pinned down. Marvin Kalb, the former television correspondent, who now directs a press institute at Harvard, put it bluntly in a comment on the press's performance here: "There's very little hard information, but there's a burning journalistic desire to prove Bill Clinton guilty."

In fairness to my colleagues, I ought to add that there is a perfectly understandable reason to ride this story hard. It is a great story in human terms. If I had been on it as a front-line reporter or editor, I think I would have been sorely tempted to push at the edge of what is responsible journalism. But one thing is not so excusable. That is the press's slowness in understanding the implications for everyone so civil liberties in the way the Independent Counsel was conducting this investigation. Leonard Witt of Minnesota Public Radio pointed out what was done to Monica Lewinsky here: "First phone conversations were illegally taped. Then those illegal tapes were used by the nation's most powerful prosecutor as an excuse to bug this woman's luncheon conversation. Days later at another restaurant half a dozen Federal agents whisked her away and grilled her for nine hours to get her to turn states evidence against her friends and acquaintances. If this were not enough, this intimate, private information was exposed to the whole world." Mr. Witt went on to suggest that "if these dirty-trick and sexual-investigation tactics were used against an editor or publisher in a libel case, there would be an outcry from every corner of the free press. Righteous indignation about these tactics and 'the trampling of freedom' would echo from editorial pages around the country." Can anyone doubt that Mr. Witt is right? I certainly do not. The first time the press got exercised about constitutional rights in this saga was when Sidney Blumenthal was subpoenaed and asked about his contacts with the press.

Nor do I regard as adequate the excuse often given for sensationalism and vulgarity: that the audience wants it. The executive vice president of CBS News, Jon Klein, put it: "We make shows for a mass audience. Right there, you begin to make a bargain with the devil." Now it is true that the press is inescapably part of the society in which it functions. If local television news dwells on the criminal and the gory, as it does, it must be because such degraded programming attracts viewers. But our business, including television, has a higher calling than to play to the lowest common denomina-

A frivolous, mercenary press—a press that appealed to the worst in us—would do terrible damage to the relationship between citizen and government that has kept this country free.

tor. British television has a less educated audience than ours. Yet both the BBC and commercial channels have infinitely better news programs, with correspondents around the world in places that our networks have abandoned. And they have a fair proportion of entertainment that is not insulting to the viewers' intelligence.

I have suggested some reasons for the press's dubious performance on the Clinton-Lewinsky story, relying largely on criticism from voices in the press itself. But I believe there are some longer-term factors at work here, too.

One is that the press has overdone its aggressive posture toward politicians. It is as if every flaw were Watergate. Instead of investigative journalism we have attack journalism, with a lot less investment in time and money and a lot less care. The attitude can be almost cynical—they all do it—and it breeds dangerous public cynicism about politics.

A particular vice of the attack posture is the end of respect for privacy. Not so long ago the press took the view that even politicians were entitled to private lives. It went so far that reporters and photographers hid from the public the fact that President Franklin Roosevelt spent most of his time in a wheelchair. When a photographer newly assigned to the White House took a picture of the President in a wheelchair, others removed the film from his camera. Even before the Lewinsky business, it was plain that, today, anything that might show a President in a bad light is fair game. The irony is that the press over recent decades built the President into a mythic figure, the center of our national drama—and then, having done that, stripped away the privacy needed to make the job bearable.

One more fault that has been growing over the years is self-importance: a hubris that I find troubling in journalists. We take ourselves terribly seriously. We speak in oracular tones. We purport to be providing not merely news but Truth. The great columnist of this century, Walter Lippmann, who was as much a philosopher as a journalist, spoke of journalism as a flashlight that illuminated something for a brief moment and then moved on. For today's editors and reporters and columnists to have higher ambitions is fine, but a little modesty is in order. The fact that television makes your face recognizable does not make you a philosopher king.

The press has real power in our system now, more than James Madison could have imagined. That is no doubt one reason for its unpopularity. Distrusting power is a profound American tradition, and a healthy one. The perception of press power in Watergate led to a public backlash. That seems to me all the more reason to recognize the limits of our wisdom—to avoid arrogance.

You must not think that because I worry about slipshod journalism, the dumbing-down of the press, disrespect for privacy and the rest, I favor television or newspapers that offer the people every day the equivalent of Plato's "Republic." Entertainment is inescapably part of our business, and anyway I would not want to escape. The press can be, and should be, enjoyable as well as informative.

Nor do I think that there was a golden age of the press in this country—in Madison's time, say. In fact, newspapers then were unreliable and highly partisan; some editors were paid by political parties. Those were the papers that Jefferson knew when he said, famously: "Were it left to me to decide whether we should have a government without newspapers or newspapers without a government, I should not hesitate a moment to prefer the latter." But after he had been President for six years he wrote to a friend: "Nothing can now be believed which is seen in a newspaper. Truth itself becomes suspicious by being put into that polluted vehicle."

The press of today, for all its faults, has given some fine examples of performing its Madisonian function. The war in Bosnia is a notable case. Successive Presidents, George Bush and Bill Clinton, wanted to duck responsibility for stopping the genocide, and hence wanted the American public to pay no attention to it. The press made that impossible. Correspondents living under the gun, in great danger, brought home to Americans the meaning of the "ethnic cleansing" carried out by the Bosnian Serbs: concentration camps, mass rape and murder.

"Bosnia was saved by journalists," its Prime Minister, Haris Siladzic, said on a recent visit to Washington. He meant American journalists: Roy Gutman of *Newsday*, Peter Jennings of ABC News, Christiane Amanpour of CNN, John Burns of the *New York Times* and others. They brought home the reality of what was happening. I think the press's unrelenting attention to the war finally forced the Clinton Administration to do what it did at Dayton: bring about an agreement that stopped the fighting and has begun, at last, to ease the divisions in Bosnia.

The question is whether we are going to have a press of the kind that told the truth—the difficult truth—about Vietnam and Bosnia, or a press that is a purveyor of tittle-tattle.

The truth is that democracy cannot function in this vast country without a press committed to its highest purpose— and, today, without a powerful press. The penny papers of Madison's day could not do the job. The great aggregations of power in industry and government demand a weightier press to hold them accountable. The pace of events, the shrinking world, the dangers and opportunities of new technology all demand more from our profession. A frivolous, mercenary press—a press that appealed to the worst in us— would do terrible damage to the relationship between citizen and government that has kept this country free.

What happens to the press now matters greatly to all of us, for it is one element in an institutional crisis. James Carey, a professor at the Columbia School of Journalism, said what I believe:

"Our political institutions have been in a slow-motion free-fall for a couple of decades, their authority, vitality—in a word their legitimacy—are slowly being eroded. A strong presidency, an independent judiciary, a self-serving Congress, and a free press are our most precious institutions. The republican ideals embedded in them provide the foundation for a democratic state and free public life.

"The actors driving the current scandal in Washington—lawyers who show contempt for the law, journalists who revel in voyeurism and political vigilantes ready to profit from any dishonor—seem no longer to understand this vow to hold the republic in their imaginations. They have created new rites for prescience and indignation but not for democratic politics."

Ladies and gentlemen, that is what is at stake when the American press adopts the pose of a cynic—when it regards everyone in office as presumptively corrupt, when it neglects the real problems of the country to demeaning gossip, when it reduces all issues to shouting matches between ideologues. I hope that we still have it in us to return to the vision of James Madison.

III. Civil Rights and Equal Opportunity

Combating Discrimination[1]

Janet Reno

U.S. attorney general, 1993– ; born Miami, FL, July 21, 1938; A.B., Cornell University, 1960; LL.B., Harvard University, 1963; associate partner, Brigham and Brigham, 1963–67; partner, Lewis and Reno, 1967–71; staff director, Judiciary Committee of the Florida House of Representatives, 1971–72; assistant state attorney, Florida, 1973–76; partner, Steel, Hector & Davis, 1976–78; attorney general, Dade County, FL, 1978–93; president, Florida Prosecuting Attorneys Association, 1984–85; member, American Bar Association's Special Committee on Criminal Justice in a Free Society, 1986–88; member, Task Force on Minorities and the Justice System, 1992; Herbert Harley Award, American Judicature Society, 1981; Medal of Honor, Florida Bar Association, 1990.

Editors' introduction: On what would have been the 68th birthday of civil rights leader Martin Luther King Jr., Attorney General Janet Reno spoke at the 16th Street Baptist Church in Birmingham, Alabama, where 34 years earlier a bomb killed four children attending Sunday school. Opposing the dismantling of affirmative action policies and practices, Reno insisted that the nation continue to "protect our civil rights" and "eliminate hatred from this land."

Janet Reno's speech: Thank you so much. I am so very honored to be here today at the 16th Street Baptist Church. And, Reverend Hamlin, I want to thank you for making me feel so welcome. Thank you for making me feel so welcome today and at home.

I am humbled by the opportunity to speak to you today, a day of such special importance to all this nation, the birth date of Dr. Martin Luther King. I wish every American could spend time, as I have this morning, walking through the Civil Rights Institute across the street reading and rereading some of Dr. King's speeches, hearing them directly as he said them and trying to imagine what those days of April and May and September of 1963 were like.

Martin Luther King was a man who saw wrong and never ceased trying to right it. He felt the weight of oppression and he

---

1. Delivered at the 16th Street Baptist Church in Birmingham, Alabama, onJanuary 15, 1997, at 10:30 a.m. Reprinted with permission of Janet Reno.

was never ever broken by it. His life embodied and he helped to define the true spirit of this great nation, our quest for justice. And he was able to express his outrage in yearning for justice so forcefully and so eloquently that he reached into the soul of America and America responded.

Dr. King had the strength of spirit to withstand jail and march in the midst of angry racism and he had the courage to battle hate with love. He did all this to bring America together as never before.

It was here in Birmingham and here at the 16th Street Baptist Church that America witnessed some of the most heroic efforts and some of the lowest, darkest moments of the civil rights struggle. It was here in this church 34 years ago that an ugly, horrible racist attack took the innocent lives of four young girls who were getting ready to participate in their first adult service. They were growing up. I'm honored that Altha Robertson and Commissioner Chris McNair and Ms. McNair and the Collins family are here with us today.

Let me say to you today what Dr. King said 34 ago. Death is not an end for these girls. They are living still in our memory and their power still moves us.

It was from this very church earlier in that same year that thousands of young people, children really, assembled for a nonviolent demonstration and they went to jail to protest segregation. The next day when more students and adults went to demonstrate, Bull Connor let loose his dogs, his clubs and his hoses right outside here in Kelly Ingram Park. We walked across that park this morning to imagine what it was like then and to see what it has become is a monument to Dr. King and to the people of Birmingham who care and will not stop in their quest for liberty, for justice and in the efforts to bring this nation together.

Those demonstrations broke the back of segregation in Birmingham and helped America come together. These are there to remind us of the courage of ordinary citizens who daily met with hateful, hateful prejudice. These are to remind us of what one person can do, young or old, student or preacher. Each one of us can make a difference.

Martin Luther King was right when he said that one day the South will recognize its real heroes. One of those real heroes here in Birmingham was Arthur Shores who died just late last year. As one of the only African-American practicing attorneys in Alabama in the 1940s, Mr. Shores was a lone voice in the wilderness defending the civil rights of his people. He played a critical role during the 1960s when he represented Dr. King and Fred Shuttlesworth. Dr. King, Arthur Shores, so many others, children, all are true heroes in the struggle for freedom and for civil rights for all in this country. They did so much to eliminate discrimination and hatred and to bring America together, but we must carry on.

There is today, as we try to carry on, real disagreement about what civil rights in today's world really means. There are some who think that we have gone too far, who think that we have already achieved the aims of the civil rights movement. I say that's not so. There are others who challenge the value and the fairness of the remedies of the civil rights movement. Some Americans, including some minorities, now question whether integration is still a valid goal. I fear that what national consensus we have on civil rights may be at the risk of unravel. And efforts to divide us along racial lines for political advantage or worse leave many wondering whether we'll move forward or slip backward in our common struggle for equal opportunity and fundamental fairness for every single American.

I say that we will move forward. I see the city of Birmingham saying we will move forward. We will not let be undone what those heroes in those days of the 1960s worked so hard and gave their lives and support for this nation.

But as we move forward, it is not enough to dismiss every criticism as mean-spirited racism or narrow-minded ignorance. We need to examine ourselves and our world with a critical eye and an open mind. We have to ask the difficult questions and attempt to answer them. We must talk openly about race relations in this country. We must talk with respect, we must listen with a listening ear, we must get rid of the angry rhetoric that has so marked this issue in so many instances of late.

We know that not all our ills are explained by racism and other bias, but we also know that hate and prejudice and intolerance and discrimination still persist today and we can't tolerate that.

Our challenge is to remind ourselves of our common interests, our common ground and to remind ourselves of our common dreams. At bottom, the needs of those in the black community, the Hispanic community, the Asian-American community are all the same as those in the white community. Everyone wants a healthy start for their children, a stable and crime-free neighborhood, quality education, supportive families and decent work opportunities. And remember that it was blacks and Hispanics and Asian-Americans and whites who fought so hard and some who gave their lives to defend this nation against the dark forces of tyranny as we saw in the moving ceremony this week when the seven brave soldiers were finally properly recognized.

We must recognize and reaffirm the ties that bind us and understand that we can't solve the problems of crime, of terrorism, of disease, of poverty in isolation each from the other. We must recognize our common humanity and by listening closely and reaching out to each other, we will find that there are ways to bring us together even more closely to bridge the differences that improperly separate us and to

Our challenge is to remind ourselves of our common interests, our common ground.

reaffirm our commitment to civil rights in America. We have much to do. For too often we live in our insular worlds with each of us enforcing our own voluntary racial separation. We pass each other on the streets or in the shopping mall, but we don't connect as individuals. We work together or we go to school together and we don't connect as individuals.

A 1995 *Washington Post* poll found that virtually half of those surveyed did not feel it was important that different racial or ethnic groups should live, go to school or work together so long as they were treated fairly. But this attitude comes dangerously close to the separate but equal doctrine that was so rightly rejected in *Brown vs. Board of Education.* With this separation, we risk a lack of understanding of and appreciation for the views and the perspectives of others. We risk not learning of wonderful racial, ethnic and cultural traditions that make this country strong. Dr. King knew that you could eliminate legal segregation and still not achieve integration. True integration, he believed, would be achieved by true neighbors.

Any sort of desecration of any place of worship is among the most despicable crimes.

This week especially, but in all weeks—my mother said you should never celebrate Mother's Day because every day should be Mother's Day. But this week especially I would ask each one of us to reach out across racial differences to someone you work with or go to school with but really don't know. This weekend visit a church or temple with a different congregation so that this Sunday morning is not, in Dr. King's words, the most segregated hour in America. Take these small steps in our efforts to rebuild a sense of community where diversity is valued and intolerance is unacceptable. But we must do more by reaching out to help others regardless of race or ethnic background to reweave the fabric of community around us all.

Recently I spent a Saturday working for Habitat for Humanity. By the end of the day, blacks, whites, and Cuban-Americans had paint on their face, plaster in their hair and a new spirit in their hearts. Each of us can reach out to lend a hand, lift a spirit and bring America together.

President Clinton has made it a cornerstone of his agenda for the next term to unify the nation around its core values. He has pledged to bring us together, to bring the diverse strands of our people together and to foster an environment of reconciliation and mutual respect. The part says revolution, but the final word is reconciliation. These values are at the heart of civil rights and shape our civil rights agendas for the next term.

In this past year, we have seen a clear example of the challenges we still face to protect our civil rights and to eliminate hatred from this land. The senseless rash of church burnings that have victimized and traumatized congregations and communities has stirred the national conscience. Any sort of desecration of any place of worship is among the most despicable crimes, reaching to the most deeply felt of all American tenets, freedom of religion. But the destruction particularly by fire of an African-American church resonates especially deeply in this country, harkening back to the bleak period when the bombing here at the 16th Street Baptist Church was one of many. And it is for these and many more reasons that the President has made it a top priority to prosecute those responsible for these [outrages,] to prevent future damages of houses of worship and to help communities and congregations in their efforts to rebuild.

We have deployed over 200 ATF and FBI investigations around the country to investigate these arsons. The National Church Arson Task Force is co-chaired by Assistant Attorney General Deval Patrick and Assistant Treasury Secretary James Johnson, and it has responded to these crimes by bringing together as partners the FBI, the ATF, Justice Department prosecutors, the United States attorneys have done such a wonderful job, the Community Relations Service, the Marshal Services in partnership with state and local law enforcement. We are committed to expending the necessary resources, the time and the effort to solve these crimes, and we are going to keep on working on it until we bring the people responsible for these desecrations to justice.

But there is a tremendous difference between the fires 30 years ago and those of today. Church attacks then had the support of too many people in the community. Today the reaction across this nation has been universal outrage. These attacks are rightly seen as a threat to our common sense of sanctuary. These fires have also generated a tremendous response from our community, solidarity among followers of many faiths, donations of money, church robes, hymnals, pews and pianos, countless volunteers to help in rebuilding and preventing further tragedy.

It is a wonderful experience to hear a young teenager talk with pride of her trip to the South to help rebuild one of the churches attacked and to hear her talk of the welcome that she was given by that community.

This past year I traveled down a little old dirt road in South Carolina with the President to see the site of a church that was burned, only a magnificent oak tree which had half covered the church still stood. But then we went further down that road to dedicate the new church. The people of that community, black and white, came together to speak out against the hatred that had spawned that fire. Haters are cowards. When they are confronted, they will often back down. It is so important for all America to speak with one voice and consistently against the hate and the bigotry that is sometimes in our midst.

And there is a common thread through this nation. As I turned and walked off the platform after the church dedication, a woman burst through the lines and came up and gave

It is so important for all America to speak with one voice and consistently against the hate and the bigotry that is sometimes in our midst.

me a big hug and said, "Hello, Janet. I used to live in Miami. You got me child support. And I want you to see the two young men you got child support for. And they are taller than me".

Our experience with church fires shows us at the very same time how much we have achieved and yet how much, much more we have to do. Yes, we have seen remarkable progress in our efforts to bridge the gap between our ideals and the harsh reality of the daily experience of many citizens. Our national journey has taken us from segregated classrooms to integrated ones, from Jim Crow laws to civil rights laws for women, minorities and persons with disabilities, from literacy tests for voting to minority representation here in Alabama at every level of government, including the mayor of Birmingham and Congressman Hilliard in the Alabama Congressional Delegation. And the political inclusion that has been brought about by the Voting Rights Act has led to so much in our progress.

Racial prejudice and the corrosive effects of discrimination are still with us.

Just today the federal government is announcing additional resources to preserve the historic Selma-to-Montgomery trail that Dr. King and others marched along to dramatize the need for the Voting Rights Act.

We have come a long way, but 30 years after the passage of the Voting Rights Act and 40 years after [*Brown vs. Board of Education,*] racial prejudice and the corrosive effects of discrimination are still with us.

We cannot say that we have completed our journey when even today blacks and Hispanics and in many cases women still have a harder time of getting into college, renting an apartment, getting a job or obtaining a loan.

We have not completed our journey when the unemployment rate for black males is still twice as high as it is for white males. Even college-educated black, Hispanic, Asian-American men and women of every race and ethnic background are paid less than comparably educated, comparably trained white men. That's not right.

These problems are doubly difficult for black and Hispanic men and women who also have disabilities. Worst of all, reports of violent hate crimes against minorities and gays and lesbians are disturbingly high. If some of the church fires are any indication, hate itself has become more brazen.

We have changed our laws, but we have not always changed our ways. Old habits die hard. Attitudes evolve slowly. We must do more, much more to open the doors of opportunity so that every American can share in and fully contribute to America's magnificent bounty.

The Department of Justice is committed to our mission which is, simply stated, to enforce the civil rights laws of this nation as vigorously and as faithfully as possible without fear or favor. I care so deeply about this mission which is one of the highest priorities of the Department of Justice. I'm one of the most fortunate people in the world in this last term to have Deval Patrick as the Assistant Attorney General in charge of the Civil Rights Division. He is one of the finest people I have ever known and one of the great public servants I have ever had the opportunity to work with.

He will be leaving at the end of this month to return to Boston to be with his family, and I think this nation, and I know I will, will miss his leadership, his vision, his intelligence and his courage.

The Division, the Civil Rights Division, had a reception for him yesterday and they promised him that they would not let our efforts to enforce the civil rights laws of this country be diminished in any way. And I think that's going to be their ultimate tribute to Deval Patrick.

We will be ever vigilant and ever forceful in bringing our cases, and I would like to highlight four areas which reflect our commitment to combating discrimination and to building trust and understanding among all Americans.

First is fair housing and fair lending, including business lending. Second is employment and affirmative action. Third is education. And fourth is the building of trust between law enforcement and the minority community.

In the next four years, I want to expand on our success in the area of fair lending and fair housing. Home ownership has profound significance in this country, and it is still at the center of the American dream. Yet many Americans are kept from that dream when they can't get a home mortgage and when they are denied home mortgages or property insurance on account of their race or national origin.

For years, disparities were explained in the industry as being justified solely by differences in creditworthiness. But the studies over the last several years have too often proved that explanation is flat and simply wrong.

Black and Hispanic applicants for loans are being denied financing at a much greater rate than white applicants with virtually identical qualifications. Some banks have simply not done business in minority neighborhoods, while others charge higher rates or add extra charges to their loans in minority areas.

We have used a two-prong approach to address this problem. First we have worked with the banking industry that wants to do right to reform their practices, and, secondly, for those who thumbed their noses, we have sued them and we are going to do whatever is necessary.

We are not asking banks to make bad loans. We are telling them that there is some business there that's good business that should not have been rejected on the grounds of race or national origin. And we are working with them to train their employees in practices and procedures that ensure that there is no discrimination. The results of these efforts have been remarkable in a very short period of time.

Black and Hispanic applicants for loans are being denied financing at a much greater rate than white applicants with virtually identical qualifications.

Access to capital is one of the most formidable barriers to the formation and development of minority businesses.

In part due to what we have done and due in part to other factors, we have expanded the availability of loans to minorities. Between 1992 and 1995, the numbers of home loans to minorities grew more than 100 percent, twice the growth rate for home loans generally. Here in Alabama, the number of home loans to minority borrowers increased 122 percent from 1992 to 1995, nearly three times the increase in lending to borrowers in the Alabama market as a whole.

We are also increasing our fair housing activity in Alabama and around the nation. The Civil Rights Division sent fair housing testers to Montgomery. Last summer we filed a record-setting 1.8 million dollar settlement for housing discrimination against the owner of a number of apartment complexes in Mobile. We also work closely with fair housing groups that recently have been established in Birmingham and Montgomery. This type of work is taking place across the country. We will continue to try to eliminate discrimination in the housing and lending market so that all Americans can pursue their dream of home ownership.

I want to expand our fair lending work into the area of business lending. Access to capital is one of the most formidable barriers to the formation and development of minority businesses. Several studies have shown that minority applicants for business loans are more likely to be rejected, and when accepted, receive smaller loan amounts than white applicants with identical borrowing credentials. One recent Colorado study found that African-Americans were three times more likely to be rejected for business loans than whites, and that Hispanic owners were one and a half times more likely to be denied a business loan. That's not right, and the Department of Justice is exploring ways that we can effectively confront discrimination in this arena.

In the next four years we will oppose efforts to limit our ability as a society to address unequal opportunity in the economy. We must do more to tap the inherent potential in every one of our citizens. For far too many, the promise of economic opportunity has a very hollow ring. All too often we learn of blatant discriminatory conduct in the employment context, discrimination based on race, gender or sexual orientation. But also there are more subtle influences of subjective factors making it more likely that we will hire and promote others like us with whom we may feel more comfortable. Social ties are often more important than actual experience and qualifications.

Some of the starkest evidence of this type of behavior comes from testing studies where white males receive 50 percent more job offers than minorities with the same qualifications applying for the same job. And the report of the Glass Ceiling Commission demonstrates that once minorities are in the workplace, their advancement is often hampered by discrimination.

The EEOC is the prime federal agency that sues over employment discrimination in the private sector. The Justice Department has responsibility over discrimination by public employers. But it is important to have a clear picture of discrimination in the workplace so that it can be addressed by the government as a whole.

The reality of current and ongoing discrimination was at the very heart of the President's decision to continue to support affirmative action.

In July of 1995, the President made clear that as a nation, we will not abandon our commitment to equal opportunity. But he also made clear that we need to refine the tool of affirmative action so that it can be used fairly and effectively to help our society achieve its goal of integration and the elimination of discrimination. He said that we needed to mend, not end, affirmative action.

At the same time, the Supreme Court ruled in the Adarand case that when the federal government uses affirmative action, it has to do so in an especially careful way. But in writing for the court, Justice Sandra Day O'Connor recognized the unhappy persistence of both the practice and the lingering effects of racial discrimination against minority groups. She confirmed that under the Constitution, government has an obligation to address it and we will not shrink from that obligation.

This is one reason why we think California's Proposition 209, which establishes a sweeping ban on affirmative action in the state, is both unconstitutional and bad policy. It would prevent local jurisdictions and state agencies from recognizing the need for additional, well-fashioned affirmative action measures to overcome the effects of past discrimination and bring minorities into the economic mainstream. It would prevent victims of racial discrimination and gender discrimination from obtaining relief from local governments and state agencies short of amending the state constitution.

By singling out race and gender for this distortion of the ordinary political process, Proposition 209 denies equal protection of the laws. A federal judge just enjoined the state from implementing the California initiative. We agree with the court, and the Department of Justice will defend that decision.

It is also why efforts in Congress to curtail affirmative action by the federal government are misguided and counterproductive towards our efforts of bringing this nation together and ensuring liberty and equality for all.

The Justice Department in light of the Adarand decision is already making certain that federal government programs now in place are fair and flexible and meet the constitutional standard described by Justice O'Connor. And the President and I will continue to oppose at every step of the way any wholesale ban on affirmative action in federal law.

Education depends on dialogue, not just between students and teacher, but between the student and his or her classmates.

I recognize that there are those who believe that affirmative action is unfair. They feel that they are being forced to pay for others' past sins and that affirmative action gives special preferences to minority groups and women. However, the fact that many minorities and women are still struggling at the bottom of the economic ladder suggests that this criticism misses the mark. Society's reality belies all the purported special treatment for minorities. Concerns about affirmative action must be addressed, but all too often these concerns are based on misperceptions about what the programs are all about. The abuses can and will be fixed. But when affirmative action is done right, there are no quotas, there are no preferences for the unqualified, and the programs end when the objectives have been achieved. When affirmative action is done right, it ensures equal opportunity. When affirmative action is done right, it corrects for the effects of both past and continuing discrimination. And when affirmative action is done right, it is an important tool in reaching our goal of an America coming together. Because of our efforts to eliminate discrimination and provide equal opportunity to all, our nation's workplaces are much more diverse than they ever were and our nation's economy is stronger for the effort.

Of course, equal opportunity in the economic sphere can only be achieved if our citizens are prepared to take advantage of these opportunities. In the next four years, the civil rights agenda must also include ensuring that educational institutions are equally accessible to women and to minorities.

As a nation, we have made great strides in broadening opportunities in higher education. Just since 1990, the numbers of Hispanics enrolled in colleges and universities has increased by 35 percent, Asian-Americans by 35 percent; and since 1990, African-Americans' enrollment in higher education has increased by 16 percent. The number of minorities graduating from colleges and universities is also rising, and that benefits all America for that fuels the economy, provides the people with skills who can run this engine that fuels the economy that maintains this nation as a great nation.

Greater integration has meant a better education for all of the students involved. Education depends on dialogue, not just between students and teacher, but between the student and his or her classmates. For over 20 years, our laws have recognized the important value of diversity in education.

Last year, however, a federal appeals court in Texas ruled that this is no longer good law. This is the Hopwood case which ruled that diversity did not justify affirmative action in education. We disagree strongly with that decision. The Supreme Court declined to take the case on procedure grounds, so the issue is still an open one. We continue to believe that if the setting in which the students learn looks more like the world, their education will be better and stronger and prepare them better for the future.

It may also be useful to ask, what do we mean when we say someone is qualified or more qualified for admission to college or to graduate school. We are making judgments about people before they have really had a chance to do anything. Education is the first rung on the ladder of opportunity. Getting an education is how you get ahead. And I just don't think it makes sense to deny that chance to someone based solely on a one-size-fits-all test. You have to look, not just at test scores, but at what that individual will bring to that school and to that community and to this nation and you have to look at what the benefits of integration will bring to society as a whole.

Let me give you just one example of a broader view of merit and the benefits of diversity. A study of University of California Medical School graduates examined where doctors practiced after graduation. A much higher percentage of minority graduates than white graduates practiced in areas that were underserved by the medical profession. Because that medical school is diverse, California has better medical care.

Abraham Lincoln said that a house divided cannot stand and that a nation divided cannot stand. I believe so strongly that we cannot have a divided nation, one exposed to education and the other not. We have to do more so that every student has access to education. Because that young man who is the first in his family to go to college will likely become a father, and his son or daughter and this nation will be the beneficiaries.

We must also reemphasize quality in education as well as racial integration as goals of the post-Brown struggle. A place in an integrated classroom is worth having only if it provides our children with a true opportunity to learn. We have to do more to address the inequality among the schools in our communities for it is unfortunately true that because of economic inequality, many predominantly minority schools tend to receive much inferior resources than those received by predominantly white schools. We need to find ways to develop and to finance city school systems that will keep families, both black and white, in the public school and give them an education that will help them meet the challenges of this next exciting century of the information age.

These are daunting challenges. But if 40 years ago those children and their parents in Topeka, Kansas, and in Little Rock, Arkansas and Clarendon County, South Carolina, had the strength and the courage to face down an intractable establishment, hell bent on segregation, then I am not ready to say that today's challenges are beyond our grasp, and I don't think America is either.

Another crucial item on the agenda for the next four years is an effort to build a greater sense of community and trust between law enforcement and the minority community. There is no other area where the potential for misunderstanding and miscommunication can have such dangerous consequences. Just in the past year, we have seen in St. Petersburg the danger of pent-up frustrations and a breakdown in community relations. And yet, at the same time, we must recognize that minorities are disproportionately victims of crime. Nothing is more important than a safe environment. The quality of the school a child attends will matter less if she is not safe in getting there or while she is at school. So it is an absolute imperative that we establish better trust, cooperation and communication between the community and the police.

We must continue to encourage diversity and understanding in all law enforcement.

There are several ways we can set about doing that. First, through community policing, we bring law enforcement to the neighborhood level. We have police officers who are committed to serve the community, who reach out to the neighbors, who involve them in identifying the problems in the community and establishing priorities and in working together to achieve solutions. That police officer, rather than creating division, reaches out to build trust. He becomes the mentor. The elderly woman who would not walk out from behind her door because she is afraid now walks down to the community center to tell people what she thinks should be done, and we see communities coming together when community police reach out in thoughtfulness and respect and involve the people of this country in building security for us all.

Second we must continue to encourage diversity and understanding in all law enforcement. In years past, too many police departments had no black or Hispanic officers, few had women officers. Now we have not just men in blue, but women in blue. Not just whites, but people of all colors. People who patrol the neighborhoods they grew up in, people who know the languages spoken there, men and women our youth can look up to as role models. And these police officers are teaching each other how to value and to appreciate the diversity and the wonder of the tradition of the neighbors they serve.

Third, we must continue our vigorous enforcement of civil rights laws. This must be combined with additional effective training efforts.

There are approximately 690,000 law enforcement officers in this country. The vast majority are honest, hard working and law abiding. They put their lives on the line every day for us in the pursuit of justice. Yet police chiefs and rank-and-file officers alike tell me to maintain the confidence in the community, we must take decisive action against those few officers who abuse their power and deny citizens their constitutional rights by use of excessive force or harassment. The Department of Justice plays a crucial role here through the use of civil rights prosecutions and criminal sanctions, and we will use our criminal and civil authority when the evidence and when the law justifies it and we will pursue each allegation. But at the same time we are working with law enforcement agencies in training programs that teach officers how to better serve their community, how to involve the community and how to make a difference.

So we have come a long way since Dr. King reached into the soul of America, challenged its conscience and brought us together as never before. But at the same time, hate, discrimination and intolerance still raised their heads and efforts to divide us rise up.

We must today and every day rededicate ourselves to meeting Dr. King's challenge, his challenge to our conscience to seek freedom, liberty and justice for all, to come together as one nation while cherishing the racial and ethnic traditions and cultures that make this nation so wonderfully and so magnificently diverse. To some it is tempting in an uncertain and rapidly changing world economy to turn inward to protect what they have and to let others fend for themselves. Others just throw up their hands and say I'm just one person, I can't make a difference. But Americans throughout this nation are making a difference as they reach out. Here in Birmingham this morning you can feel the excitement as people look on your city, a tiny new city rising around the park. They look at their history and build on the history to make sure that what happened in 1963 will never happen again. They are coming together to give children a future, to bring people out from behind closed doors, to involve America in the process of community and to provide the glue that brings us together.

In Dorchester, Massachusetts, I stand with religious leaders and young African-American students and white police officers as they have joined together to significantly reduce the incidence of youth violence in that community.

Now some of you may say but I'm too old, I can't make a difference. Remember the 84 year-old man who once stood up in a meeting and said do you know how old I am and what I do three mornings a week? I'm 84 and I volunteer as a teacher's aide. And the young woman next to him stood up and said I'm the first grade teacher for whom he volunteers. And the children with learning disability can't wait for their time with him because he has the patience of Job and those who are gifted can't wait for their time with him because he challenges them far beyond what I can with the number in my class.

Come with me to dispute resolution programs in Washington, D.C. public schools where white and black students are learning to live together where they're working together to

To some it is tempting in an uncertain and rapidly changing world economy to turn inward to protect what they have and to let others fend for themselves.

resolve the disputes without knives and guns and fists. Come with me across this country and you will see so much of America coming together and reaching out and making a difference in making this a more peaceful nation that is together. Take part and take hope.

But remember the children of Birmingham, remember those four girls, and let us focus for this next time on the children of America, the right to a mortgage, the right to equal opportunity for a home. Equal opportunity for an education won't mean very much if that young person does not live to seize that opportunity. Let us come together as one nation to say that we will stop youth violence in this nation. We will stop youth killing. We will work together to give them their foundation in which they can grow as strong, constructive human beings. This nation is coming together to do that.

You can hear Dr. King telling us we're not moving fast enough. Let us walk out of here today and think of what each one of us can do to make a difference in the lives of all Americans and in the name of the children who walked out the door of this church or the children who died here, let us give all American children a future of peace, of liberty, of freedom, and of justice for all.

Lessons on Race[2]

Newt Gingrich

Speaker of the U.S. House of Representatives, 1995–98; born Harrisburg, PA, June 17, 1943; B.A, Emory University, 1965; M.A., 1968, and Ph.D. in history, 1971, Tulane University; assistant professor, West Georgia College, Carrollton, 1970–78; representative (R) from Georgia, U.S. House of Representatives, 1979–98; House Minority Whip, 1989–94; co-founder, Earning by Learning; fundraiser, Paralympics, Cobb YWCA Battered Women's Shelter, Georgia Breast Cancer Society, American Cancer Society, Boy Scouts of America, and Roswell Vietnam War Memorial; Time *"Man of the Year," 1995; co-author,* Window of Opportunity *(1984),* 1945 *(1995), and* Meltdown on Main Street: Why Small Business Is Leading the Revolution Against Big Government *(1996); co-editor,* Contract with America *(1994); author,* To Renew America *(1995) and* Lessons Learned the Hard Way: A Personal Report *(1998).*

Editors' introduction: On June 18, 1997, Newt Gingrich addressed orphans, donors, supporters, members of Congress, and volunteers at the Oliver Project Awards gala in Washington, D.C.; the gala was sponsored by the Orphan Foundation. Gingrich's purpose was "to create a vision of equal opportunity for every American regardless of background." The speech was carried by C-SPAN.

Newt Gingrich's speech: Thank you, Jim Taylor, for that very nice introduction. Even more, thank you and the GATE-WAY 2000 Foundation for underwriting the scholarships for these remarkable young people. I would also like to thank Eileen McCaffrey as President of the Orphan Foundation of America for her leadership in organizing the Fourth Annual OLIVER Project in support of foster youth attending college.

The Orphan Foundation is but one part of a worldwide movement toward helping people. We are a movement of people who believe that combining the wisdom of the founding fathers, with the opportunities of the Information Age and the world market, will help each person exercise their Creator-endowed right to pursue happiness and will eventually lead to freedom, prosperity and safety everywhere. It seems to me that that is a good description of what Eileen, Jim and everyone associated with the success of this year's OLIVER Project hope to achieve.

---

2. Delivered in Washington, D.C., on June 18, 1997, at 8:00 p.m.
Reprinted with permission of Newt Gingrich.

When we look around this room, and we see children of many, many hues, we learn, frankly, that it is the common bonds of experience which truly bring us together.

I understand that the young people honored here tonight were in foster care for a long time. Thankfully, you were able to reach out on your own to private organizations like the Orphan Foundation to find mentors and parents that have been more helpful in brightening your future than any government bureaucracy.

For example, David DiBernardo, now a freshman at Slippery Rock University in Pennsylvania survived twenty-nine foster care placements before he found the Orphan Foundation. This illustrates the fact that investing in our youth and strengthening permanent families is not accomplished by any government program—it happens one child at a time.

It is essential that we learn from organizations like The Orphan Foundation and specifically the OLIVER Project, which honors foster youth attending college. Their goal is to replicate the OLIVER Project in the states for high school students.

As we pursue these endeavors to brighten the future of every young American, it is important that we listen and learn from the real experts: the young people here with us tonight. For example, Elizabeth DeBroux, a senior at Oglethorpe University in Atlanta, and her friends can advise us in Georgia on the most effective policies to help young people.

The Orphan Foundation has the right idea and is the right model: It saw a need and chose to provide an opportunity. You have seen what these young people have managed to accomplish so far. You have faith in them that they will be achievers. You have assisted them in helping them make their dreams come true. You have given them a precious opportunity to now have the tools to exercise their Creator-endowed right to pursue happiness. In your eyes, there is no black or white or any other color. There is only a genuine need and the possibility to offer an opportunity. What you are doing is uniquely American—in more ways than you may realize. When we look around this room, and we see children of many, many hues, we learn, frankly, that it is the common bonds of experience which truly bring us together. These bonds have as much influence on our lives, our successes and our ultimate futures than something that is as ultimately superficial as race.

Consider the experience of the orphan: Whether because of war, famine, accident, irresponsibility or illness, a child is suddenly alone in the world. The obstacles that child has to overcome and the opportunities that organizations such as the Orphan Foundation provide for that child—those experiences shape them in a particular way. And so one orphan—black, white, Asian, Muslim, Christian . . . or whatever combination of those characteristics you can imagine—can look to another and say, "Yes, I've been down the same road that you've traveled and regardless of how you may look or how you may worship, I can see that you and I share the same experience."

This is a particularly apt metaphor for America writ large. America is a nation of immigrants. In certain ways, the experience of the immigrant and the experience of the orphan mirror one another. We have, in America, people who have, for various reasons come to America for a better opportunity. Before there was a nation called the United States, Pilgrims, fleeing religious persecution, landed in a place they called the New World. In the 1800s the Irish came to these shores fleeing a famine which had devastated their country. As recently as the 1970s, Vietnamese fled a homeland wounded by decades of war. These and so many others saw hope and opportunity in America. They came here for a chance to succeed. They made the conscious decision to become part of a new family—to become Americans. And becoming an American is a unique experience, which comes with certain responsibilities, certain habits that one has to absorb and accept to successfully finish the process.

An American is not "French" the way the French are or "German" the way Germans are. You can live in either of those countries for years and never *become* French or German. I think one of the reasons Tiger Woods has had such a big impact is because he is an American. He defines himself as an American. I think we need to be prepared to say, the truth is we want all Americans to be, quite simply, Americans. That doesn't deprive anyone of the right to sense further define their heritage—I go to celebrations such as the Greek festival in my district every year. It doesn't deprive us of the right to have ethnic pride, to have some sense of our origins. But it is wrong for some Americans to begin creating subgroups to which they have a higher loyalty than to America at large. The genius of America has always been its ability to draw people from everywhere and to give all of them an opportunity to pursue happiness in a way that no other society has been able to manage.

That is a particularly useful way of discussing the question of race which I raised at the beginning of the year, when I was re-elected Speaker, and which the President addressed this past weekend in California. This question of race is at the heart of America's darkest moments—slavery, the Civil War, segregation—and yet dealing with it in the public sphere also produced two of our most brilliant and influential leaders—Abraham Lincoln and Martin Luther King, Jr. Such has been the tragedy and the triumph of race in America. As W. E. B. DuBois observed, the 20th century has in some ways been defined by the "color line." As we move into a new century, we have to look at what has worked when it comes to race, what hasn't and what lessons we should learn. Because, as the old adage goes, there is no

We need to be prepared to say, the truth is we want all Americans to be, quite simply, Americans.

surer sign of insanity than doing the same thing over and over again—and expecting a different result each time.

Looking to the new rather than repeat a failed pattern is a very American truth. To those who doubt whether America holds promise even in the most hostile of circumstances, we need only turn to the *Narrative of the Life of Frederick Douglass, An American Slave*—his autobiography. While the question of a federal apology for slavery can be discussed by reasonable people of all persuasions, let us not forget someone like Douglass who didn't wait for an apology. He allowed bonds neither physical nor mental to prevent him in one lifetime to go from being a slave to becoming an adviser to the President. That is quintessentially an American story. That is a story like many others in this unique nation. It stands as one of many historic lessons which all Americans can benefit from learning. Slavery was an awful period in this country's existence—one which we as a country—must never forget. That's why I was glad that J. C. Watts introduced his "June Teenth" resolution yesterday, observing the day many African-Americans celebrate as the traditional end of slavery. The more Americans learn about America—the triumphs and the tragedies—the more we mature as a nation. But while Americans must respect the past, part of being an American is about looking forward.

We will not be successful in moving our society forward if we submerge individuals into groups.

The scholarships being awarded here tonight are a good place to continue the dialogue on race—because they are awards of pure achievement, pure merit rewarding individuals for their superior work as individuals. They are not being granted because somebody felt sorry for you or thought you needed assistance because you were a particular race or gender. You are being rewarded for your hard work as individuals. That is the way we must approach the issue of opportunity. We will not be successful in moving our society forward if we submerge individuals into groups.

Unfortunately, government policy has concentrated on groupings over the last 30 years. The results of the group-think approach are in and they have proven tragic. Let me draw a distinction. I was an Army brat. I was born in Harrisburg, PA. I grew up in an integrated institution. I went to the South as a teenager and was in Columbus, Georgia when there was still legal segregation. Segregation was the legal imposition by the state of a set of unfair rules. Ending segregation was an inherently political fight. It made perfect sense for people who wanted to advance the cause of freedom and end government-imposed segregation to focus on politics and government. Since the rules of segregation were focused on a specific group, it made sense that the focus was on removing the impediments at the group level.

Having ended segregation, however, the next struggle, frankly, is and has been economic and educational achievement. Government is a peculiarly ineffective institution in those areas. This is a lesson we now tell the Chinese, we tell the Russians, we say everywhere around the planet. Centralized, bureaucratic, command-and-control systems don't work. Well, guess what? They don't work very well in the inner cities of Washington, D. C., New York . . . or Detroit, either. And they have proven tragically not to work on Indian reservations.

We need to treat individuals as individuals and we need to address discrete problems for the problems they are—and not presume them to be part of an intractable racial issue which will never be torn out.

Consider education as an example. Following the removal of racial quotas in the University of California system, Berkeley experienced a precipitous drop in accepted black students for their fall classes. The old way of thinking assumes this to be a racial problem that must be addressed in a race-specific manner. That is exactly the wrong kind of thinking. If in fact, enough young people are not being educated well enough to get into Berkeley, the focus should be on what's wrong with the schools that are producing them and how we improve those schools. And if the need is for more tutoring . . . and if the need is for better education . . . if the need is for a way to dramatically overhaul the schools—then let's overhaul the schools.

Similarly, if there are not enough young blacks in particular—young Hispanics to a lesser extent—going out and creating small businesses, then let's look at what are the inhibitions to creating small businesses. All of the set-asides in the world will not change Anacostia or other such pockets of poverty. We have to have a profound fundamental rethinking of the assumptions that have failed for 30 years.

As you look at the success of West Indian, first-generation immigrants or of Koreans or you look at the success, for that matter, of people who have come here from Africa in the last thirty years, the fact is a surprising number of people of color rise surprisingly rapidly. And by rising I mean get wealthier, buy property, have freedom and go on nice vacations. They rise very rapidly. They rise because they have the right habits, skills and networking ability. But if you trap people into public housing with anti-work and anti-achievement regulations, send them to schools that fail, teach them a set of habits about not working, create an environment where no one near them gets up on Monday to go to a job, have nobody in the neighborhood who opens a small business, it shouldn't shock you that we end up with cycles of despair which repeat for generations.

What we've done is artificially create, both on Indian reservations and in the inner city, zones of despair and depression where people have no hope. So we need to talk about a very different model. The President's commission needs to begin with this new, more powerful approach. In America everyone is an individual. Everyone in America has the Creator-endowed right to pursue happiness. In America, we pragmatically solve problems by asking, "Why isn't this happening?" For example, "Why aren't children learning in a particular neighborhood?" Then systematically break the problem into components and solve it. In many cases, a solution will require a replacement rather than a repair. That's why we developed a replacement for the failed welfare system. You couldn't repair the old welfare system of passivity and lifetime dependency. It had to be replaced with a different model that emphasized training work and self-help. I would argue the same is true with much of the public housing rules. You can't repair them. You have got to replace them with a different model.

If you do create a replacement system at a practical level, what behaviors are you trying to encourage among large numbers of people? You want to make it easy to open a small business. Most big cities make it hard. Hernando DeSoto 15 years ago wrote "The Other Path." It is based on anti-job rules in Lima, Peru. It applies as well to Washington, D. C., Atlanta, Miami, New York, Los Angeles and virtually all large American cities. So the very place we want more business—we're going to face this problem of local anti-job taxes and rules now. I'm the leading advocate for tax breaks for Washington, D. C. We have nearly 580 million in tax breaks (over ten years) in the tax bill for our nation's capital. We have fought hard to protect these tax breaks. Yet D. C. *city* taxes are one-third higher than the surrounding counties' taxes. Now, it is not hard for any student of Adam Smith to figure out why, if you are a rational small businessperson, you go to Prince George's County. It's safer, it's cheaper and the local government doesn't make it so difficult for the entrepreneur to succeed.

If you're not willing to confront the central need to reform and replace the systems that have failed, they will continue to fail.

It doesn't matter how many quotas you have. If you're not willing to confront the central need to reform and replace the systems that have failed, they will continue to fail. I would hope the President's commission will have the moral courage to erase the assumption that we are a "group" society. If they will look to Canada right now, they will see profound reasons for Americans to want to avoid our decaying into a series of groups. I hope this commission will decide that its goal must be to have every American succeed as an individual within the framework of their Creator-endowed rights.

We must focus on individuals and their personal educational and economic achievements. Obsessing on race will not allow us to move beyond race. We must follow the example of the Orphan Foundation and recognize specific needs and provide principles that will allow Americans of all backgrounds to open the doors of opportunity.

We have to start with the development of a solid foundation—with an economic and social pillar—which will allow us to build a true opportunity society. We must emphasize continuing economic growth with low inflation and rising take-home pay. Within this economic growth we must emphasize creating opportunities for minorities to create new small businesses. Our goal should be to encourage at least a three-fold growth in black-owned small businesses over the next few years. This will require reductions in taxation, litigation and regulation to make it dramatically easier to launch small businesses. It also will require an aggressive outreach program to encourage minority individuals to create their own business as an alternative to working for others.

In addition to expanded economic opportunity we should insist on solving other challenges which affect all Americans but bear particularly harshly on minority populations. I imagine it is January 1, 2001, the first day of a new century and a new millennium. It is a Monday morning. Imagine waking up in an America that was virtually drug-free, in which practically every child was learning at their best rate, and in which almost all children were born into or adopted into families that could nurture and raise them.

I am not describing a utopia. This is the America I went to high school in in 1960. Drug use was marginal. There was an expectation you could read the diploma before they gave it to you. Self-esteem was earned not given. Young males knew that fatherhood was a responsibility not just a biological side effect of hedonism.

All of America will be better of if we create a drug-free, learning-oriented America of children growing up in families—minority Americans in general and black Americans in particular—would find their lives dramatically improved by these changes.

Stopping drug addiction, drug-related violence and drug-generated wealth will do more to improve the lives of young blacks and the prospects of poor neighborhoods than all of the quotas and set-asides combined. When neighborhoods are drug-free and crime free, businesses will return, jobs will reappear and economic opportunity will be re-established.

True learning is infinitely more powerful than social promotion combined with quotas and set-asides. Every child of every background in every neighborhood deserves their full rights to pursue happiness as their Creator endowed them. Recently, I attended an eighth grade graduation at St. Augustine private school here in Washington. Ninety-eight percent of the private school children will graduate. The public schools, which cost three to four times as much, will graduate less than half as many of their entering children. Saving the children who are dropping out requires new approaches not new quotas.

We know we can dramatically reduce single teen pregnancy because it is being done. Kay Granger, former mayor of Fort Worth and now a freshman member of Congress, worked on a YWCA project for 800-at-risk teenage girls. Statistically 70% should have become pregnant. The program taught these young girls ambition, integrity and motivation. Instead of 560 becoming pregnant, only two did. We *can* break the cycles of dependency and despair in our poor neighborhoods.

This is not a proposal for a massive new government program. If centralized bureaucracies in Washington could have stopped drugs, guaranteed learning and ended single teen pregnancy, the job would have been done—we have created the bureaucracy and spent the money. It was just the wrong model.

America is a great country filled with good people. Tocqueville pointed out in the 1840s that volunteerism, local leadership and faith-based charities were the unique attributes that gave America its dynamic character. Marvin Olasky recaptured these principles of American success in his 1994 book *The Tragedy of American Compassion.*

Instead of focusing on broad sweeping generalizations about race, the President's commission needs to focus on practical, doable, immediate action steps that can solve America's problems. If Americans get busy enough working together to achieve real goals, racism will recede. Perspiration and teamwork will dissolve racism faster than therapy and dialogue.

I'm sure most of you saw the Bulls-Jazz championship game last week. In the closing moments, when Michael Jordan looked to find an open man for a winning shot, he didn't look for the closest black player. He looked for the nearest Chicago jersey. That happened to be Steve Kerr who is white. This is the example for society to follow: A group of individuals so focused on a common goal of winning—that they don't have time to worry about what color the other guy is. I will also remind everyone here and watching on C-SPAN that Michael Jordan tragically lost his father a few years ago. Steve Kerr, while a college freshman, lost his father to Middle East violence. They are also good examples of overcoming adversity and triumphing in the face of it.

We thank the President for wishing to continue the dialogue on race last weekend. But frankly, there has been much talk on this issue and very little action of the sort which will dramatically change people's lives. Let me now suggest ten practical steps which, started today can build a better America and, in the process, close the racial divide:

LEARNING—We must create better opportunities for all children to learn by breaking the stranglehold of the teachers' unions and giving parents the financial opportunity to choose the public, private or parochial school that's best for their children (as outlined in Majority Leader Armey's Educational Opportunity Scholarships for District of Columbia students).

SMALL BUSINESS—We must set a goal of tripling the number of minority-owned small businesses by bringing successful small business leaders together to identify—and then eliminate—the government-imposed barriers to entrepreneurship.

URBAN RENEWAL—We must create 100 Renewal Communities in impoverished areas through targeted, pro-growth tax benefits, regulatory relief, low-income scholarships, savings accounts, Brownfields clean-up and home-ownership opportunities (as outlined in Jim Talent and J. C. Watts' American Community Renewal Act).

CIVIL RIGHTS—The Equal Employment Opportunity Commission should clear its existing backlog of discrimination cases by enforcing existing civil rights laws, rather than trying to create new ones by regulatory decree.

EQUAL OPPORTUNITY—We must make America a country with equal opportunity for all and special privilege for none by treating all individuals as equals before the law and doing away with quotas, preferences and set-asides in government contracts, hiring and university admissions (as outlined in the Canady-McConnell-Hatch Civil Rights Act of 1997).

RACIAL CLASSIFICATION—We must break down rigid racial classifications. A first step could be to add a "multiracial" category to the census and other government forms to begin to phase out the outdated, divisive and rigid classification of Americans as "blacks" or "whites" or other single races. Ultimately, our goal is to have one classification—"American."

HOME OWNERSHIP—We must ease the path toward home ownership by giving local communities and housing authorities the flexibility and authority to more effectively and efficiently house low-income Americans (as outlined in the Housing Opportunity and Responsibility Act). We must also expand faith-based charities such as Habitat for Humanity, which grow families as well as build homes

VIOLENT CRIME—We must make our cities safe and secure places to live and work through community policing, tougher sentences for violent criminals and innovative anti-crime programs (as outlined in the Juvenile Crime Control Act of 1997). We must also dramatically expand the community-based anti-drug coalition efforts and insist on a victory plan for the war on drugs.

ECONOMIC GROWTH—We must expand economic opportunities for all Americans by promoting continued economic growth with low inflation and rising take-home pay, through tax cuts, tax simplifications, litigation reform, less regulation and overhaul of the burden of government on small busi-

For welfare-to-work to be successful, work needs to be available.

nesses. After all, for welfare-to-work to be successful, work needs to be available.

WELFARE REFORM—We must take the next step in welfare reform by fostering and promoting innovative local job training, and entry-level employment programs to move welfare recipients into the workforce (as outlined in the Personal Responsibility Act of 1996 and the welfare-to-work initiatives of Governor George Bush of Texas and others).

These ten steps are examples of the kind of practical, down-to-earth, problem-solving efforts which will improve the lives of all Americans, but have an especially important and dramatic impact on the lives of poor Americans and minority communities.

I hope the President's commission will establish a goal of practical reforms and practical changes and will hold hearings designed to elicit pragmatic, down-to-earth proposals for real change.

The commission would do well to start right here with the Orphan Foundation. This is a uniquely American institution—in your generosity of spirit, in your inner strength and in your boundless optimism. But most of all, you are uniquely American because in giving these and many other young people the rarest of treasures—a sense of hope, a sense of place and a sense of possibility—you are in fact helping show them what it means to be citizens and part of the American family. And those are the greatest gifts of all. You are part of a worldwide movement of freedom and faith. You are all making our jobs a little bit easier. I thank the Foundation for its work; I salute this year's scholarship winners and I thank you for allowing me to join you this evening.

Understanding and Empathy[3]

Albert Gore Jr.

Vice president of the United States, 1993– ; born Washington, D.C., March 31, 1948; B.A., Harvard University, 1969; U.S. Army, 1969–71; reporter, the Tennessean, 1971–76; home builder and land developer, Tanglewood Home Builders Co., 1971–76; Student, Vanderbilt University's Graduate School of Religion, 1971–72; student, Vanderbilt University Law School, 1974–76; representative (D) from Tennessee, U.S. House of Representatives, 1977–85; U.S. senator (D) from Tennessee, 1985–93; author, Earth in the Balance: Ecology and the Human Spirit (1992).

Editors' introduction: Albert Gore Jr. spoke on January 19, 1998, at the Ebenezer Baptist Church in Atlanta, Georgia, where civil rights leader Martin Luther King Jr. had served as pastor. With affirmative action policies and practices throughout the country being challenged in the courts and in the Congress, Gore used this historic setting to advocate a new initiative by the Clinton administration on civil rights. In an uncharacteristic, emotionally charged delivery, Gore opposed those who would "roll back equal opportunity." "Let us not weary," he urged, "as we address the unfinished agenda."

Albert Gore Jr.'s speech: Today, we honor the memory of Martin Luther King Jr., and rededicate ourselves to his work. Thirty years ago, the first eulogies to Dr. King recalled what was said in Genesis by the brothers of Joseph: "Behold, this dreamer cometh. Come now therefore, and let us slay him, and cast him into some pit . . . and we shall see what will become of his dreams."

Thirty years later, that is still the question: what will become of Dr. King's dream?

It is ironic that some of the modern apostles of apathy now misappropriate Dr. King's own words to support their belief that the struggle for justice in which he led us is nearly over—and that the time has come for our policies to be, in their phrase, "color-blind."

Let's start at the beginning: what is racism? Is it merely a mistake in reasoning, an erroneous conclusion based on faulty logic which, once corrected, can be banished from human society? Or is it something deeper and more powerful, more threatening and more persistent?

What is racism? Is it merely a mistake in reasoning, an erroneous conclusion based on faulty logic which, once corrected, can be banished from human society?

---

3. Delivered at the Ebenezer Baptist Church in Atlanta, Georgia, on January 19, 1998.

Dr. King taught us that as human beings, we are vulnerable to the sin of racism. As a young man, he studied the teachings of the theologian Reinhold Neibuhr, who had written that it is foolish to regard racism, in his words, "as a mere vestige of barbarism when it is in fact a perpetual source of conflict in human life." Neibuhr criticized those who "wrongly drew the conclusion . . . that racial prejudice is a form of ignorance which could be progressively dispelled by enlightenment. Racial prejudice is indeed a form of irrationality;" he said, "but it is not as capricious as modern universalists assume."

What is it about human nature that creates this persistent vulnerability to the sin of racism?

First and foremost, the Bible teaches us, in the words of the Apostle John: "If we say that we have no sin, we deceive ourselves and the truth is not in us."

But the Bible also teaches that we have the capacity to overcome evil with good. We're called upon to choose. In the words of the famous hymn:

"Once to every man and nation
Comes the moment to decide
In the strife for truth and falsehood
For the good or evil side."

There is a tendency, rooted in human nature, to group up with those who look like ourselves. In the Apocrypha, which is part of Catholic scripture, it is written: "flesh consorteth according to kind, and a man will cleave to his like."

So even though we understand that diversity is an enriching and ennobling strength, in creating an integrated society, it is foolish and naive to imagine that our differences will disappear and relinquish their claims upon us. Indeed, our challenge is to appreciate and celebrate our differences, as a necessary prelude to transcending them in order to join together in celebrating what we all have in common as children of God.

That does not mean that we ignore difference. Indeed, we ignore it at our peril. Dr. John Hope Franklin has taught that the most important lesson of his long single life of scholarship is that race is always present. Pretending it isn't is naive. But if properly acknowledged and sensibly dealt with, race can be transcended.

It is far from easy to acknowledge and celebrate differences while simultaneously transcending them, because differences among people automatically carry the potential for unleashing an impulse to compare, to magnify whatever feelings of insecurity, or abandonment, or loss each individual feels in his or her soul.

Why did Cain slay Abel?

He felt "disrespected"—because God regarded his offerings *differently* from those of Abel. "It came to pass . . . that Cain rose up against Abel his brother, and slew him."

In creating an integrated society, it is foolish and naive to imagine that our differences will disappear.

Why was Joseph, resplendent in his coat of many colors, thrown into that pit and left for dead by his brothers?

They felt "disrespected" because their father regarded them *differently* from Joseph. Why do so many young men on the streets with empty lives and loaded guns slay their brothers? They tell us time and again that their brothers "disrespected" them. And often what they are really feeling is that their fathers disrespected them by abandoning their mothers and them.

Those who are quick to feel disrespected often have a spiritual vacuum in their lives, because they feel disconnected to the love of their Father in Heaven. False gods force their way into the hole in their hearts. They search for meaning and respect in trivial forms of group identification. Rival gangs adopt rival colors. The slight difference between a blue bandana and a red bandana has led to the senseless loss of many lives.

What is the difference between Hutus and Tutsis? Outsiders who visit Rwanda have difficulty telling them apart. But their slight differences have served as a trigger for an horrific genocide.

Look at Bosnia. There, too, outsiders can't tell the different groups apart. Look at Northern Ireland, the Middle East, Chechnya, Nogorno-Karabakkh, and a hundred other places that dot the broken landscape of our hurting world. In all these places, slight differences have served as an excuse to unleash the evil that lies coiled in the human soul.

Sometimes it seems that the smaller the difference, the more explosive the violence. At the beginning of this century, our greatest scientist, Albert Einstein, taught us that the most powerful and destructive force on earth is found in the smallest container so small we can't even see it with the naked eye—the atom. Controlling our vulnerability to racism is every bit as crucial to the future of humankind as controlling the atom.

Our nation was founded on the basis of a highly sophisticated understanding of human nature, which took our vulnerability to sin into account. That's why we have checks and balances, in a Constitution that has been emulated by freedom loving people all over this earth.

One of our founders, James Madison, wrote these words: "So strong is this propensity of mankind to fall into mutual animosities that . . . the most frivolous and fanciful distinctions have been sufficient to kindle their unfriendly passions and excite their most violent conflicts. . . . The latent causes . . . are . . . sown in the nature of man; and . . . cannot be removed. . . . Relief is only to be sought in . . . controlling its effects. . . . The majority . . . must be rendered . . . unable to . . . carry into effect schemes of oppression."

> *Rival gangs adopt rival colors. The slight difference between a blue bandana and a red bandana has led to the senseless loss of many lives.*

As we have struggled throughout our history to perfect our union, slavery and other manifestations of virulent racism have stained our national conscience.

When the Cherokees were forced on their fateful trail of tears. When Mexican-Americans were forcibly removed from farms and ranches. When Irish immigrants escaping famine encountered signs in Boston saying "no dogs or Irish allowed." When innocent and loyal Japanese-Americans were imprisoned at the outset of World War II, and when Hispanic heroes of World War II—who helped all our soldiers end the Holocaust against millions of European Jews and the mass murder of hundreds of thousands of Chinese— came home, they were denied burial in military cemeteries.

But in the aftermath of that war—a war in which Americans of all racial and ethnic backgrounds joined together to defeat the racist rulers of Nazi Germany and Imperial Japan—minority groups were emboldened to insist that America live up to our values. Thurgood Marshall led the charge in our courts. And the mass movement led by Dr. Martin Luther King Jr. gave us a chance to redeem our nation's soul. And much progress has been made.

We've left Egypt, but don't tell me we've arrived in Canaan.

Yet now we hear voices in America arguing that Dr. King's struggle is over—that we've reached the promised land. Maybe they're just carried away by the arrival of the Millennium. Maybe they are deluding themselves that when the calendar turns to the year 2000, man will be perfected.

These people who now call for the end of policies to promote equal opportunity say there's been so much progress that no more such efforts are justified. But they fail to recognize that the tap root of racism is almost 400 years long.

When I was eight years old, in Carthage, Tennessee, my family and I lived in a little house on Fisher Avenue, halfway up a hill. At the top of the hill was a big old mansion. One day, as the property was changing hands, the neighbors were invited to an open house. My father said: "Come, son, I want to show you something." And we walked up the hill and into the front door.

But instead of dwelling in the parlor, or the ornate dining room, or on the grand staircase, my father took me down to the basement and pointed to the dark, dank stone walls— and the cold metal rings in a row.

Slave rings.

We've left Egypt, but don't tell me we've arrived in Canaan.

Don't tell me that our persistent vulnerability to racism has suddenly disappeared, and that we now live in a color-blind society.

What would Dr. King see if he were here with us and walked out of this church, taking us on a tour of America in 1998?

I believe Dr. King would be proud that in the past 30 years, we have cut in half the gap between black earnings and white earnings. But I believe he would not let us forget that the wealth of black and Hispanic households still averages less than one-tenth that of white households.

I believe he would be proud that African-American employment is at its highest level in history, and African-American poverty is at its lowest level in history; Thanks to President Clinton, all Americans are rising with the tide of a stronger economy. But I believe he would not let us forget us that African Americans earn roughly 62 cents on each dollar that white Americans earn; he would not let us forget that black unemployment is still twice as high as unemployment for whites.

I believe Dr. King would be proud that the gap in high school graduation between blacks and whites has now been virtually eliminated—and that more African Americans are going to college than ever before in American history. But I believe he would not let us forget that the drop-out rate among Hispanic Americans is still eight points higher, with barely half finishing high school, and far fewer going on to college.

If he were here today, I believe he would be proud that this administration has appointed more blacks, more Hispanics, more Asian Americans and Native Americans to Cabinet positions and judgeships and other high posts than ever before in our history. But I believe he would not let us forget that in so many places and professions, the glass ceiling still has not been shattered.

I believe he would be proud to see how much we have done to banish discrimination from our laws. But I believe he would tell us that we still have much to do in banishing discrimination from our hearts. And I believe he would tell us that we still have much to do to enforce the laws that are on our books.

That is why I am pleased to announce today that President Clinton and I are proposing, as part of his initiative on race, the largest single increase in the enforcement of our civil rights laws in nearly two decades. Through new reforms and through heightened commitment to enforcement, we will seek to prevent discrimination before it occurs, and punish those who do discriminate in employment, in education, in housing, in health care, in access for those with disabilities.

I believe Dr. King would be proud of how diverse American culture has become—with people of all races and ethnicities listening to each other's music, reading each other's books, living and working together. But I believe he would be disappointed by how destructive and dangerous some of our culture has become—with guns, drugs, and violence against women too often taking the place of family, faith, and community. I think he would find unacceptable the number of broken homes and the failure of too many fathers to accept responsibility for their children. I think he would be heart-broken to see the devastation in too many inner-city communities, with boards still covering the windows and doors of some places burned in anger and grief three decades ago.

In the movie *Grand Canyon*, the character played by Danny Glover surveys a desolate portion of South Central Los Angeles and says, "It's not supposed to be this way."

Two thousand years ago, the Apostle Paul explained why it is this way: "All have turned aside, together they have gone wrong."

So it is appropriate on this day for us to focus on the work that remains to be done.

I believe Dr. King would urge us to get busy and that he would be proud that for people of all races, creeds, and colors, his birthday is a day of national reconciliation and service. But I believe he would be genuinely surprised that, as mayor Campbell said, some who actively oppose his agenda roll his words and phrases off their tongues even as they try to roll back equal opportunity.

The phrase "the content of our character" takes on a different meaning when it is used by those who pretend that that is all we need to establish a color-blind society. They use their color blind the way duck hunters use a duck blind. They hide behind the phrase and just hope that we, like the ducks, won't be able to see through it.

They're in favor of affirmative action if you can dunk the basketball or sink a three-point shot. But they're not in favor of it if you merely have the potential to be a leader in your community and bring people together, to teach people who are hungry for knowledge, to heal families who need medical care. So I say: we see through your color blind.

Amazing Grace also saved me;

Was color-blind but now I see.

The Gospel of Luke tells us of Jesus's reaction to people who willfully refuse to see the evidence before their eyes: "When ye see a cloud rise out of the West, straightway ye say, there cometh a shower; and so it is. And when ye see the South wind blow, ye say, there will be heat; and it cometh to pass. Ye hypocrites, ye can discern the face of the sky and of the Earth; how is it that you do not discern this time?"

"Man sees on the outside, God sees on the inside."

I believe God has a plan for the United States of America, and has since our founding.

Our mission has always been to advance the cause of liberty and to prove that religious, political, and economic freedom [is] the natural birthright of all men and women, and that freedom unlocks a higher fraction of the human potential than any other way of organizing human society.

Religious, political, and economic freedom [is] the natural birthright of all men and women.

I believe in my heart that our nation also has another, closely-related mission—one that we did not fully understand when we counted each slave as three-fifths of a person—a mission we began to glimpse through a glass, darkly, as the terrible Civil War approached.

I believe that God has given the people of our nation not only a chance, but a mission to prove to men and women throughout this world that people of different racial and ethnic backgrounds, of all faiths and creeds, can not only work and live together, but can enrich and ennoble both themselves and our common purpose.

We learned in school about the "lowest common denominator"; America is about the highest common denominator.

That is why Dr. King loved this country. He often spoke about "the glory of America, with all its faults." Even as he was persecuted, even as he was jailed, even as he was hunted, he spoke of the "glory of America, with all its faults." During the bus boycott, he said, "We are not wrong, God Almighty is wrong."

When the Supreme Court then struck down segregated transportation, Dr. King said: "That wasn't a victory for colored folks. Oh no, don't make the victory that small; that was a victory for justice and goodwill!"

And from the steps of the Lincoln Memorial, he told us of his dream that America would "live out the true meaning of its creed."

He was a patriot who always believed, as we do today, that America is indeed, the last, best hope of humankind. So just as we reproach the apostles of apathy who tell us our work is done, let us condemn those who spread hatred of America—those disciples of division who preach a separatist philosophy and call people of a different race "devils." To them, I commend the words of Dr. King when he said: "Let us not seek to satisfy our thirst for freedom by drinking from the cup of bitterness and hatred."

The alternatives to bitterness and hatred are understanding and empathy. And we must rise to the challenge with our hearts as well as our minds. We must use, in Niebuhr's phrase, "every strategem of education and every resource of religion" to promote understanding and mutual respect. And in our hearts, we must nurture empathy.

In 1957, Dr. King quoted Gandhi in saying that "the appeal of reason is more to the head, but the penetration of the heart comes from suffering. It opens up the inner understanding in man."

Dr. King said of his approach to the white majority: "The Negro all over the South must come to the point that he can say to his white brother: We will match your capacity to inflict suffering with our capacity to endure suffering. We will meet your physical force with soul force." We will not hate you, but we will not obey your evil laws.

We learned in school about the "lowest common denominator"; America is about the highest common denominator.

Many ridiculed his reliance on what he called "the weapon of non-violent protest." But the white majority, I promise you, came to understand his humanity and the justice of his cause through his reliance on "soul force."

In my tradition, we believe the world has been transformed by the willingness of Jesus Christ to suffer on the cross. Suffering binds us together, and enables us to see what we all have in common, and what we are called upon to do.

It can be summed up simply, as it was in the Gospel of Matthew: "Thou shalt love the Lord thy God with all thy heart, and with all thy soul, and with all thy mind. This is the first and greatest commandment. And the second is like unto it, thou shalt love thy neighbor as thyself."

So let us not be weary in well-doing as we address the unfinished agenda. Let us make Dr. King's dream our agenda for action. And remember, in the words of the hymn he loved:
"In Christ there is no East or West,
In him, no South or North,
but one great fellowship of love
throughout the whole wide earth.
Join hands, disciples of the faith,
whate'er your race may be,
who serves my father as a child
is surely kin to me."

White Feminism, Liberal Racism, and Welfare Reform[4]

Gwendolyn Mink

Professor of politics, University of California at Santa Cruz, 1980– ; student, University of Chicago, 1970–72; B.A. with Highest Honors, University of California at Berkeley, 1974; Ph.D. in government, Cornell University, 1982; author, Old Labor and New Immigrants in American Political Development *(1986);* Wages of Motherhood: Inequality in the Welfare State, 1917–1942 *(1995);* Welfare's End *(1998); co-editor (with Wilma Mankiller, Marysa Navarro, Barbara Smith, and Gloria Steinem),* Reader's Companion to U.S. Women's History *(1998); winner, Victoria Schuck Award for best book on women and politics, American Political Science Association, 1996; co-chair, Women's Committee of One Hundred, a feminist mobilization against punitive welfare reform.*

Editors' introduction: In her book *Welfare's End,* Gwendolyn Mink supports the civil rights of poor women. On November 7, 1997, in Chicago, Illinois, she addressed some 150 students, faculty, and community members at the Dean's Symposium concerning the need to protect benefits for poor women. She asks: "How might feminists of all races have intervened differently in the welfare debate?"

Gwendolyn Mink's speech: More than 95 percent of adult welfare recipients are women. This is not surprising, since women are usually their families' care-givers. What is surprising is that during two years of formal legislative debate about ending welfare, the adverse consequences of such a decision for poor women were scarcely mentioned. Even in liberal circles, where tears flowed prodigiously for poor children, few rued the effects of punitive welfare provisions on poor women.

Some feminist activists did regard Republican welfare proposals as an attack on poor single mothers. The Women's Committee of One Hundred, for example, campaigned against those proposals, stressing the importance of welfare to poor women's rights and survival. Speaking of "welfare as women's issue," we argued that "a war against poor women is a war against *all* women."

This was a strategically clever rallying cry; but it failed to rally many women—even feminists. In fact, the war against

---

4. Delivered in Chicago, Illinois, on November 7, 1997, at 2 p.m.
Reprinted with permission.

Welfare reform failed to arouse many white feminists to make a differ- ence—to defend poor women's citizenship and security against legislative attack.

poor women was just that: a war against poor women. And it was a war in which many white, middle class feminists participated on the anti-welfare side. Some examples: On Capitol Hill, all white women in the U. S. Senate—including four Democratic women who call themselves feminists— voted *for* the new welfare law when it first came to the floor in the Summer of 1995. In the House, only a half dozen white women voted for a substitute bill that would have pre- served the welfare entitlement without time limits in 1995; and in 1996, only one white Democratic woman voted against a substitute bill that revoked poor mothers' entitle- ment to cash assistance. Meanwhile, across the country, a NOW-LDEF appeal for funds to support an economic justice litigator aroused so much hate mail that NOW-LDEF stopped doing direct mail on the welfare issue.

Feminist Members of Congress did not write the Personal Responsibility Act, of course. Nor did members of the National Organization for Women or contributors to Emily's List comprise the driving force behind the most brutal provi- sions of the new welfare law. My point is not that white fem- inists were uniquely responsible for how welfare has been reformed. It is that they were uniquely positioned to make a difference. They have made a difference in many arenas across the years, even during inauspicious Republican presi- dencies—reforming rape laws, winning recognition of sexual harassment as a form of sex discrimination, and securing passage of a federal law against domestic violence. They cer- tainly could have made a difference when a friendly Demo- cratic president begun casting about for ways to reform welfare in 1993; and while they could not have changed Republican intentions in the 104th Congress, they surely could have pressured the Democrat they helped elect to the White House to veto the Republican bill.

But welfare reform failed to arouse many white feminists to make a difference—to defend poor women's citizenship and security against legislative attack. Instead, white and middle class solipsism enforced silence among many white femi- nists; this silence gave permission to policy-makers to treat punitive welfare reform as a no-lose situation. Welfare reform did not bear directly on the lives of most white, mid- dle class feminists—and so they did not mobilize their net- works and raise their voices as they so often do to defend abortion rights or to protest domestic violence. So much for sisterhood.

Silence among feminists was not the only problem, how- ever. When they did enter the public debate, many white feminists echoed welfare foes. At the same time white femi- nists were silent about the effects of new welfare provisions on poor women's rights—rights to sexual privacy, reproduc- tive choice, and family liberty, for example—they were vocal about the need to reform welfare so as to improve the per-

sonal and family practices of poor single mothers. Around
Capitol Hill, for example, white feminist legislators could be
heard lamenting that "they" have too many babies; that
"we" need to do something about "their" illegitimacy; and
that "work" is better than welfare. Out of this myth-monger-
ing, feminists in Congress- like feminists across the country—entered the welfare debate on the side of coercive
reform.

The point I want to make is that the Republicans won their
war against poor single mothers with white feminist com-
plicity. The new welfare law reflects a consensus that there's
something wrong with mothers who need welfare and that
cash assistance should require their reform. The two pillars
of the new welfare law—work and marriage—were born
from this consensus. Work requirements and sanctions
against non-marital childrearing may be Republican and
patriarchal in execution, but they are Democratic and feminist in inspiration.

How is it that feminists participated in the most aggressive
assault against women's rights and gender equality in this
century? Why were so many white feminists unconcerned
that welfare reform stripped poor single mothers not only of
cash assistance, but of basic civil rights, as well? These questions raise a larger question of ideology and policy: how
might feminists have framed a defense of poor single mothers' right to welfare?

For anyone committed to reaching equality, the answers to
these questions matter a lot. In the absence of widespread
feminist opposition to the welfare reform principles of the
Personal Responsibility Act, the legislative record is devoid of
a counter-narrative that might temper administrative and
judicial enforcement of the new law. Moreover, it is devoid of
any discursive precedent for woman-friendly, equal-
ity-enhancing amendments to the new law. Since white feminists did not contest or disturb the Republican welfare
paradigm, about all they can do now to fix the new welfare
mess is urge that more money be spent on job training and
child care and that broader exceptions for battered women
be adopted. These are important goals, but they do not repair
the damage wrought by the new welfare law on the lives and
rights of poor single mothers.

The new welfare law—the Personal Responsibility Act of
1996—distinguishes poor single mothers as a separate caste,
subject to a separate system of law. Poor single mothers are
the only people in America forced by law to work outside the
home. They are the only people in America whose decisions
to bear children are punished by government. They are the
only people in America of whom government may demand
the details of intimate relationships in exchange for food,
medical, and cash assistance. And they are the only mothers

*How is it that
feminists partici-
pated in the
most aggressive
assault against
women's rights
and gender
equality in this
century?*

in America compelled by law to make room for biological fathers in their families.

Given the harms visited upon poor single mothers, why didn't white feminists mobilize against the welfare law? Why were there no candlelight vigils like there were against O. J. Simpson? Why were there no marches like there have been to celebrate *Roe v. Wade*? Why were no boycotts waged like they were against *The People vs. Larry Flynt*?

I think white feminists, who are the mainstream of the women's movement, view mothers who need welfare as mothers who need feminism. They see welfare mothers as victims—of patriarchy, maybe of racism, possibly of false consciousness. They don't see welfare mothers as feminist agents of their own lives—as women who are entitled to and capable of making independent and honorable choices about what kind of work they will do and how many children they will have and whether they will marry. As a result, when many white feminists weighed into the welfare debate, it was to prescribe reforms to assimilate welfare mothers to white feminists' own goals—to independence through paid employment, and to family equity through child support enforcement.

White feminists were not the only ones to prescribe the assimilation of welfare mothers to middle class feminist norms. Eleanor Holmes Norton sometimes spoke of the "pathology" of non-marital motherhood among poor Black women, for example, while Maxine Waters occasionally called for more aggressive social work intervention into poor single mothers' lives. But women of color feminists were far more interested in mitigating the effects of poverty on poor mothers and children than in engineering the moral and cultural circumstances under which poor mothers raise their children. Thus women of color in Congress, including Norton and Waters, argued strenuously to preserve the welfare entitlement—something their white sisters did not do. Instead, hiding behind "constituent pressures," white feminists like Barbara Boxer and Nina Lowey said they "had to" vote for punitive welfare reform—and that they anyway had already "done a lot for women" by voting right on abortion.

These sorts of trade-offs—between voting right on abortion and voting wrong on welfare—do indeed reflect constituent pressures, including pressures brought by women voters, of whom there are far more white women than women of color and far more middle class women than poor. They also reflect the bias of electoral feminism—especially Emily's List—which measures a woman candidate's feminism solely on the basis of her position on abortion. White feminist goals supply the content of white feminist constituent pressures and campaign contribution decisions. These goals reflect white feminists' experiences—middle class experiences privileged by white skin. Far from humbled by their limited, even parochial, experiences, white feminists typically translate their goals and experiences into political claims and social expectations in the name of all women. White, middle class feminists are of course ideologically varied—and have been across two centuries of U. S. feminism. Nevertheless, they too often have assumed that their own gender experiences stand for all women's experiences and thus too often have presumed to speak for all women across the privileges and disabilities of class and color.

White feminists have fought valiantly to win rights and opportunities in the name of all woman. But for women who are not white and middle class, some of these rights and opportunities come at a price. That price is conformity to choices as white feminists would make them. I've shared many podiums with white, middle class feminists who argue that while *all* women have rights, *poor* women ought to exercise their rights not as they *themselves* choose but as *white feminists* do. According to this view, women ought to choose fertility control rather than childbirth if they are poor; ought to associate at least economically with the fathers of their children; ought to choose child care provided by others over child-raising performed by themselves; ought to work outside the home. These white feminist prescriptions for poor single mothers who need welfare bleed into negative judgments of poor single mothers' choices when those choices are at odds with white feminist prescriptions. White feminist prescriptions and judgments are often well-intentioned, but they often are also racist, or at least have racist effects.

At this point in the 20th century, racism within white feminism sounds like an oxymoron—or so most white feminists would have us believe. Most white feminists believe themselves to be committed anti-racists; many of the academically-inclined even theorize an organic relationship between anti-racism and the feminist project. If the standard for racism is David Duke and the Aryan Nation, then white feminism is surely not racist. But racism takes different forms. Alexander Saxton named them "hard racism" and "soft racism" in his history of the 19th century white republic. I'll call their late 20th century descendants easy racism and liberal racism.

The hard racism of exclusionists and exterminators persists in our time, but it has also become easier to fight: we have laws thut punish lynching, for example; we use the Constitution to prohibit government from forcibly segregating people or denying their rights on the basis of race; and, at least for now, we have laws that make discrimination by schools and employers potentially quite costly. The hard racism of today—the most difficult racism—is liberal racism: it is the racism of people who say they are not racists. This racism is elusive—hard to pin down, because often couched in the language of merit and neutrality; hard to prove because

The hard racism of today—the most difficult racism—is liberal racism: it is the racism of people who say they are not racists.

coded into proxy issues like welfare, immigration, and crime. It's the kind of racism that makes something like affirmative action necessary, because it's the kind of racism people practice while claiming to treat people equally.

Liberal racists run the gamut, from conservatives who insist on "color-blind" laws and practices, to liberals and lefties who celebrate multiculturalism and inclusivity. What mskes all these folks liberals is their professed faith in individual possibility. What makes some liberals racists is their expectation that we will all be equal when we are all alike. What makes other liberals racists is the way they embrace difference: sometimes exoticizing it, sometimes appropriating it, always genuflecting before it—but never relinquishing the privilege of setting the standard against which difference is defined.

Among feminists, the liberal racism of many white feminists accounts for some of our bitterest divisions. Most white feminists are committed to being "inclusive"—by which they mean telling the stories of more and different groups of women. But the addition of other women's stories does not necessarily change how they tell *white* women's story, does not move white women off center-stage, and does not alter their understanding of gender in the relations of inequality. So, for example, although the story of women of color in the U. S. is in part the story of subordination by white women and feminists, many white feminists cannot accept a narrative of feminist history in which white feminists are not always heroes. Nor can they accept an analysis of gender as part of a matrix of oppression, rather than as the root oppression from which all other oppressions derive. Most feminists are eager to enlarge the canvas; fewer are willing to change the picture.

Most white feminists were unwilling to change the picture when it came to welfare reform, as well. On Main Street and in the halls of Congress, white, middle class feminists generally insisted that their prescriptions for their own liberation suit the circumstances of mothers who are single and poor.

This stalled white feminist opposition to welfare reform. It also turned many feminists into latter-day materialists . . . as welfare mothers became objects of feminist reform rather than agents of feminist solidarity. Maternalist reformers of the early 20th century invented welfare to teach immigrant women how to be good mothers. Many late twentieth century white feminists conspired to reform welfare to teach poor mothers of color how to be good feminists.

White feminists influenced welfare reform legislation in two major ways. The first had to do with work requirements. The second had to do with paternity establishment and child support enforcement.

Although there is plenty of evidence that women in general and feminists in particular don't like the draconian aspects of

Most feminists are eager to enlarge the canvas; fewer are willing to change the picture.

the new welfare law, they do not necessarily eschew the law's core assumptions. One of the core assumptions is that poor single mothers should move from welfare to work.

White feminists did not invent the "work" solution to welfare. But their emphasis on women's right to work outside the home—in tandem with women's increased presence in the labor force—gave cover to conservatives eager to require wage-work of single mothers even as they championed the traditional family. Moreover, it legitimated the view popular among many white feminists, that wage-earning is "good for" mothers who need welfare.

Most of the policy claims made by second wave feminists have emphasized women's right to participate in men's world and have made work outside the home a defining element of women's full and equal citizenship. White middle-class feminists responded to their particular historical experiences, experiences drawn by an ethos of domesticity which confined middle class white women to the home. As they entered the labor market, these women did not spurn family work; rather, they found their energy doubly taxed by the dual responsibility of earning and caring. Accordingly, many feminists called for labor market policies addressing the family needs that fall disproportionately on women—parental leave and child care policies, for example. Their concern has been to ease the contradictions between wage-work and family life. Their focus has been how family needs impede opportunities and achievements in the labor market; their goals have been labor policies that relieve women's family responsibilities (e.g., child care) and strengthen women's rights in the workplace (e.g., wage equity). They have not been so interested in winning social policies to support women where we meet our family responsibilities: in the home.

The popular feminist claim that women earn independence, autonomy, and equality through wages historically has divided feminists along class and race lines, as women of color and poor white women have not usually earned equality from sweated labor. To the contrary. Especially for women of color, wage work has been a mark of inequality: expected by the white society for whom they work; necessary because their male kin cannot find jobs or cannot earn family-supporting wages; and exploitative because their earnings keep them poor. Thus, the right to care for their own children—to work inside the home—has been a touchstone goal of their struggles for equality. The fact that women are positioned divergently in the nexus among care-giving, wage-earning, and inequality separated feminists one from another on the welfare issue; separate many white feminists from many feminists of color; and separated employed middle class feminists from mothers who need welfare.

Out of second-wave feminism's emphasis on winning rights in the workplace emerged, *sotto voce*, a feminist expectation that women *ought* to work outside the home and an assumption that *any* job outside the home—including caring for other people's children—is more socially productive than caring for one's own. Although feminism is fundamentally about winning women choices, our labor market bias has put much of feminism not on the side of vocational choice—the choice to work inside or outside the home—but on the side of wage-earning for all women. Thus, most congressional feminists, along with many white feminists across the country, have conflated their *right* to work outside the home with poor single mothers' *obligation* to do so. Thus many feminists agreed with Republicans that poor single mothers should "move from welfare to work."

The labor market focus of second wave feminism has accomplished much for women—most importantly establishing equality claims for women as wage-earners. Contemporary feminist calls for further labor market reforms—for an increased minimum wage, gender-sensitive unemployment insurance, comparable worth, child care—rightly point out the persisting impediments to women's equality as labor market citizens. The problem is not with the specific content of feminist agendas but with their one-sidedness and prescriptivity.

Applying white, middle class feminist principles to poor single mothers' lives, many white feminists have worked ardently to attenuate the new welfare law's harshest provisions. But they do not refute the idea that poor single mothers *should* seek work outside the home. Except among welfare rights activists and a handful of feminists, no one has defended poor mothers' right to raise their children, and no one has questioned the assumption that poor single mothers should *have to*—should be compelled by law to—work outside the home.

When welfare rules indenture poor mothers as unpaid servants of local governments (in workfare programs), it is mothers of color who are disproportionately harmed.

White feminists' enlistment in work-ethical welfare reform reflected their gender goals and biases. In the welfare context, these goals and biases have racial effects. Although work requirements aim indiscriminately at all poor single mothers, it is mothers of color who bear their heaviest weight. African American and Latina mothers are disproportionately poor, and, accordingly, are disproportionately enrolled on welfare: in 1994, adult recipients in AFDC families were 37.4 percent white, 36.4 percent Black, 19.9 percent Latina, 2.9 percent Asian, and 1.3 percent Native American. So when welfare rules indenture poor mothers as unpaid servants of local governments (in workfare programs), it is mothers of color who are disproportionately harmed. And when time limits require poor mothers to forsake their children for the labor market, it is mothers of color who are disproportionately deprived of their right to manage their

family's lives and it is children of color who are disproportionately deprived of their mothers' care.

White feminists did not clamor to end the welfare entitlement; and many expressed deep disagreement with Republican plans to de-fund job training, vocational education, and
child care. But their conflation of gender equality with labor
market equality—of independence from men with independence as wage-earners—put them into conversation with
conservatives intent on repealing welfare. So, too, did their
insistence on tough child support provisions.

Feminists in Congress have been particularly emphatic
about "making fathers pay" for children through increased
federal involvement in the establishment and enforcement of
child support orders. In fact, without white, middle class
feminist interventions, especially in the House of Representatives, paternity-based child support would not be the major
pillar of the new welfare policy that it has become. The only
reason the Personal Responsibility Act contains child support
provisions is because feminists in Congress embarrassed
Republicans into adopting them.

These provisions impose stringent national conditions on
non-marital childrearing. Under the mandatory establishment of paternity provision, welfare eligibility depends upon
a mother's willingness to reveal the identity of her child's
father. Since the purpose of paternity establishment is to
assign child support obligations to biological fathers, the provision also requires mothers to cooperate in establishing,
modifying, and enforcing the support orders for their children. The law requires states to reduce a family's welfare
grant by at least 25 percent when a mother fails to comply
with these rules and permits states to deny the family's grant
altogether.

The view that the dereliction of fathers creates or feeds
mothers' need for welfare is quite popular among white feminists. Finding the costs of childbearing that fall disproportionately on women a wellspring of gender inequality, many
feminists want men to provide for their biological children,
even if they have no relationship with them. Incautious pursuit of this objective aligned white feminists behind a policy
that endangers the rights of poor single mothers.

Paternity establishment rules compel non-marital mothers
to disclose private matters in exchange for cash and medical
assistance—to answer questions like whom did you sleep
with? how often? when? where? how? . . . Meanwhile, child
support rules require non-marital mothers to associate with
biological fathers, and in so doing to stoke such fathers'
claims to parental rights. In these and other ways, paternity
establishment and child support provisions set poor single
mothers apart from other mothers, subjecting them to a separate system of law. While they beef up services that
deserted middle class mothers may *choose* to enlist, they

impose such services on—and compel intimate revelations from—poor mothers who have chosen to parent alone.

Middle class feminist energy behind stringent paternity establishment and child support enforcement is no doubt animated in part by exasperation with some men's cost-free exploitation of the sexual revolution. From this perspective, men ought to be held responsible for the procreative consequences of their heightened access to women's bodies. The quest for fairness in procreative relations drives the increasingly punitive proposals designed to force fathers to meet their obligations to children. But it doesn't explain why middle class feminists believe material coercion is an acceptable means to paternal responsibility.

A reading of congressional debates suggests that the main impetus behind middle class feminists' advocacy of punitive paternity establishment and child support enforcement rules are their own class and marital experiences. When middle class women think of the circumstances that might lead them to welfare, they think of divorce—from middle class men who then refuse to chip in for the core and maintenance of children. California Congresswoman Lynn Woolsey, who is white, is a case in point. Something of a Beltway icon during the welfare debate, she described herself and was described by others as "a typical welfare mother." Thirty years earlier, she had had to turn to welfare following her divorce from a man she describes as "very successful." Though she had a support order, she "never received a penny in child support." Woolsey's story provided a useful strategic intervention into the welfare debate, countering the stereotypic image of welfare mothers as Black and unmarried. But marking one mother's story, however uplifting, as representative of a whole population invites the kind of solipsism that produces one-size-fits-all policy prescriptions. Such prescriptions are not only unworkable, they also neglect the needs of people who must and do live their lives differently.

The compulsory features of paternity establishment and child support enforcement may be unremarkable to a divorced mother with a support order: she escapes compulsion by choosing to pursue child support, and what matters to her is that the support order be enforced. But some mothers do not have support orders because they do not want them—do not want to identify fathers; do not want fathers involved with children; do not want to expose their children to danger; do not want to expose fathers to harsh penalties when they cannot pay what a court tells them they owe; do not want to discourage fathers from participating in the lives of their children if they cannot pay the state's price for the pleasure.

"Making fathers pay" may promote the economic and justice interests of many custodial mothers. But *making mothers* make fathers pay means making mothers pay for subsistence with their own rights—and safety. The issue is not whether government should assist mothers in collecting payments from fathers. Of course it should. Neither is the issue whether child support enforcement provisions in welfare policy help mothers who have or desire child support awards. Of course they do. Nor is the issue whether it is a good thing for children to have active fathers—of course it can be. The issue is coercion, coercion directed toward the mother who has eschewed patriarchal conventions—whether by choice or from necessity. It is also coercion directed toward the mother whose deviation from patriarchal norms has been linked to her racial and cultural standing.

Paternity establishment and child support became strategies for welfare reform not because of the unjust effects of divorce on mothers but because of the allegedly unsavory behavior of mothers of non-marital children. It is non-marital childbearing, not divorce, that has been blamed for social pathologies like crime and dependency. The preamble to the new welfare law legislates precisely this point of view. Such patriarchal reasoning leaches into racial argument, as welfare discourse specifically correlates non-marital childbearing rates among African Americans with social and moral decay.

Like work requirements, the coercive aspects of paternity establishment and child support policy are aimed against single mothers in general. However, like work requirements, they have decidedly racial effects. The mandatory maternal cooperation rule targets mothers who are not and have not been married, as well as mothers who do not have and do not want child support. Non-marital mothers are the bulls-eye, and among non-marital mothers receiving welfare, only 28.4 percent are white. This means that the new welfare law's invasions of associational and privacy rights will dispro-portionately harm mothers of color. Inspired by white feminist outrage against middle class "deadbeat dads," the paternity establishment and child support provisions both reflect and entrench inequalities among women.

How might feminists of all races have intervened differently in the welfare debate? We could have begun with the feminist method—with listening to welfare mothers' stories rather than inferring from our own. And we could have begun by defending poor mothers' rights as we would defend our own—by resisting any reforms that coerce poor mothers to surrender rights in exchange for cash assistance.

We did, indeed, need to end welfare—but as poor single mothers experienced it, not as middle class moralizers imagined it. *Why* we end welfare dictates *how* we end it— whether we end it by subordinating poor single mothers or by improving their prospects for equality.

Why *we end welfare dictates* how *we end it.*

In theory . . . all care-giving is work.

Equality requires us to expose and repudiate the assumptions embedded in welfare law and rife in the welfare debate. We can do this most effectively by establishing a new presumption—namely, that poor single women who give care to their children are mothers whose care-giving *is work*.

Once we establish that *all* care-giving is work, whatever the racial, marital, or class status of the care-giver, we can build a case for economic arrangements that enable poor single mothers to do their jobs. We all know that family work—household management and parenting—takes skill, energy, time and responsibility. We know this because people who can afford it *pay* other people to do this work. Many wage-earning mothers pay for child care; upper class mothers who work outside the home pay for nannies; very wealthy mothers who don't even work outside the home pay household workers to assist them with their various tasks. Moreover, even when we are not paying surrogates to do our family care-giving, we pay people to perform activities in the labor market that care-givers also do in the home. We pay drivers to take us places—bus drivers, taxi drivers, limousine drivers; we pay nurses to make us feel better and help us get well; we pay psychologists to help us with our troubles; we pay teachers to explain our lessons; we pay cooks and waitresses to prepare and serve our food. If economists can measure the value of this work when it is performed for other people's families, why can't we impute value to it when it is performed for one's own?

Were we to end welfare as poor single mothers know it, we would redefine welfare. In place of stingy benefits doled out begrudgingly to needy mothers, welfare would become an income owed to non-market, care-giving workers—owed to anyone who bears sole responsibility for children (or for other dependent family members). We could model this income on survivors' insurance, so that it would be nationally uniform, paid automatically to categorically eligible care-givers, and unconditioned by the race, class, and moral value society assigns to individual women.

All family care-givers are owed this income in theory, for all care-giving is work. However, the cardinal purpose of such an income should be to redress the unique inequality of care-givers—usually mothers—who are parenting alone. Such care-givers shoulder the dual responsibilities of providing care for children and financing it. While some single mothers may be able to afford both responsibilities, most cannot, because they are time-poor, cash-poor, or both. A care-giver's income would relieve the disproportionate burdens that fall on single mothers and in so doing would lessen inequalities among women based on class and marital status, and between male and female parents based on default social roles. Although paid to single care-givers only, this income support would assure a safety net to all care-givers, guaranteeing a means to survive if ever they need or choose to parent—or to care for other family members—alone. The extension of the safety net to care-givers as independent citizens would underwrite equality as it would enable adults to exit untenable—and often violent—relationships of economic dependency and to retain reproductive and vocational choices when they do.

We need to end welfare in this way to enable equality—in the safety net, between the genders, among women, and under the Constitution. Income support for all care-givers who are going it alone would permit solo parents to decide how best to manage their responsibilities to children. It would (eventually) undermine the sexual division of labor, for some men will be enticed to do family care-giving work once they understand it to have economic value. Offering an income to all solo care-givers in a unitary system—to non-marital mothers as well as to widowed ones—would erase invidious moral distinctions among mothers and eliminate their racial effects. Further, universal income support for single parents would restore mothers' constitutional rights—to not marry, to bear children, and to parent them, even if they are poor. It would promote occupational freedom, by rewarding work even when work cannot be exchanged for wages. So redefined, welfare would become a sign not of dependency but of independence, a means not to moral regulation but to social and political equality.

Ending welfare this way will remedy inequality where it is most gendered—in the care-giving relations of social reproduction. Yet, it will not be enough to end welfare by replacing it with a care-givers' income. The end of welfare—the goal of feminist social policy—must be to enhance women's choices across their full spectrum. We need to improve women's opportunities as *both* non-market and market workers, so that care-givers' choice to work inside the home is backed up by the possibility of choosing not to. We must, then, also win labor market reforms to make outside work feasible even for mothers who are parenting alone. Unless we make outside work affordable for solo care-givers, a care-givers' income would constrain choice by favoring care-giving over wage-earning.

The end of welfare, then, includes "making work pay," not only by remunerating care-giving work but also by making participation in the labor market equitable and rewarding for women, especially mothers. To make work pay we must improve women's position in the labor market: through a minimum wage that provides an income at least at the poverty threshold; comparable worth policies that correct the low economic value assigned to women's jobs; unemployment insurance reforms covering women's gendered reasons for losing or leaving jobs (lack of child care and pregnancy, for example); paid family leave; guaranteed child care; uni-

The end of welfare—the goal of feminist social policy—must be to enhance women's choices across their full spectrum.

versal health care; full employment policy; a massive investment in education and vocational training; and aggressive enforcement of anti-discrimination laws.

This end to welfare will take us down many paths, in recognition of women's diverse experiences of gender and diverse hopes for equality.

IV. Legacies of War

Banning Landmines[1]

Jody Williams

Coordinator, International Campaign to Ban Landmines; born 1950; graduated Johns Hopkins School of Advanced International Studies; coordinated the Nicaragua-Honduras Education Project; associate director of Medical Aid to El Salvador, a Los Angeles-based humanitarian relief organization; advocate on issues relating to US policy toward Central America; began working for Vietnam Veterans of America Foundation, 1991, to bring together a coalition to ban antipersonnel landmines; has spoken world-wide on the landmine crisis; co-authored After the Guns Fall Silent: The Enduring Legacy of Landmines *(1995).*

Editors' introduction: In 1997, the Nobel Foundation bestowed the Nobel Peace Prize jointly on the International Campaign to Ban Landmines—a coalition of some 1,000 world organizations—and its coordinator, Jody Williams. Beginning in 1991, Williams's campaign has convinced 123 nations to endorse a treaty to eliminate landmines that kill and maim thousands of persons each year. Williams proclaimed that "landmines have been used since the U.S. Civil War, since the Crimean War. Yet we are taking them out of arsenals of the world."

Jody Williams's speech: Your Majesties, Honorable Members of the Nobel Committee, Excellencies and Honored Guests:

It is a privilege to be here today, together with other representatives of the International Campaign to Ban Landmines, to receive jointly the 1997 Nobel Peace Prize. Our appreciation goes to those who nominated us and to the Nobel Committee for choosing this year to recognize, from among so many other nominees who have worked diligently for peace, the work of the International Campaign.

I am deeply honored—but whatever personal recognition derives from this award, I believe that this high tribute is the result of the truly historic achievement of this humanitarian effort to rid the world of one indiscriminate weapon. In the words of the Nobel Committee, the International Campaign "started a process which in the space of a few years changed a ban on antipersonnel mines from a vision to a feasible reality." Further, the

---

1. Lecture delivered in Oslo, Norway, on December 10, 1997, upon accepting the Nobel Peace Prize awarded by The Nobel Foundation. Reprinted with permission of Jody Williams. Copyright © The Nobel Foundation.

effort to rid the world of one indiscriminate weapon. In the words of the Nobel Committee, the International Campaign "started a process which in the space of a few years changed a ban on antipersonnel mines from a vision to a feasible reality." Further, the Committee noted that the Campaign has been able to "express and mediate a broad range of popular commitment in an unprecedented way. With the governments of several small and medium-sized countries taking the issue up . . . this work has grown into a convincing example of an effective policy for peace."

The desire to ban land mines is not new. In the late 1970s, the International Committee of the Red Cross, along with a handful of non-governmental organizations (NGOs), pressed the world to look at weapons that were particularly injurious and/or indiscriminate. One of the weapons of special concern was landmines. People often ask why the focus on this one weapon. How is the landmine different from any other conventional weapon?

Landmines distinguish themselves because once they have been sown, once the soldier walks away from the weapon, the landmine cannot tell the difference between a soldier or a civilian—a woman, a child, a grandmother going out to collect firewood to make the family meal. The crux of the problem is that while the use of the weapon might be militarily justifiable during the day of the battle, or even the two weeks of the battle, or maybe even the two months of the battle, once peace is declared the landmine does not recognize that peace. The landmine is eternally prepared to take victims. In common parlance, it is the perfect soldier, the "eternal sentry." The war ends, the landmine goes on killing.

Since World War II most of the conflicts in the world have been internal conflicts. The weapon of choice in those wars has all too often been landmines—to such a degree that what we find today are tens of millions of landmines contaminating approximately 70 countries around the world. The overwhelming majority of those countries are found in the developing world, primarily in those countries that do not have the resources to clean up the mess, to care for the tens of thousands of landmine victims. The end result is an international community now faced with a global humanitarian crisis.

Let me take a moment to give a few examples of the degree of the epidemic. Today Cambodia has somewhere between four and six million landmines, which can be found in over 50 percent of its national territory. Afghanistan is littered with perhaps nine million landmines. The U. S. military has said that during the height of the Russian invasion and ensuing war in that country, up to 30 million mines were scattered throughout Afghanistan. In the few years of the fighting in the former Yugoslavia, some six million landmines were sown throughout various sections of the coun-

The landmine cannot tell the difference between a soldier or a civilian.

try—Angola nine million, Mozambique a million, Somalia a million—I could go on, but it gets tedious. Not only do we have to worry about the mines already in the ground, we must be concerned about those that are stockpiled and ready for use. Estimates range between one and two hundred million mines in stockpiles around the world.

When the ICRC pressed in the 1970s for the governments of the world to consider increased restrictions or elimination of particularly injurious or indiscriminate weapons, there was little support for a ban of landmines. The end result of several years of negotiations was the 1980 Convention on Conventional Weapons (CCW). What that treaty did was attempt to regulate the use of landmines. While the Convention tried to tell commanders in the field when it was okay to use the weapon and when it was not okay to use the weapon, it also allowed them to make decisions about the applicability of the law in the midst of battle. Unfortunately, in the heat of battle, the laws of war do not exactly come to mind. When you are trying to save your skin you use anything and everything at your disposal to do so.

Throughout these years the Cold War raged on, and internal conflicts that often were proxy wars of the Super Powers proliferated. Finally with the collapse of the Soviet Bloc, people began to look at war and peace differently. Without the overarching threat of nuclear holocaust, people started to look at how wars had actually been fought during the Cold War. What they found was that in the internal conflcts fought during that time, the most insidious weapon of all was the antipersonnel landmine—and that it contaminated the globe in epidemic proportion.

As relative peace broke out with the end of the Cold War, the U. N. was able to go into these nations that had been torn by internal strife, and what they found when they got there were millions and millions of landmines which affected every aspect of peacekeeping, which affected every aspect of post-conflict reconstruction of those societies. You know, if you are in Phnom Penh in Cambodia, and you are setting up the peacekeeping operations, it might seem relatively easy. But when you want to send your troops out into the hinterlands where four or six million landmines are, it becomes a problem, because the main routes are mined. Part of the peace agreement was to bring the hundreds of thousands of refugees back into the country so that they could participate in the voting, in the new democracy being forged in Cambodia. Part of the plan to bring them back included giving each family enough land so that they could be self-sufficient, so they wouldn't be a drain on the country, so that they could contribute to reconstruction. What they found: So many landmines they couldn't give land to the families. What did they get? Fifty dollars and a year's supply of rice. That is the impact of landmines.

It was the NGOs, the non-governmental organizations, who began to seriously think about trying to deal with the root of the problem—to eliminate the problem, it would be necessary to eliminate the weapon. The work of NGOs across the board was affected by the landmines in the developing world. Children's groups, development organizations, refugee organizations, medical and humanitarian relief groups—all had to make huge adjustments in their programs to try to deal with the landmine crisis and its impact on the people they were trying to help. It was also in this period that the first NGO humanitarian demining organizations were born—to try to return contaminated land to rural communities.

It was a handful of NGOs, with their roots in humanitarian and human rights work, which began to come together, in late 1991 and early 1992, in an organized effort to ban antipersonnel landmines. In October of 1992, Handicap International, Human Rights Watch, medico international, Mines Advisory Group, Physicians for Human Rights and Vietnam Veterans of America Foundation came together to issue a "Joint Call to Ban Antipersonnel Landmines." These organizations, which became the steering committee of the International Campaign to Ban Landmines called for an end to the use, production, trade and stockpiling of antipersonnel landmines. The call also pressed governments to increase resources for humanitarian mine clearance and for victim assistance.

From this inauspicious beginning, the International Campaign has become an unprecedented coalition of 1,000 organizations working together in 60 countries to achieve the common goal of a ban of antipersonnel landmines. And as the Campaign grew, the steering committee was expanded to represent the continuing growth and diversity of those who had come together in this global movement. We added the Afghan and Cambodian Campaigns and Radda Barnen in 1996, and the South African Campaign and Kenya Coaltion early this year as we continued to press toward our goal. And in six years we did it. In September of this year, 89 countries came together—here in Oslo—and finished the negotiations of a ban treaty based on a draft drawn up by Austria only at the beginning of this year. Just last week in Ottawa, Canada, 121 countries came together again to sign that ban treaty. And as a clear indication of the political will to bring this treaty into force as soon as possible, three countries ratified the treaty upon signature—Canada, Mauritius and Ireland.

In its first years, the International Campaign developed primarily in the North—in the countries which had been significant producers of antipersonnel landmines. The strategy was to press for national, regional and international measures to ban landmines. Part of this strategy was to get the governments of the world to review the CCW and in the review process—try to get them to ban the weapon through that convention. We did not succeed. But over the two and one-half years of the review process, with the pressure that we were able to generate—the heightened international attention to the issue—began to raise the stakes, so that different governments wanted to be seen as leaders on what the world was increasingly recognizing as a global humanitarian crisis.

The early lead had been taken in the United States, with the first legislated moratorium on exports in 1992. And while the author of that legislation, Senator Leahy, has continued to fight tirelessly to ban the weapon in the U. S., increasingly other nations far surpassed that early leadership. In March of 1995, Belgium became the first country to ban the use, production, trade . . . and stockpiling domestically. Other countries followed suit: Austria, Norway, Sweden, and others. So even as the CCW review was ending in failure, increasingly governments were calling for a ban. What had once been called a utopian goal of NGOs was gaining in strength and momentum.

While we still had that momentum, in the waning months of the CCW review, we decided to try to get the individual governments which had taken action or had called for a ban to come together in a self-identifying bloc. There is, after all, strength in numbers. So during the final days of the CCW we invited them to a meeting and they actually came. A handful of governments agreed to sit down with us and talk about where the movement to ban landmines would go next. Historically, NGOs and governments have too often seen each other as adversaries, not colleagues, and we were shocked that they came. Seven or nine came to the first meeting, 14 to the second, and 17 to the third. By the time we had concluded the third meeting, with the conclusion of the Review Conference on May 3rd of 1996, the Canadian government had offered to host a governmental meeting in October of last year, in which pro-ban governments would come together and strategize about how to bring about a ban. The CCW review process had not produced the results we sought, so what do we do next?

From the third to the fifth of October we met in Ottawa. It was a very fascinating meeting. There were 50 governments there as full participants and 24 observers. The International Campaign was also participating in the Conference. The primary objectives of the conference were to develop an Ottawa Declaration, which states would sign signalling their intention to ban landmines, and an "Agenda for Action," which outlined concrete steps on the road to a ban. We were all prepared for that, but few were prepared for the concluding comments by Lloyd Axworthy, the Foreign Minister of Canada. Foreign Minister Axworthy stood up and congratulated everybody for formulating the Ottawa Declaration and the Agenda for Action, which were clearly seen as giving teeth to

Historically, [non-governmental organizations] and governments have too often seen each other as adversaries, not colleagues.

the ban movement. But the Foreign Minister did not end with congratulations. He ended with a challenge. The Canadian government challenged the world to return to Canada in a year to sign an international treaty banning antipersonnel landmines.

Members of the International Campaign to Ban Landmines erupted into cheers. The silence of the governments in the room was defeaning. Even the truly pro-ban states were horrified by the challenge. Canada had stepped outside of diplomatic process and procedure and put them between a rock and a hard place. They had said they were pro-ban. They had come to Ottawa to develop a road map to create a ban treaty and had signed a Declaration of intent. What could they do? They had to respond. It was really breath-taking. We stood up and cheered while the governments were moaning. But once they recovered from that initial shock, the governments that really wanted to see a ban treaty as soon as possible, rose to the challenge and negotiated a ban treaty in record time.

What has become known as the Ottawa Process began with the Axworthy Challenge. The treaty itself was based upon a ban treaty drafted by Austria and developed in a series of meetings in Vienna, in Bonn, in Brussels, which culminated in the three-week long treaty negotiating conference held in Oslo in September. The treaty negotiations were historic. They were historic for a number of reasons. For the first time, smaller and middle-sized powers had come together, to work in close cooperation with the non-governmental organizations of the International Campaign to Ban Landmines, to negotiate a treaty which would remove from the world's arsenals a weapon in widespread use. For the first time, smaller and middle-sized powers had not yielded ground to intense pressure from a superpower to weaken the treaty to accomodate the policies of that one country. Perhaps for the first time, negotiations ended with a treaty stronger than the draft on which the negotiations were based! The treaty had not been held hostage to rule by consensus, which would have inevitably resulted in a gutted treaty.

The Oslo negotiations gave the world a treaty banning antipersonnel landmines which is remarkably free of loopholes and exceptions. It is a treaty which bans the use, production, trade . . . and stockpiling of antipersonnel landmines. It is a treaty which requires states to destroy their stockpiles within four years of its entering into force. It is a treaty which requires mine clearance within ten years. It calls upon states to increase assistance for mine clearance and for victim assistance.

It is not a perfect treaty—the Campaign has concerns about the provision allowing for antihandling devices on antivehicle mines; we are concerned about mines kept for training purposes; we would like to see the treaty directly apply to nonstate actors and we would like stronger language regarding victim assistance. But, given the close cooperation with governments which resulted in the treaty itself, we are certain that these issues can be addressed through the annual meetings and review conferences provided for in the treaty.

As I have already noted, last week in Ottawa, 121 countries signed the treaty. Three ratified it simultaneously—signaling the political will of the international community to bring this treaty into force as soon as possible. It is remarkable. Landmines have been used since the U. S. Civil War, since the Crimean War yet we are taking them out of arsenals of the world. It is amazing. It is historic. It proves that civil society and governments do not have to see themselves as adversaries. It demonstrates that small and middle powers can work together with civil society and address humanitarian concerns with breathtaking speed. It shows that such a partnership is a new kind of "superpower" in the post-Cold War world.

It is fair to say that the International Campaign to Ban Landmines made a difference. And the real prize is the treaty. What we are most proud of is the treaty. It would be foolish to say that we are not deeply honored by being awarded the Nobel Peace Prize. Of course, we are. But the receipt of the Nobel Peace Prize is recognition of the accomplishment of this Campaign. It is recognition of the fact that NGOs have worked in close cooperation with governments for the first time on an arms control issue, with the United Nations, with the International Committee of the Red Cross.

Together, we have set a precedent. Together, we have changed history. The closing remarks of the French ambassador in Oslo to me were the best. She said, "This is historic not just because of the treaty. This is historic because, for the first time, the leaders of states have come together to answer the will of civil society."

For that, the International Campaign thanks them—for together we have given the world the possibility of one day living on a truly mine-free planet.

Thank you.

The Moral Legacy of the Cold War[2]

George Lee Butler

Vice president of business development, Peter Kiewit Sons, Inc., and president of Kiewit Energy Group, 1994– ; graduate, U.S. Air Force Academy, 1961; Master's degree in international affairs, University of Paris, France; officer in the U.S. Air Force, 1961–94; Director for Strategic Plans and Policy, Joint Chiefs of Staff; retired from military, 1994; Advanced Management Program, Harvard Business School; chairman, BioClean Fuels, Inc.; chairman, Clean Fuels Foundation; Council on Foreign Relations; Committee on International Security and Arms Control for the National Academy of Sciences; numerous Omaha, Nebraska civic organizations.

Editors' introduction: Former General George Lee Butler addressed 200 members of the Henry L. Stimson Center, government officials, academicians, foreign policy experts, and journalists in the historic Car Barn, Georgetown, on the occasion of receiving the Stimson Center's award for Distinguished Public Service. General Butler's purpose was "to further public and government interest in and support for eliminating nuclear weapons." He received "worldwide, positive reaction to the speech," although he expressed disappointment at the quality of the debate that followed publicly. The speech was covered by representatives from radio and television. General Butler gave a "companion speech" on nuclear abolition to the National Press Club, December 4, 1996.

George Lee Butler's speech: Thank you, and good afternoon, ladies and gentlemen. What a great joy it is for Dorene and myself to be once again in the company of so many dear friends and colleagues, and equally a privilege for me to address such a distinguished audience. I am honored by your presence and most indebted to the Stimson Center for today's events. I leave it to the judgment of their selection committee that I have done anything to merit such recognition. For my part, I feel unduly honored by an award given in the name of a man of such Olympian achievement. My reservations are compounded by the fact that the first recipient of this award was my dear friend and personal hero, Secretary Bill Perry. Indeed, you could well have retired the award after

---

2. Delivered in Washington, D.C., on January 8, 1997, at 1:00 p.m. Reprinted by permission of George Lee Butler.

that Inaugural presentation given the exceedingly high standard he has set in serving the public interest.

Beyond a very modest sense of personal gratification and the presence of a highly respected audience, what does draw me to this podium is a powerful sense of intellectual kinship with Secretary Stimson on an issue that in the closing years of our respective public service became a consuming concern. Permit me to quote briefly from a memorandum that many of you will find familiar. It is from the Secretary to President Truman, dated September 11, 1945. "If the atomic bomb were merely another—though more devastating—military weapon to be assimilated into our pattern of international relations, it would be one thing. We could then follow the old custom of secrecy and . . . military superiority, relying on international caution to prescribe the future use of the weapon . . . but I think the bomb instead constitutes merely a first step in a new control by man over the forces of nature too revolutionary and dangerous to fit into the old concepts. I think it really caps the climax of the race between man's growing technical power for destructiveness and his psychological power of self-control—his moral power."

This prescient insight gives perfect expression to the growing sense of alarm which over the course of my long experience in the nuclear arena evolved ultimately to a singular goal: to bend every effort, within my power and authority, to promote the conditions and attitudes which might someday free mankind from the scourge of nuclear weapons.

To my utter astonishment and profound gratitude, the opportunity to advance that agenda came in the form of two wholly unanticipated and unlikely eventualities. One, of historic consequence, was the end of the Cold War; the other, of little moment, was my appointment as the commander of America's strategic nuclear forces. I was electrified by the prospects presented by the sudden shattering of the cold war paradigm. And on entering my new office, I was seized by the opportunity to promote fundamental changes in nuclear weapons policy, force structure, planning and operational practice.

Two days after taking the helm of Strategic Air Command, I called together my senior staff of 20 generals and one admiral, and over the course of what I am sure for all of them was a mystifying and deeply unsettling discussion, I presented my case that with the end of the Cold War, SAC's mission was effectively complete. I began to prepare them for a dramatic shift in strategic direction, to think in terms of less rather than more, to argue for smaller forces, fewer targets, reduced alert postures and accelerated arms control agreements.

This was a wrenching readjustment. It prompted angry debate, bruised feelings and the early termination of a dozen promising careers. But in the final analysis, I could have not

The bomb . . . constitutes merely a first step in a new control by man over the forces of nature too revolutionary and dangerous to fit into the old concepts.

been prouder of a staff that over the course of a few short months endorsed the cancellation of $40 billion of strategic nuclear force modernization programs; that supported my recommendations to convert the B-2 to a primarily conventional role and to stand the entire bomber force down from 30 years of alert; that did pioneering analysis in developing notional nuclear war plans numbering down to hundreds of targets; and perhaps most notably, unanimously supported my decision to recommend that Strategic Air Command itself be disestablished after 46 years at the nuclear ramparts.

This was an extraordinary period, a promising start to a wholesale realignment of America's national security policy and practice. And in the ensuing months there has been much to record and to applaud, thanks to a host of agencies and initiatives. Conversely, there is yet no cause for celebration nor satisfaction. The harsh truth is that six years after the end of the Cold War we are still prisoner to its psychology of distrust, still enmeshed in the vocabulary of mutual assured destruction, still in the thrall of the nuclear era. Worse, strategists persist in conjuring worlds which spiral toward chaos, and concocting threats which they assert can only be discouraged or expunged by the existence or employment of nuclear weapons.

It is well that Secretary Stimson did not survive to witness this folly. I can readily imagine his dismay at witnessing mankind's miraculous reprieve from nuclear disaster only to risk losing the race between self-destructiveness and self-control, permitting technological prowess and mistrust triumph over morality and the rule of law. For my own part, I find it unconscionable, and for that reason I felt increasingly the moral imperative to reenter the public arena.

That resolve was crystallized by an invitation from the Government of Australia in late 1995 to join the Canberra Commission on the Elimination of Nuclear Weapons. I was deeply moved by Prime Minister Keating's forceful condemnation of the resumption of French nuclear testing, and his courageous effort to bring focus to the ensuing international outcry.

I come away from the Canberra Commission experience with decidedly mixed feelings. On the one hand, I was enormously enriched by this year-long association with men and women of such great stature. I was equally gratified by the unanimity of view and the forceful logic of our report. It captured in measured, balanced, and reasoned terms the essence of my own conclusions about the risks and penalties associated with nuclear weapons. Most importantly, it set forth a practical, realistic blueprint for working toward their elimination.

Subsequently, however, I became increasingly disturbed that the report failed to ignite the interest and debate which its subject so urgently warrants, thus faring littler better than the Stimson Center study before it. After long reflection I concluded that because of my unique experience, if our message was to be heard it would require a very direct and public intervention on my part. That decision ultimately led me to the National Press Club where, in early December, I gave an intensely personal expression of my views on the case for the elimination of nuclear weapons.

After a lifetime of public service, that was a defining moment for me and, by extension, for my family who, as always, are caught up in the consequences of my beliefs. But, as always, they understood the demands of conscience which compelled my actions. I believe my family also shares my sense of wonder at the reaction my views, joined with those of dozens of respected military colleagues such as General Andrew Goodpaster, have provoked. As I survey the response of what appears to be a rather astonished world, I am by turns encouraged, disappointed and dismayed.

Encouraged, by the flood of supportive calls and letters I have received from every corner of the planet because the issue has now been widely joined, with great interest and intensity, and because I can discern the makings of an emerging global consensus that the risks posed by nuclear weapons far outweigh their presumed benefits.

Disappointed, thus far, by the quality of the debate, by those pundits who simply sniffed imperiously at the goal of elimination, aired their stock Cold War rhetoric, hurled a personal epithet or two, and settled smugly back into their world of exaggerated threats and bygone enemies. And by critics who attacked my views by misrepresenting them, such as suggesting that I am proposing unilateral disarmament or a pace of reduction that would jeopardize the security of the nuclear weapon states.

And finally, dismayed that even among more serious commentators the lessons of 50 years at the nuclear brink can still be so grievously misread; that the assertions and assumptions underpinning an era of desperate threats and risks prevail unchallenged; that a handful of nations cling to the impossible notion that the power of nuclear weapons is so immense their use can be threatened with impunity, yet their proliferation contained.

Albert Einstein recognized this hazardous but very human tendency many years ago, when he warned that "the unleashed power of the atom has changed everything save our modes of thinking, and thus we drift toward unparalleled catastrophe."

How else to explain the assertion that nuclear weapons will infallibly deter major war, in a world that survived the Cuban Missile Crisis no thanks to deterrence, but only by the grace of God? How else to accept the proposition that any civilized nation would respond to the act of a madman by adopting his methods? How otherwise to fathom a historical view that can witness the collapse of communism but fail to imagine a world rid of nuclear weapons? Or finally, to account for the assumption that because we are condemned to live with the knowledge of how to fabricate nuclear weapons, we are powerless to mount a global framework of verification and sanctions which will greatly reduce the likelihood or adequately deal with the consequences of cheating in a world free of nuclear weapons.

Many well meaning friends have counseled me that by championing elimination I risk setting the bar too high, providing an easy target for the cynical and diverting attention from the more immediately achievable. My response is that elimination is the only defensible goal and that goal matters enormously. First and foremost, all of the declared nuclear weapon states are formally committed to nuclear abolition in the letter and the spirit of the nonproliferation treaty. Every President of the United States since Dwight Eisenhower has publicly endorsed elimination. A clear and unequivocal commitment to elimination, sustained by concrete policy and measurable milestones, is essential to give credibility and substance to this long-standing declaratory position. Such a commitment goes far beyond simply seizing the moral high ground. It focuses analysis on a precise end state; all force postures above zero simply become way points along a path leading toward elimination. It shifts the locus of policy attention from numbers to the security climate essential to permit successive reductions. It conditions government at all levels to create and respond to every opportunity for shrinking arsenals, cutting infrastructure and curtailing modernization. It sets the stage for rigorous enforcement of nonproliferation regimes and unrelenting pressures to reduce nuclear arsenals on a global basis. I say again, the goal matters enormously and the only defensible goal is elimination.

But hear me say clearly, and unreservedly, that no one is more conscious than am I that realistic prospects for elimination will evolve over many years. I was in the public arena for too long ever to make the perfect the enemy of the good. I hasten to add, however, my strong conviction that we are far too timorous in imagining the good, we are still too rigidly conditioned by an arms control mentality deeply rooted in the Cold War. We fall too readily into the intellectual trap of judging the goal of elimination against current political conditions. We forget too quickly how seemingly intractable conflicts can suddenly yield under the weight of reason or with a change of leadership. We have lost sight too soon that in the blink of an historical eye the world we knew for a traumatic half-century has been utterly transformed.

How better then, you may well ask, to proceed. As I noted earlier, my own prescription is carefully detailed in the report of the Canberra Commission. It begins not with a call for greater reductions, but rather to initiate immediate, multilateral negotiations toward ending the most regrettable and risk-laden operational practice of the Cold War era: land and sea-based ballistic missiles standing nuclear alert. Why is it that five years after removing bombers, the most stable element of the nuclear triad, from alert, we keep missiles—with their 30-minute flight time—on effectively hair-trigger postures? What possibly can justify this continuing exposure to the associated operational and logistical risks? What could be more corrosive to building and sustaining security relationships built on trust? What could undercut more overtly the credibility of our leadership in advancing a nonproliferation treaty premised on a solemn obligation to eliminate nuclear arsenals?

There are a host of other measures outlined in the Canberra Commission report which should also be given immediate consideration. But this is not the time nor place to debate alternative agendas, although thoughtful debate is both urgent and essential. What matters more is the much larger and defining question upon which the debate must ultimately turn: above all nations, how should the United States see its responsibility for dealing with the conflicted moral legacy of the Cold War? Russia, with its history of authoritarian rule and a staggering burden of social transformation, is ill-equipped to lead on this issue. It falls unavoidably to us to work painfully back through the tangled moral web of this frightful 50-year gauntlet, born of the hellish confluence of two unprecedented historical currents: the bi-polar collision of ideology, and the unleashing of the power of the atom.

Above all nations, how should the United States see its responsibility for dealing with the conflicted moral legacy of the Cold War?

As a democracy, the consequences of these cataclysmic forced confronted us with a tortuous and seemingly inextricable dilemma: how to put at the service of our national survival, a weapon whose sheer destructiveness was antithetical to the very values upon which our society was based. Over time, as arsenals multiplied on both sides and the rhetoric of mutual annihilation grew more heated, we were forced to think about the unthinkable, justify the unjustifiable, rationalize the irrational. Ultimately, we contrived a new and desperate theology to ease our moral anguish, and we called it *deterrence.*

I spent much of my military career serving the ends of deterrence, as did millions of others. I want very much to believe that in the end that it was the nuclear force that I and others commanded and operated that prevented World War III and created the conditions leading to the collapse of the Soviet Empire. But, in truth, I do not and I cannot know that. It will be decades before the hideously complex era of the Cold War is adequately understood, with its bewildering interactions of human fears and inhuman technology. Nor would it much matter that informed assessments are still well beyond our intellectual reach—except for the crucial and alarming fact that, forgetting the desperate circumstances which gave it birth, and long after their miraculous resolution, we continue to espouse deterrence as if it were now an infallible panacea. And worse, others are listening, have converted to our theology, are building their arsenals, are poised to rekindle the nuclear arms race—and to reawaken the specter of nuclear war.

What a stunning, perverse turn of events. In the words of my friend Jonathan Schell, we face the dismal prospect that, "the Cold War was not the apogee of the age of nuclear weapons, to be succeeded by an age of nuclear disarmament. Instead, it may well prove to have simply been a period of initiation, in which not only Americans and Russians, but Indians and Pakistanis, Israelis and Iraqis, were adapting to the horror of threatening the deaths of millions of people, were learning to think about the unthinkable. If this is so, will history judge that the Cold War proved only a sort of modern-day Trojan Horse, whereby nuclear weapons were smuggled into the life of the world, made an acceptable part of the way the world works? Surely not, surely we still comprehend that to threaten the deaths of tens of hundreds of millions of people presages an atrocity beyond anything in the record of mankind? Or have we, in a silent and incomprehensible moral revolution, come to regard such threats as ordinary—as normal and proper policy for any self-respecting nation."

> *Will history judge that the Cold War proved only a sort of modern-day Trojan Horse?*

This cannot be the moral legacy of the Cold War. And it is our responsibility to ensure that it will not be. We have won, through Herculean courage and sacrifice, the opportunity to reset mankind's moral compass, to renew belief in a world free from fear and deprivation, to win global affirmation for the sanctity of life, the right of liberty, and the opportunity to pursue a joyous existence.

Winston Churchill once remarked about the nuclear era that "the stone age may return on the gleaming wings of science." Secretary Stimson might well have added, "and the way made straight by a failure of moral power."

It is time to heed Secretary Stimson's admonition, before his prophecy becomes a numbing reality. For me, his words provide renewed inspiration. For the nuclear powers, they are a mandate for action. For America, they are an obligation to lead. Thank you for honoring me with this award and with your company. And may God bless, keep, and guide our great nation.

Peace and Reconciliation in Northern Ireland[3]

George Mitchell

Special Counsel, Verner, Liipfert, Bernhard, McPherson & Hand; born Waterville, Maine, 1933; B.A., Bowdoin College, 1954; Counterintelligence Corps in U.S. Army in Berlin, 1954– 56; law degree, Georgetown University, 1960; trial attorney in the Antitrust Division of the U.S. Justice Department, 1960– 62; executive assistant to Democratic U.S. Senator Edmund S. Muskie in 1962; partner, Jensen, Baird, Gardner, Donovan, and Henry, 1965–77; chairman of the Maine State Democratic Committee, 1966–68; assistant attorney for Cumberland County, Maine, 1971; U.S. attorney for Maine, 1977–79; judge of the U.S. District Court for Northern Maine, 1979; U.S. Senator (D) from Maine, 1980–95; majority leader of the U.S. Senate, 1988; board of directors, the Xerox Corporation; special advisor to the President of the U.S. on economic initiatives in Ireland, 1995– ; Philadelphia Liberty Medal for work in brokering Northern Ireland peace agreement, 1998; honorary Doctor in Laws degree, Trinity College, Dublin, 1998.

Editors' introduction: Former United States Senator George Mitchell spent 22 months supervising negotiations for peace in Northern Ireland, an initiative that established the machinery for self-government in the region. When addressing some 125 supporters of the American-Ireland Fund at the National Building Museum, in Washington, D.C., he declared that "there will be peace and reconciliation in Northern Ireland."

George Mitchell's speech: I'm grateful for this award. The American-Ireland Fund is an important force for good in Ireland. I commend you for your efforts and I encourage you to continue them.

As you know, I've spent most of the past two years in Northern Ireland. On my trips back to the U.S., I've been asked two questions, over and over again, by Americans who care about Ireland: Why are you doing this? And, What can I do to help?

Tonight, I'll try to answer both of those questions.

Why am I doing this?

---

3. Delivered in Washington, D.C., on March 13, 1997, at 7:00 p.m. Reprinted by permission of George Mitchell.

I've asked myself that question many times. To answer it, I must go back nearly 20 years, before I'd ever been to Ireland, before I'd ever thought seriously about Northern Ireland.

Before I entered the United States Senate I had the privilege of serving as a Federal Judge. In that position I had great power. The power I most enjoyed exercising was when I presided over what are called naturalization ceremonies. They're citizenship ceremonies. A group of people who'd come from every part of the world, who'd gone through all the required procedures, gathered before me in a federal courtroom. There I administered to them the oath of allegiance to the United States and, by the power vested in me under our constitution and laws I made them Americans.

It was always emotional for me, because my mother was an immigrant from Lebanon, my father the orphan son of immigrants from Ireland. They had no education and they worked hard all their lives at difficult and low-paying jobs. But because of their efforts, and, more importantly, because of the openness of American society, I, their son, was able to become the majority leader of the United States Senate.

No one can really have a chance in a society dominated by fear and violence.

After every naturalization ceremony, I spoke personally with each new American, individually or in family groups. I asked them where they came from, how they came, why they came. Their stories were as different as their countries of origin. But they were all inspiring, and through them ran a common theme, best expressed by a young Asian. When I asked why he had come, he replied, in slow and halting English, "I came because here in America everybody has a chance."

A young man who'd been an American for just a few minutes summed up the meaning of our country in a single sentence. Here, everybody has a chance.

I was one of those who had a chance, and I thank God for my good fortune. Now, by an accident of fate, in a way that I did not seek or expect, I have been given the opportunity to help others to have a chance. That they are in Ireland, the land of my father's heritage, is just a fortuitous coincidence. That I am able to help, even if in just a small way, is what matters.

No one can really have a chance in a society dominated by fear and violence. And so I, who have been helped by so many, now must do what I can to help others to try to end the violence, to banish the fear, to hasten the day when all the people of Northern Ireland can lead lives of peace, reconciliation and opportunity.

Let me say, as clearly and as emphatically as I can: There will be peace and reconciliation in Northern Ireland. I don't know exactly when it will come. But I am convinced that it is inevitable, for one over-riding reason: It is the will of the overwhelming majority of the people of Northern Ireland.

They remain divided along sectarian lines, and they mistrust each other. But they share a fervent desire not to return
to the violence which for so long has filled their lives with
fear and anxiety.

It will take a very long time for the mistrust to end. But it
need not take a long time for the violence to end. Once it
does, once people can live free of fear, then gradually the
walls of division will come down. Walls that exist on the
ground, and in people's minds, will come down, brick by
brick, person by person, slowly but inevitably.

Over the past two years I've come to know the people of
Northern Ireland. They're energetic, intelligent and productive. I admire and like them. They deserve better than the
troubles they have. But there is only one way to achieve that
better life.

There is no alternative to democratic, meaningful, inclusive
dialogue. For that to come about, there must be an end to
violence and to intransigence. They are the twin demons of
Northern Ireland—violence and intransigence. They feed off
each other in a deadly ritual in which most of the victims are
innocent.

There are those who don't want anything to change, ever.
They want to recreate a past that can never be recreated. But
their way will only guarantee never-ending conflict. It will
insure that the next half century is as full of death and fear
as was the past half century.

The people of Northern Ireland must make it clear to their
leaders that they oppose intransigence, that they want meaningful negotiation. Not capitulation; not the surrender of
conviction. But good-faith negotiation that places the interest
of the people, the interest of peace, above personal or political considerations. Good faith negotiation can produce an
agreed settlement that will command the support of the
majority in Northern Ireland, including the majority in each
community. I know in my heart that it can be done.

With an end to intransigence must come a total and final
repudiation of violence. There is no justification for violence,
or the threat of violence. To those of you who ask: What can
I do? Here is my answer: You, the leaders of the Irish-Ameri-
can community, must say that you condemn violence, that
you demand its end, that you will not support those who
engage in or support or condone violence. You must say it
publicly, you must say it loudly, you must say it forcefully.
And you must say it over and over again.

Violence is wrong. It is counterproductive. It deepens divisions. It increases hatred. It hurts innocent people. It makes
peace and reconciliation more difficult to attain. It must end.

Let me be clear on one more point. They may be twin
demons but there is no moral equivalence between intransigence and violence. They are both wrong. But as bad as

*There is no alter-
native to demo-
cratic,
meaningful,
inclusive
dialogue.*

intransigence is, violence is worse. Intransigence takes away people's hopes. Violence takes away their lives.

There exists an historic opportunity to end centuries of conflict in Northern Ireland. If it is not seized now, it may be years before it returns, and the failure could cost many their lives.

Peace and reconciliation in Northern Ireland is a worthy cause. It deserves your attention and support. You can make a difference. What you say is heard, what you do matters.

As you leave tonight, ask yourself this question: Wouldn't it be a wonderful thing if, on St. Patrick's day next year, rather than praying for peace and reconciliation in Northern Ireland, we were celebrating its existence?

If you agree, then beginning tomorrow, do all you can to make it happen. When you do, you will reap the greatest of all rewards: You will have earned the title of peacemaker.

NATO Expansion[4]

Madeleine Albright

U.S. Secretary of State 1997–; National Security Council staff 1997–; born, Prague, Czechoslovakia, May 15, 1937; B.A., Wellesley College, M.A. and Ph.D., Columbia University; professor, Georgetown University, 1982–93; Permanent U.S. Ambassador to the United Nations, 1993–97.

Editors' introduction: President Clinton formally submitted to the U.S. Senate for ratification the documents for the admission of Poland, Hungary, and the Czech Republic to North Atlantic Treaty Organization (NATO). In the speech below, Secretary Madeleine Albright addressed the New Atlantic Initiative Conference concerning the North Atlantic Treaty in relation to these three countries. Foreign ministers from these three Central European states attended the conference. In the address, Secretary Albright maintained that "it will be in our interest to have a vigorous and larger alliance with those European democracies that share our values and our determination to defend them."

Madeleine Albright's speech: Thank you very much. Goodness, I hate to begin this by denying a compliment, but it's not quite true. I think there was great support for expanding NATO before I came on the scene. It's very hard to get up here and say, "I loved your introductions, but it's not true."

Christopher, thank you very much; and let me welcome my colleague Foreign Ministers Geremek, Kovacs, Mikhailova and Sedivy to Washington. And let me thank John O'Sullivan, Jeffrey Gedmin and everyone at the New Atlantic Initiative for all you have done to strengthen America's partnership with its friends and allies in Europe, old and new.

As I was thinking about this speech, I remembered a chart of European organizations that I actually asked to be created that's making its rounds around the State Department. It consists of not two or three but 13 colored overlapping circles, with the names of countries grouped according to the institutions to which they belong. There's NATO and the EU; the Council of Europe and the Council of Baltic States; the Central European Free Trade Association and the Nordic Council; the Partnership for Peace and the EAPC; the NATO–Russia PJC and the Southeastern European Cooperative Initiative; the NATO–Ukraine Commission and the Western

---

4. Delivered in Washington; D.C., on February 9, 1998.

European Union. And then, of course, there is OSCE, which includes them all.

Now, here I am addressing the New Atlantic Initiative; I'll probably have to throw in something about the New Transatlantic Agenda, and I guess you want me to explain how all this Euro-architecture fits together. Unfortunately, I have concluded that you have to be either a genius or French to keep it all straight.

(Laughter.)

Which reminds me of an inscrutable comment a French diplomat actually made once in response to an American proposal: "It will work in practice, yes. But will it work in theory?"

(Laughter.)

In all seriousness, the development of these old and new organizations in Europe is part of a truly hopeful global trend that our country has done more than any other to shape. In every part of the world, we have encouraged the growth of institutions that bring nations closer together around basic principles of democracy, free markets, respect for the law and a commitment to peace.

America's place—and I believe, correctly—is at the center of this emerging international system. And our challenge is to see that the connections around the center, between regions and among the most prominent nations, are strong and dynamic, resilient and sure. But it is equally our goal to ensure that the community we are building is open to all those nations, large and small, distant and near, that are willing to play by its rules.

There was a time not long ago when we did not see this as clearly as we do today. Until World War II, we didn't really think that most of the world was truly part of our world. This attitude even applied to the half of Europe that lay east of Germany and Austria. Central Europe and Eastern Europe was once a quaint, exotic mystery to most Americans. We wondered at King Zog of Albania; we puzzled about Admiral Horthy, ruler of landlocked Hungary; we laughed with the Marx Brothers as they sang "Hail, Hail Fredonia."

Jan Masaryk, the son of Czechoslovakia's first president, used to tell a story about a U.S. Senator who asked him, "How's your father; does he still play the violin?" To which Jan replied, "Sir, I fear you are making a small mistake. You are perhaps thinking of Paderewski and not Masaryk. Paderewski plays piano, not the violin, and was president not of Czechoslovakia, but of Poland. Of our presidents, Benes was the only one who played. But he played neither the violin nor the piano, but football. In all other respects, your information is correct."

(Laughter.)

It took the horror of World War II and the Holocaust to get across the message that this region mattered; that it was the battleground and burial ground for Europe's big powers; that the people of Paris and London could neither be safe nor free as long as the people of Warsaw and Riga and Sofia were robbed of their independence, sent away in boxcars, and gunned down in forests.

President Bush certainly understood this when, after the fall of the Berlin Wall, he inspired us to seek a Europe whole and free. And President Clinton understood it when, in 1993, he set in motion a process that would bring that ideal to life.

Part of our challenge was to adapt NATO to master the demands of the world not as it has been, but as it is and will be. This meant adopting a new strategic concept, streamlining NATO's commands, accepting new missions and asking our European allies to accept new responsibilities. It also meant welcoming Europe's new democracies as partners, and some eventually as members, in a way that preserves NATO's integrity and strength. For NATO, like any organization, is defined not just by its mission, but by its makeup. The preeminent security institution in an undivided Europe cannot maintain the Iron Curtain as its permanent eastern frontier.

And so last July, after three years of careful study, President Clinton and his fellow NATO leaders invited three new democracies—Poland, Hungary and the Czech Republic—to join our alliance, while holding the door open to others. This month, Canada and Denmark became the first NATO members to ratify the admission of our future central European allies. On Wednesday, President Clinton will send the instruments of ratification to the United States Senate.

The strategic rationale for this policy is straightforward. First, a larger NATO will make us safer by expanding the area of Europe where wars do not happen. By making it clear that we will fight, if necessary, to defend our new allies, we make it less likely that we will ever be called upon to do so. It is true that no part of Europe faces an immediate threat of armed attack. But this does not mean we face no dangers in Europe. There is the obvious risk of ethnic conflict. There is the growing threat posed by rogue states with dangerous weapons. There are still questions about the future of Russia.

And while we cannot know what other dangers might arise in 10 or 20 or 50 years from now, we know enough from history and human experience to believe that a grave threat, if allowed to arise, would arise. Whatever the future may hold, it will not be in our interest to have a group of vulnerable, excluded nations sitting in the heart of Europe. It will be in our interest to have a vigorous and larger alliance with those European democracies that share our values and our determination to defend them.

A second reason why enlargement passes the test of national interest is that it will make NATO stronger and more cohesive. Our Central European friends are passionately

Whatever the future may hold, it will not be in our interest to have a group of vulnerable, excluded nations sitting in the heart of Europe.

committed to NATO. Experience has taught them to believe in a strong American role in Europe. They will add strategic depth to NATO, not to mention 200,000 troops. Their forces have risked their lives alongside ours from the Gulf War to Bosnia. Without the bases Hungary has already provided to NATO, our troops could not have deployed to Bosnia as safely as they did. Here are three qualified European democracies that want us to let them be good allies. We can and should say yes.

A third reason to support a larger NATO is that the very promise of it has given the nations of Central and Eastern Europe an incentive to solve their own problems. Aspiring allies have strengthened democratic institutions; made sure soldiers serve civilians, not the other way around; and resolved virtually every old ethnic and border dispute in the region.

I have been a student of Central European history, and I have lived some of it myself. When I see Romanians and Hungarians building a real friendship after centuries of enmity; when I see Poles, Ukrainians and Lithuanians forming joint military units after years of suspicion; when I see Czechs and Germans overcoming decades of mistrust; when I see Central Europeans confident enough to improve their political and economic ties with Russia, I know something amazing is happening. NATO is doing for Europe's east precisely what it did for Europe's west after World War II.

I know that there are serious critics who have had legitimate concerns about our policy. We have grappled with many of the same concerns. Some revolve around the cost of a larger NATO, which will be real. But NATO has now approved estimates which make clear that the costs will be manageable, that they will be met, and that they will be shared fairly.

I certainly understand the concern some have expressed about Russian opposition to a larger NATO. But as Secretary of State, I can tell you that Russia's disagreement on this issue has not in any way hurt our ability to work together on other issues. On the contrary, we have made progress on arms control; Russia now has a permanent relationship with NATO; it has improved its ties with the Baltic states, even as those nations have made clear their desire to join NATO. Russia has a better relationship with Central Europe now than at any time in history; and the differences we still have with Russia would certainly not disappear if we suddenly changed our minds about enlargement.

We need to keep Russia's objections in perspective. They are the product of old misperceptions about NATO and old ways of thinking about its former satellites. Instead of changing our policies to accommodate Russia's outdated fears, we need to concentrate on encouraging Russia's more modern aspirations.

Others have argued that we should let the European Union do the job of reuniting Europe, or at least tell Central European countries that they cannot join NATO until they join the EU. I want the EU to expand as rapidly as possible. But the EU is not in the business of providing security; NATO is. And we saw in Bosnia what a difference that makes.

As for tying membership in one institution to membership in another, it is not in America's interest to subordinate critical security decisions of NATO to another institution. We are a leader in NATO; we're not even members of the EU. The qualifications for joining the EU are vastly different from the qualifications for becoming a member of NATO. Forcing the two processes to move in lockstep makes no sense, neither for the EU nor for NATO.

Others ask why we need to enlarge NATO when we already have NATO's Partnership for Peace. When the Partnership for Peace was established in 1994, I went to Central Europe with General Shalikashvili and with my good friend, Charles Gati, who is with us here today, to explain its purpose. I can tell you the Partnership was never intended to be an alternative to a larger NATO. On the contrary, it has always provided both the opportunity to cooperate with NATO, and a program for preparing to join. That is why so many nations have participated in it so enthusiastically, whether they aspire to membership or not. If we want the Partnership to thrive, the last thing we should do is to tell some of its members that they can never be allies, no matter how much progress they make.

NATO is a military alliance, not a social club; but neither is it an in-bred aristocracy. That is one reason why today every NATO ally agrees that NATO doors must remain open after the first three new allies join. Let us be clear—we have made no decisions about who the next members of NATO should be or when they might join. But let us also have some humility before the future.

How many people—even in this room of experts—predicted in 1949 that Germany would so soon be a member of the Alliance? Who could have known in 1988 that in just ten years, members of the old Warsaw Pact would be in a position to join NATO? Who can tell today what Europe will look like in even a few years? We should not erect artificial roadblocks today that will prevent qualified nations from contributing to NATO tomorrow.

This Administration opposes any effort in the Senate to mandate a pause in the process of NATO enlargement. This would be totally unnecessary, since the Senate would, in any case, need to give its advice and consent to any new round of enlargement. It would also harm American interests by surrendering our leverage and flexibility, fracturing the consensus NATO has reached on its open door, and diminishing the

NATO is a military alliance, not a social club; but neither is it an in-bred aristocracy.

incentive Central European countries now have to cooperate with the Alliance.

Some critics have said NATO enlargement would draw a destabilizing dividing line in Europe. A larger NATO with an open door will not. One round of enlargement with a mandated pause would. President Clinton and I will keep on addressing these concerns, and others, in the days ahead. The debate has been joined, and it will continue.

But already an extraordinary coalition has come together to say NATO enlargement is right and smart for America. It includes American veterans, who do not want their country to have to fight another war in Europe; American business, which understands the link between security and prosperity; American labor, which aided freedom's victory in Europe and wants it to endure. It includes every living former Secretary of State, a half a dozen former National Security Advisors and five Chairmen of the Joint Chiefs.

The debate about a larger NATO might easily have provided an opportunity for skeptics to praise isolationism. Instead, it has given the American people and the Congress an opportunity to bury it. And I have confidence that is what will happen.

If the Senate says yes to a larger NATO .. . that will be a vote for continued American engagement in Europe.

If the Senate says yes to a larger NATO—and I believe it will—that will be a vote for continued American engagement in Europe. It will be a signal that America will defend its values, protect its interests, stand by its allies and keep its word.

We'll need that same spirit to prevail when the Congress faces its other foreign policy tests this year. For example, the President and I are asking the Congress to pay what our country owes to the International Monetary Fund and to the United Nations. At issue is a very simple question. Will we stand alone in the face of crises from Gulf to Rwanda to Indonesia, asking American soldiers to take all the risks and American taxpayers to pay all the bills? Or will we support organizations that allow us to share the burdens of leadership with others? This is not least an issue in our relationship with Europe. When we challenge our allies to meet their responsibilities to us, it hurts our case when we are seen as not meeting ours.

Another important choice before the Congress is whether it will support continued implementation of the Dayton Accords. I trust the Congress will agree that our mission in Bosnia is very much related to our goals of NATO enlargement. For NATO could not have credibly set out on an effort to prevent future conflict in Central Europe had it not acted decisively to end the very real bloodshed it encountered in the Balkans.

Our effort in Bosnia has met with growing success. Multi-ethnic institutions are beginning to function. Economic growth is accelerating. War criminals are being arrested. Refugees are slowly beginning to return. A new Bosnian Serb government has acted swiftly on its pledge to start implementing Dayton. Far from the endless quagmire some people feared, we have been able to reduce our troop presence as the peace process has taken hold.

I know this region all too well to have any illusions about the difficulties that still lie ahead. But I also think it is time for the skeptics to be a bit more humble, as well. After all, a few years ago they were sure NATO could not stop the war in Bosnia. They were certain NATO could not implement Dayton without taking massive casualties. They knew for a fact that Bosnian Serbs would never choose leaders committed to peace. They have been mistaken so many times, I think we should at least give them an award for consistency.

My message to the Congress and to the American people is that we should be consistent, and persistent, in our support for those in Bosnia who are taking risks for peace. For the evidence is growing that peace will be sustained if we sustain the effort that has brought us thus far.

America is strongest when our leaders focus not on partisan differences, but on unifying concerns. We have seen that strength increasingly in our effort to help build a new structure for the security and prosperity of Europe. And we see it today in U. S. policy towards Iraq.

The Administration does not agree with those who suggest we should deploy hundreds of thousands of American troops to engage unilaterally in a ground war, aimed at goals that could not be achieved during Operation Desert Storm. But we do agree fully with the bipartisan leadership of Congress that Iraq cannot be allowed to get away with its flagrant violation of UN Security Council resolutions.

Our approach to Iraq begins with the knowledge that Saddam Hussein is an aggressor who has used weapons of mass destruction before and, if allowed, would surely use or threaten to use them again.

When the Gulf War ended, the UN Security Council established a Special Commission, or UNSCOM, to ensure that Saddam would not have this opportunity. But from the outset, Iraqi officials concealed information and did all they could to evade UNSCOM's requirements. UNSCOM nonetheless accomplished a great deal, destroying more weapons of mass destruction than were demolished in the entire Gulf War.

In recent years, as UNSCOM has learned more about Iraqi methods of concealment, we have seen develop a high stakes game of cat and mouse. UNSCOM has become increasingly creative in its inspection strategy, and therefore more threatening to Saddam. And as UNSCOM has moved closer to discovering information that Iraq wants to hide, Baghdad has grown more belligerent—repeatedly blocking inspection teams, challenging UNSCOM's authority, and refusing access to dozens of suspected sites. Iraq now threatens to eject UNSCOM altogether if UN sanctions are not lifted.

Clearly, if UNSCOM is to uncover the full truth about Iraq's weapons of mass destruction programs, it must have unrestricted access to locations, people and documents that may be related to those programs. But as UNSCOM's Chairman Richard Butler attests, Iraq is making it impossible for the Commission to do its job.

Saddam's dream is the world's nightmare: to gain the lifting of UN sanctions, without losing his capacity to build and use weapons of mass destruction. In pursuing this fantasy, Saddam has thwarted efforts to resolve the crisis diplomatically and made military action more likely.

The trans atlantic partnership is our strategic base—the drivewheel of progress on every world-scale issue when we agree, and the brake when we do not.

During my recent meetings in Europe and the Gulf, I emphasized that we cannot tolerate Saddam's continued defiance. The threat posed by weapons of mass destruction in the hands of Saddam Hussein is too real. The risk to our friends and allies, and to our armed forces in the region, is too high. And the danger that others will emulate Saddam's example if he does not pay a penalty for his actions is too great.

I have been heartened by the support our position has received. In almost every part of the world, there is a determination that Iraq comply with the UN Security Council resolutions and that it provide unfettered access to UN weapons inspectors. There is agreement that responsibility for the current impasse and its potential consequences rests with Iraq alone. And there is an understanding that, unless Iraq's policies change, we will have no choice but to take strong measures—not pinpricks, but substantial strikes to reduce significantly Saddam's capacity to reconstitute his weapons of mass destruction and their delivery systems and to diminish the threat he poses to Iraq's neighbors and the world. Do not doubt; we have the authority to do this, the responsibility to do this, and the means and the will.

It may seem to you that my comments about Iraq have little to do with the earlier part of my speech, but that is not true. I wanted to talk about Iraq in part because the Central European Foreign Ministers are here today. Their countries were once on the outside looking in when the great powers responded to global crises. They will soon be on the inside, looking forward with us. The Iraq crisis has long been their concern. And I'm pleased to announce that in my meeting that concluded just ten minutes before I came here, they quickly responded to my request for their support, subject to relevant consultations with their governments. As we, they would prefer a diplomatic solution. And in the Security Council, through the years that I was there, each of them stood with us to maintain sanctions. They all said they are ready to support us, as appropriate, should military action become necessary.

It is my great hope that Poland, Hungary and the Czech Republic will be part of a transatlantic partnership that is not only broader, but deeper as well; a partnership that is a force for peace from the Middle East to Central Africa; a partnership that has overcome barriers to trade across the Atlantic; a partnership strong enough to protect the environment and defeat international crime; a partnership that is united in its effort to stop the spread of weapons of mass destruction, the overriding security interest of our time.

However old or new the challenges we face, there is still one relationship that more than any other will determine whether we meet them successfully, and that is our relationship with Europe. The transatlantic partnership is our strategic base—the drivewheel of progress on every world-scale issue when we agree, and the brake when we do not.

In cultivating that partnership and extending it to those free nations that were too long denied its benefits, I pledge my continued best efforts, and respectfully solicit all of yours.

Thank you very much.

(Applause.)

MR. DEMUTH: Secretary Albright has time for just two questions. If any in the center group would like to address questions to her, please just step to the microphone in the center.

QUESTION: I would like to ask you what America is going to do if some European states hesitate to give their—to agree with NATO expansion; maybe Turkey or Greece, because they like to play their own national interests by hesitating.

SECRETARY ALBRIGHT: I answer many questions this way, and I'm pleased to answer this one. I think it is a hypothetical question, because I do think that in the meetings that I have been in with all NATO partners, they understand that no matter what specific national interest issues they may have, the expansion of NATO is in everybody's national interest. In the internal discussions that we have had, I think there has been broad-based support.

QUESTION: Madame Secretary, the Slovak Republic was not among the first countries to be invited to join NATO in the first round. Do you think one of the reasons was that the Slovak Republic is not a qualified Eastern European democracy? And if so, can you explain why? Thank you.

SECRETARY ALBRIGHT: I think it is a cause of sadness to many people in this room that the Slovak Republic was not part of the original group of first invitees. I think that the reason it was not, the determination was made that it had not met a number of the criteria that have been looked at, or guidelines that have been looked at for membership in NATO.

And among those are a functioning market system, a functioning democracy, the control of the civilian over the military, and generally a set of guidelines that we had all looked at, all NATO, in terms of who was qualified. And the determination was made that at this time, Slovakia was not.

Thank you all very much.

Could NATO Expansion Lead to Nuclear War?[5]

Daniel Patrick Moynihan

U.S. Senator (D) from New York, 1976– ; born, 1927; U.S. Navy, 1944–47; retired Naval Reserve, 1966; bachelor's degree, Tufts University; studied at London School of Economics as a Fulbright Scholar; M.A. and Ph.D., Tufts University Fletcher School of Law and Diplomacy; Averell Harriman's gubernatorial campaign staff, 1954; Governor Harriman's staff to 1958; beginning 1961 assistant to the Secretary of Labor, and later Assistant Secretary of Labor for Policy Planning and Research; director of the Joint Center for Urban Studies, Massachusetts Institute of Technology and Harvard University, 1966; taught at Harvard University, Syracuse University, Russell Sage College, and Cornell University; U.S. Ambassador to India, 1973-75; U.S. Permanent Representative to the United Nations, 1975–76; U.S. Senate, 1976– ; U.S. Senate committees: Finance, Environment and Public Works, Rules and Administration, Taxation, and Library of Congress; 62 honorary degrees; author of 17 books, including Miles to Go: A Personal History of Social Policy *(1996); International League of Human Rights Award, 1975; John LaFarge Award for Interracial Justice, 1980; Cartwright Prize for outstanding contributions to medicine.*

Editors' introduction: Senator Daniel Patrick Moynihan addressed some 500 correspondents from throughout the world on the 150th anniversary session of the Associated Press. His topic was the dangerous implications of accessing Poland, Hungary, and the Czech Republic to the North Atlantic Treaty Organization (NATO). In the *Congressional Record*, April 27, 1998, in introducing this speech text, Senator Moynihan wrote that Russia issued a national security memorandum in December, 1997, in which that country, while admitting that its "armed forces have seriously declined," warned, "Don't forget . . . we have nuclear weapons, and don't think that we will not use them if our country is in danger."

Daniel Patrick Moynihan's speech: As some of you may have learned, things are a bit confusing in Washington just now.

I have had some personal experience of this.

---

5. Delivered in Dallas, Texas, on April 20, 1998, at noon. Reprinted by permission of Daniel Patrick Moynihan.

Some while ago, I was most generously invited by the President to a formal White House dinner. Our daughter had never been to one of these affairs, and so off we went, making our way past one Secret Service checkpoint after another, until at last we arrived at the East entrance where a bright young Agent, clipboard in hand, leaned through the car window and proclaimed, "Good evening, Senator Thurmond."

Next came my birthday, March 16, and a letter from the Vice President which began:

"Dear Daniel:

I was very pleased to learn about the recent birth of your twins. Tipper joins me in sending our warmest congratulations and best wishes to you. We know that everyone close to you shares the excitement of the new additions to your family."

The more, then, do I welcome this opportunity to talk to people who make it their business to get their facts straight.

The Associated Press at 150! Conceived by David Hale of the *Journal of Commerce*, still flourishing on West Street in Manhattan, meeting with editors from five other New York dailies. It happens that at that time there was another such organization, operating out of Brussels. This was the network of correspondence bureaus which Karl Marx and Frederich Engels had established connecting various European capitals. Soon they had a Communist League across Europe, and in 1848, issued the celebrated Communist Manifesto.

There is a sense in which the age that followed was a competition between the ideas embodied in these respective organizations. As an early AP correspondent, Lawrence A. Gobright put it, "My business is to communicate facts." To the Marxists and the other ideologues that would follow, facts were merely an epiphenomenon of vast historical forces, which could and should be shaped to great historical ends. That much grief came of the latter is well known. Lesser known, perhaps, is the achievement of the Associated Press and the ideals *it* represented in large polities in which democratic politics become possible because people basically have the same information, and accordingly, can reach common understandings.

This was the beginning of modernization. We go straight from Hale and Raymond and Greeley to the Internet. The whole world now has the same facts.

The transition has not been smooth and, indeed, at times seemed doubtful. There were many reasons, but in essence they were those that Marx and Engels set forth, namely that the transition to a modern world meant we would enter a period of ever mounting economic crises which would eventually destroy the system that created them. For a half century, until just recently, the world has been frozen in a Cold War between the Soviet Union, committed to this proposition, and the West, led by the United States which, well, hoped it wasn't so.

There was one person, however, who you could say *knew* it wasn't so, the English economist John Maynard Keynes. In 1932 he published here in the United States a small volume entitled *Essays in Persuasion*. The whole of the Western world was then seized by a devastating economic crisis. How right Marx and Engels appeared to have been; how hopeless our own situation. Nonsense, wrote Keynes. His thesis was simple:

> "the profound conviction that the Economic Problem, as one may call it for short, the problem of want and poverty and the economic struggle between classes and nations, is nothing but a frightful muddle, a transitory and an *unnecessary* muddle. For the Western World already has the resources and the technique, if we could create the organization to use them, capable of reducing the Economic Problem, which now absorbs our moral and material energies, to a position of secondary importance."

He estimated it might take about 100 years.

Well, here we are, two thirds of the way and it begins to look as if Keynes might have been right. The past half century has been one of near continuous economic growth for the United States, and most of the industrial democracies. A story by David Skidmore on the *AP* wire last Tuesday began, "Inflation disappeared from the U.S. economy for the second time in three months in March . . ." We have full employment and steady growth. Other nations that pay attention are having the same experience.

Just last week our distinguished Secretary of the Treasury Robert E. Rubin outlined an American initiative to avoid future economic convulsions of the kind that have unsettled Asia. It is time, he said, to update the international financial institutions which Keynes, for the British, along with various Americans, established at the end of World War II. Time for international financial systems "to be as modern as the markets." Which means, as the AP would say, to get the facts out fast and straight. Work on the optimistic hypothesis, Keynes would say, and the hypothesis will tend to be realized.

A final reference to Keynes. In the preface to his essays, he has this seeming simple, but profound forecast:

> ". . . [t]he day is not far off when the Economic Problem willtake the back seat where it belongs, and that the arena of the heart and head will be occupied, or re-occupied, by our real problems—the problems of life and of human relations, of creation and behavior and religion."

Human relations, behavior, religion. Hmm. We may yet long for the age of the General Strike! For, as we look about the world, we see dreadful civil strife, ethnic warfare, religious hatred of the most appalling kind. This is seen as

The collapse of the Soviet Union in 1991 took the West almost completely by surprise.

somehow pre-modern, in that much of the most conspicuous
conflict seems to occur in pre-modern settings. But I would
offer you the thought that a number of us have been writing
about for years that it is essentially post-modern, and is not
about to go away. To be sure, we are developing international
institutions to deal with such matters, from election observers to international criminal courts. An international common law is emerging, along with an ever more elaborate
network of legal agreements. And yet, the Cold War no more
ended, with the collapse of the Soviet Union, than the first
European war in 50 years broke out in what had been Yugoslavia. I got into Sarajevo in 1992; one could feel the future.

This comes to us of a sudden, and our grasp of it all is only
just beginning to develop. For it *was* sudden, the end of the
Cold War. I spoke to your annual luncheon in 1976, almost a
quarter century ago. It was a somewhat sullen talk. I felt we
had been conceding too much to the Soviets, and for my
pains had just been fired as U.S. Representative to the United
Nations. I had previously been Ambassador to India and had
left the subcontinent asking how long could anyone seriously suggest that the Russians would hang on to, let us say,
Tajikstan. I remarked at lunch:

> "Russia, after all, is merely the last 19th century Euro-
> pean Empire left, and it is just as likely to come apart
> one of these days as did its onetime peers."

This, I argued, would come about principally from centrifu-
gal forces of ethnicity, religion, nationalism, which drive
international politics in our age. But there was something
more; the near death of the universalist Marxist belief in
world communism in the Soviet Union itself. Moscow might
then have been dispatching Cuban forces to Angola, invad-
ing Africa, if you like, but with small conviction. What I was
not able to tell you in that talk was that Arkady N.
Shevchenko, Under Secretary General of the United Nations,
a man on most anyone's short list to succeed Andrei
Gromyko as Foreign Minister of the U.S.S.R., had that winter
defected to the United States. No such event had ever
occurred. An official near the center of Kremlin policy had
looked about him and decided that the whole Soviet idea had
failed. No one in the Kremlin any longer believed in it, or, for
that matter, understood it. Dissolution was inevitable.
Shevchenko was kept "in place," in the tradecraft term, for
another two years. But his insights and forecasts were available from the first, even if few in Washington paid much
heed.

This is central. The collapse of the Soviet Union in 1991
took the West almost completely by surprise. We now have
volumes like that of former Red Army political commissar,
Dmitri Volkogonov, whose *Autopsy for an Empire* was published posthumously. It describes the stagnant decades in
which decline became irreversible. In a review in *The Wall*

Street Journal, Gabriel Schoenfeld writes that we should ask ourselves:

[W]hat failure of will led the West to behave so timidly, pursuing unobtainable friendship and detente with doddering mediocrities who engaged in the ceaseless accumulation of arms and who recklessly lit bonfires around the globe?

We have never asked this question in Washington. At least we have never answered it. Instead, we continue to act as though the Cold War is still a central reality of foreign policy, withal there has been a turnover and we now have the ball and it is time to move downfield. How else can we explain the astonishing decision to expand NATO to include three former members of the Warsaw Pact. And only the beginning. As Amos Perlmutter recently wrote in the *Washington Times*: "the second phase, sometime at the end of 1999, will usher the entry of Croatia, Slovenia, Romania, Bulgaria, and assorted new and old entities." Thereafter, the three Baltic nations and after that, who can say?

Moreover, the Resolution of Ratification now before the Senate providing for the Accession of Poland, Hungary and the Czech Republic has this singular provision.

(1) THE STRATEGIC CONCEPT OF NATO.

(A) THE FUNDAMENTAL IMPORTANCE OF COLLECTIVE DEFENSE—The Senate declares that—

(i) in order for the NATO to serve the security

interests of the United States, the core purpose of NATO must continue to be the collective defense of the territory of all NATO members; and

(ii) NATO may also, pursuant to Article 4 of the North Atlantic Treaty, on a case-by-case basis, engage in other missions when there is a consensus among its members that there is a threat to the security and interests of NATO members.

Does this not read suspiciously like a license to get into a fight just about anywhere?

The founding of NATO in 1949, then a pact of 12 nations, was an act of rare foresight and political will. Yet, it had its ambiguities. At the signing ceremony, President Truman observed that the alliance was made necessary because "one of the major powers"—the USSR—had blocked the formation of an international force provided for in Article 43 of the Charter that was to have enabled the United Nations to preserve world peace. By contrast, the *AP* account of the signing ceremony recorded that the French Foreign Minister, "speaking in his native tongue," noted that the new treaty in no way compromised his country's nonaggression pact with the Soviet Union. Rather, said the French Minister in the words of the dispatch, "This is directed against a possible future German menace. Indeed, in 1966, President Charles de Gaulle, having developed an independent atomic potential, withdrew France from NATO and unceremoniously threw our headquarters cadre out of his country.

And there were reservations. George Kennan, for one, felt economic recovery as embodied in the Marshall Plan provided the best hope of peace. The eventual incorporation of a prospering Federal Republic of Germany surely attests to this thought.

Much of this history is repeating itself, so much that it could be said we are on the verge of fighting the last war. Half a century ago the Soviets kept their Eastern neighbors out of the Marshall Plan, and so an iron curtain descended across Europe. Five decades later it is the west Europeans who are not prepared to admit the Poles, Hungarians, Czechs, Slovenes, Estonians, who have made clear their hopes to join a continental common market, the European Union, which would make for a united and secure Europe. Last fall Ambassador Richard Holbrooke noted the irony.

> "Almost a decade has gone by since the Berlin Wall fell and, instead of reaching out to Central Europe, the European Union turned toward a bizarre search for a common currency. So NATO enlargement had to fill the void."

Allow me to suggest that wandering in this void we may stumble into the of catastrophe of nuclear war with Russia.

This would come about not from Russian strength, but Russian weakness. This is an idea we find difficult to absorb, and understandably so. But we had better do.

Russians have been trying to tell us this. On December 7, 1988, Mikhail Gorbachev gave an extraordinary speech to the General Assembly of the United Nations declaring, "We in no way aspire to be the bearer of ultimate truth." The Marxist promise had failed in astonishing ways. (Thus, in 1996, a 16-year-old Russian male had only a 54 percent chance of surviving to age 60; two percentage points *less* than had he been born a century earlier!) In the meantime, ethnic hostilities, which were in theory meant to disappear, seemed to rise on every hand. In 1992, Gorbachev spoke to us in Statuary Hall in the Capitol of the problems of Russians now outside Russia:

> "One problem which is assuming an acute and at times dramatic character in Russia is that of ethnic enclaves which, thanks to the breakup of the formerly unified state organism are being violently separated from their accustomed motherland, and now find themselves on the other side of a national boundary . . ."

The situation is aggravated by the paroxysms of extreme nationalism which have here and there generated direct discrimination against minorities. Sometimes this is carried to a point which resembles apartheid. In this situation, any incautious step by anyone, however well intended it might be, can be misinterpreted and used in a way contrary to what was anticipated.

"Any incautious step." As, for example, expanding NATO to the Soviet border of Kaliningrad. Or the mayor of Moscow comparing the leader of Latvia to Pol Pot, as happened just last week.

Also last week Charles Krauthammer, blunt as ever, asked in his *Washington Post* column: "Is NATO expansion directed against Russia?" "Of course it is," he answered.

If we don't see that, surely the Russians do. This is painfully clear in their National Security Blueprint issued by President Yeltsin on December 17, 1997. It is a 14,500 word assessment of their bleak situation and their only seeming option. "The former defense system has been disrupted, and the creation of a new one is proceeding slowly. Long unprotected sections of the Russian Federation state border have appeared." What does remain and does work are the strategic nuclear forces. And so: Russia reserves the right to use all the forces and systems at its disposal, including nuclear weapons, if the unleashing of armed aggression results in a threat to the actual existence of the Russian Federation as an independent sovereign state.

Conspicuously, the Duma has yet to ratify the START II Treaty signed in 1991. In a careful argument against NATO expansion first published in *The Los Angeles Times*, Howard Baker, Sam Nunn, Brent Scoworoft and Alton Frye termed this a doctrine of "inflexible response." A generation of arms negotiations, beginning under President Eisenhower, all directed against "first use" nuclear policies seems now to have been rejected.

A *Newsday* editorial of March 15 began with George Kennan's stark assessment: "Expanding NATO would be the most fateful error of American policy in the entire post-Cold-war era." More recently Kennan has written in *World Policy Journal*:

> ". . . what is at stake in this sad state of affairs is a problem of tragic and momentous importance; for the situation now prevailing stands firmly in the way of the creation in influential American opinion of any quiet thoughtful concepts of American policy and hence of any really useful and constructive employment of the great and unique potential weight of this country in world affairs. But the national political establishment, as now existing, has shown itself totally incapable even of understanding the true dimensions of this problem, and much less in tackling it effectively; and one cannot now look to it for anything more than what it is capable of giving."

Now is the time to look to the Senate. There will be a debate. Thanks to the insistence of Senators such as John Warner, Bob Smith, and Tom Harkin, there *will* be a debate.

As of now there is not much doubt as to the outcome. This could change. Public opinion would seem to be changing. A recent Pew opinion survey found that approval for NATO expansion has dropped to 49 percent, with a large undecided element.

But should the vote go as expected, may we at very least hope that the people and that the "national political establishment," as Ambassador Kennan has it, be alert to the risk we will have taken? We might even change our mind one day. We might even recall that Article 51 of the Charter of the United Nations recognizes "the inherent right of individual or collective self-defense if an armed attack occurs against a Member of the United Nations . . ." Which includes every nation in Eastern Europe. This is grounds on which we went to war with Iraq. It is the law of nations. Concerning which at the General Assembly in 1988, Gorbachev declared "*Pacta Sunt Servanda.*" Agreements must be kept. That is all President Truman intended at that ceremony in 1949. The law of the Charter must be enforced. Such "idealism" no longer resonates with Americans. But surely it is the great standard we have given the world. Russia included. It deserves our attention.

V. In Memoriam

My Memorial Day[1]

Dawn Annette Rigdon

International Student Services Assistant, State University of West Georgia, 1997– ; born 1975; grew up in Willacoochee, GA; graduated Citizens Christian Academy, Douglas, GA, 1993; attended South Georgia College, 1994–95; B.A. in psychology, State University of West Georgia, 1997; plans to pursue advanced degree in counseling or social work.

Editors' introduction: For a Veterans Day ceremony in Washington, D.C., Dawn Annette Rigdon spoke at the Vietnam Veterans Women's Memorial. Some 175 veterans, relatives, and friends attended. The speech was carried by NBC and MSNBC. Rigdon was the first child of a veteran to speak at the Memorial. She attempted "to make everyone aware that the Vietnam conflict still affected families and children of veterans."

Dawn Annette Rigdon's speech: My name is Dawn Rigdon, and I am the daughter of a Vietnam veteran. I would like to share my story with you, and in doing so, share him. Words have failed me so often when I have thought of what I would like to say about Cpl. James H. Rigdon. He was my daddy, my foundation, my protector, my hero. He was also one of the many who returned from Vietnam to fight it every day in his waking world and every night in his dreams. His official tour of duty ended in 1967, and I am here today, 30 years later, standing without him and standing for him, doing what he could not do. I know sometimes it is easy to look at my generation in amazement. We are power-hungry and eager for what may lay around the next corner. We are seemingly non chalant about our past, and idealistic about our future. But, we are children of Vietnam veterans, and we will carry the memories and the lessons of our mothers and fathers with us.

Several months ago I was searching for somebody, or anybody, that would care about the life and the death of my father. I was 21 years old, looking for answers to a war that ended the year I was born. I found comfort in writing, and when I shared it, a whole new world was opened up to me. I found compassion and understanding and empathy from so many who only knew me from my words but who embraced me because of them. The story I share

---

1. Delivered in Washington, D.C., on November 11, 1997, at 2:30 p.m. Reprinted by permission of Dawn Annette Rigdon.

153

with you today is the first one I wrote in memory of my father. It was written earlier in the year; I call it My Memorial Day.

This time of year always makes my chest tight. It is already April and soon will be May. My Memorial Day is almost here again.

I was a busy, self involved, 18-year-old girl on May 27, 1994. I can still recall that day. It was a Friday, and after class all morning and work all day, I was looking forward to a night out with friends and the long holiday weekend ahead. Home was tense, I could feel the heaviness in the air. Daddy was in his room when I rushed home from work. This had become his habit of late. Mom was tired and distracted; those days she seemed to have several jobs, and the role of mother always seemed to spill over into peacemaker and counselor. My 15-year-old sister, Courtnie, was watching TV and talking quietly on the phone. If I had taken the time that afternoon, I may have caught a sense of something different; I did not care or notice if anything was amiss, I just wanted to leave the all controlling mood of my father behind for a little while. Before I left for the evening, though, he managed to do or say something to anger or belittle us all. My family was quietly resigned for the most part to his lashing out and his temper. Temper is really a mild word that barely belies rage.

Daddy was a Vietnam veteran who had been diagnosed with severe post-traumatic stress disorder [PTSD]; all of my life I had lived with the demons that haunted my father. He had myriad health problems that were only exacerbated by his failing body. That evening, though, I felt no sympathy for him, only impatience. His whole attitude had gone straight to hell in the last six months, and it was tiresome. I found myself coldly turning away his excuse for his behavior. Mama tried to explain that when he was angry or upset, it wasn't really him, it was the PTSD. I got tired of this excuse; on his less frequent 'good days' he was sorry and did all he could to make up for everything. These good days had all but vanished in the last few months. As I left for the evening, I marched past his recliner without even so much as a glance in his direction. I ignored him, my usual practice was to sit on the armrest of his chair and kiss his cheek good-bye. I did not care that night to hear his admonition to be careful or to wear my seatbelt. That night, the only thing I said to my father was in defense of my mother. "Why don't you leave her alone" were the last words he ever heard me speak; these words from the child that he loved so much. Had I hesitated a moment on my way out of the door I would have seen my father alive for the last time.

That night, about five minutes after I got home, my daddy stepped in the hallway, stepped back into his room, clicked the lock, and shot himself point blank through the heart. My mother and sister were busy in another room; I was talking with them from the doorway, and I was the one who heard the shot. I looked at my mom from my surreal stance in the hallway and told her I thought that daddy had just shot himself. That moment, that explosion, that ludicrous sounding sentence I uttered, changed my life forever and completely.

Daddy's note was filled with a desperate rage against a war that eventually took his life. Hanging in the corner of daddy's room were his military issue dress blues. He was buried three days later on Monday, Memorial Day, 1994. The Marines that he loved so much helped lay him to rest, and as Taps was played I listened and watched and wondered when this dream would end. At the beginning of my holiday, I had a daddy. At holiday's end, he was dead, and I was beginning to realize that I would forever be without him. On Memorial Day, I was looking over his flag-draped casket.

Three years have passed since then. Now I am a 21-year-old young lady who has moved on in many ways. Soon I will graduate from the University of West Georgia with a degree in Psychology, and graduate school is in the near future. I just bought my first new car and moved into my own place. I have a great job, a great group of friends, and a new life. Yet, I still have a great big void in my heart that is not new anymore, but it is still just as empty as it was on the first day of my new life. Sometimes I think that I have come so far and moved ahead so well. Sometimes I get angry or jealous when I see other fathers doing something for their daughters that my daddy would or could have done for me. Sometimes, I am just sad in a lonely, daddy's girl kind of way. He has missed things in my life that I really wish he could have stuck around for. After all, who better to help a broken heart or check out a funny noise coming from the car? I wonder if he would have cried at my college graduation; I have a feeling I will cry for both of us then. If I could just have him back for one day, I would regale him with hugs and kisses in between stories of new friends, places, and experiences. I would ask him why growing up is so hard, and how he thinks I am doing. These thoughts are all just a part of my memorial day.

Now, patriotic holidays are a mixed bag of emotions. Memorial Day is very important to me; I want to shout to the world that my daddy died for his country, so don't forget him. Isn't that what Memorial Day is for? Gone but not forgotten has a hollow ring when Memorial Day is just another day for so many. I urge everyone in our free nation to consider the price paid for freedom. Shattered lives, dashed hopes, and families with nothing but pictures on a wall and memories recalled in a scent or a sound; these are realities that are hard to imagine but even harder to live with. The veterans of our country deserve a hundred years' worth of Memorial Days. The very least I can do is say thank you. I

Shattered lives, dashed hopes, and families with nothing but pictures on a wall and memories recalled in a scent or a sound; these are realities that are hard to imagine but even harder to live with.

thank you all, every defender of liberty. And, to Cpl. James H. Rigdon of the United States Marine Corps, Daddy, this is for you. I love you.

Pain, Sadness, Exhaustion, and Compassion[2]

Ann C. Cunningham

Staff Operating Room Nurse, University of Virginia Medical Center; Mercy College of Nursing, San Diego, CA, 1965; U.S. Army Nurse, 1966–70; Operating Room Nurse, Vietnam, 36th Evacuation, and 12th Evacuation Hospitals, 1967–68; Operating Room Nurse, 18th Surgical Hospital, 1969–70; Army Commendation Medal; Vietnam Service Medal; YWCA Outstanding Women Nominee, 1992; Sacramento Women of History Award for Initiative, 1990; California Coordinator for Vietnam Women's Memorial, 1988–95; Virginia State Coordinator for Vietnam Women's Memorial Project, 1996– .

Editors' introduction: Nurse Ann C. Cunningham gave this address on the 15th anniversary of the dedication of the Vietnam Veterans Memorial, and the fourth anniversary of the dedication of the Vietnam Women's Memorial. She spoke in front of the Vietnam "wall," to some 7,000 veterans, family members, U.S. Senators, and U.S. Representatives. In her speech, Nurse Cunningham "conveyed what the memorial, Veterans Day, and Vietnam mean to her, as a Vietnam veteran." She was pleased with the response, particularly from veterans, the persons she was really "speaking to." One U.S. Marine veteran gave Nurse Cunningham his Purple Heart. "That was most poignant," she said. "It was a difficult speech to write," she recalled, "knowing I was the only woman speaker and the significance of the day and the Memorial for Vietnam Women Vets—who were not included in events for several years." C-SPAN carried the Veterans Day program.

Ann C. Cunningham's speech: Today is Veterans Day—a day set aside to honor the men and women who have served this country. Today is also the 15th anniversary of the dedication of the Vietnam veterans memorial—the wall—which at the time of dedication was scorned and ridiculed as a black gash of shame and today is the most visited of any memorial in Washington.

Today is also the fourth anniversary of the dedication of the Vietnam Women's Memorial, which took 10 years to build and I feel would never have been built but for the tenacity and determination of Diane Carlson Evans. People ask me

2. Delivered in Washington, D.C., on November 11, 1997, at 1:00 p.m. Reprinted by permission of Ann C. Cunningham.

which of the three women remind me of myself. They all remind me of myself at one time or another but the one I am most drawn to is the kneeling figure. If you look closely at her face you will see pain, sadness, exhaustion, and compassion reflected there.

All the women who served in Vietnam and during the Vietnam War had these traits—from the nurse in the operating room, to the nurse in the ICU unit.

From the Red Cross women who read books and wrote letters for wounded GI's, to the air traffic controllers who brought the planes home after their missions. From the women who counted and tallied up the casualties daily, to the women in special services.

Thirty years ago I was in Vietnam. I was a young, naive 22-year-old, a year and a half out of nursing school when I joined the Army Nurse Corps. I was two and a half weeks out of basic training the day I landed at Bien Hoa airbase with about half of my basic class and a greener second Lieutenant. You would never find.

I was a trained operating room nurse, but I had never seen a trauma patient, let alone a mass casualty situation. Needless to say in the next 12 months I saw many such situations. It was the best of times and the worst of times and it took me 15 years to talk about it. When the wall was dedicated, I didn't even know about it because I didn't read about Vietnam or watch Vietnam movies.

When I did see the dedication on TV, part of me was sad that I wasn't there, but in 1982 I wasn't ready to face Vietnam.

I look at the wall behind me and I see the names of people I knew—Bruce Kennedy and Charlie Warner—I grew up with in Santa Monica, CA—we all went to school together.

I look behind me and I see the names of people I served with: Leroy Pitts, Al Gaidis, Zeddie Dulin, Chuck Springer, Lowell Morgan and Phil Schmitz.

I look behind me and I see the names of women who cared enough to volunteer to help other Americans: Carol Drazba, Annie Graham, Elizabeth Jones, Hedwig Orlowski, Eleanor Alexander, Pamela Donovan, Mary Klinker and Sharon Lane.

I look behind me and I see the name of Gary Jones, a person I loved very much—we went to Vietnam, I came back and he didn't.

I look behind me and I see the name of patients we were unable to save. One, I especially remember, he is engraved in my mind forever. I was able to find his family and I wrote them a letter. His mother wrote back and these were her words: "When we received word that our son was wounded, I wanted to go to him, to somehow be there for him, but I could not be there. That is a mother's worst nightmare. You will never know what it means to us to know that before he died, someone was there to care. Thank you for all you did."

It was the best of times and the worst of times and it took me 15 years to talk about it.

I think of the friends who have died since Vietnam, whose names are not on the wall, but maybe ought to be, of B. T. Collins, whose contributions to the living and the dead will live on forever, and of Doug Colliander, who was a friend and died too soon.

I look behind me at the memorial and think of the friends who have been dead now longer than they lived and of the impact they made on my life.

To the veterans in the audience today, the veterans of World War I, World War II, Korea, Desert Storm, Somalia, Bosnia and Vietnam, especially Vietnam, I say, "Thank you for your service and your sacrifices for your country and welcome home. You are very special people. I consider it an honor to know you."

Thank you.

The Gift of Anastasia[3]

Marcy Kaptur

U.S. Representative (D) from Ohio; lifelong resident of Toledo, OH; B.A. in history, University of Wisconsin; master's degree in urban planning, University of Michigan; honorary degrees, University of Toledo and Saint Mary's College, Notre Dame; professional city and regional planner, Toledo and Lucas County, Ohio; urban policy advisor in the Carter administration; was pursuing a doctorate in urban planning and development finance at Massachusetts Institute of Technology when recruited to run for the U.S. House of Representatives; in eighth term in U.S. House; defender of American jobs, workers, and businesses; House Appropriations Committee; Subcommittee on Agriculture; founded the Job and Fair Trade Caucus; formed the Auto Parks Task Force; honorary chair, Toledo Diocese Catholic Central Cities Ministry; hosts In the National Interest, *syndicated radio program; author,* Women in Congress: A Twentieth Century Odyssey.

Editors' introduction: Representative Marcy Kaptur eulogized Mrs. Anastasia Delores Mary Rogowska Kaptur, her mother, at a funeral mass at St. Teresa of the Little Flower Catholic Church, before some 300 friends, family members, community leaders, church members, United Auto Workers members, and guests. The eulogy was co-authored by Representative Kaptur and her brother, Mr. Stephen J. Kaptur. Their purpose was to "pay tribute to her heroic life," a story of "triumph over adversity."

Marcy Kaptur's speech: Welcome to St. Teresa of the Little Flower Parish, where our family has attended for 52 years.

On behalf of my mother's son and my brother, Steve, and the Kaptur and Rogowski families, especially our loving father Stephen "Kappy" who was laid to rest 28 years ago, as well as mother's mother and father, Teofila and John, and her sister, Anna, her brothers Anthony and Stanley, all of whom preceded her in death; her sister-in-law Esther Kalinska Rogowski; her niece and goddaughter Rose Ann Rogowska Koperski and her nephew John Rogowski; her cousins Theresa and Joe Kaptur, and John and Rita Kaptur, and their children and grandchildren; and her treasured friends, Mrs. Blanche Zalipski, Mrs. Esther Dutkiewicz, Mrs. Sally Zawierucha, and Mrs. Connie (Corrie) Dutched—all of us wish to extend deepest gratitude to you, our friends, for

---

3. Delivered in Toledo, Ohio, on March 24, 1997, at 2:30 p.m. Reprinted by permission of Marcy Kaptur.

your compassion and for making the effort to celebrate the life of our most beloved mother Anastasia "Cherie" Delores Mary Rogowska Kaptur. We wish also to express the sincerest thanks to the doctors, nurses, and support staff at every level at St. Vincent's Medical Center, especially Dr. Ward Taylor, Drs. A. Zacharias and Thomas Schwann, and Drs. Phillip Horowitz and Allen Markowicz. Our family is also indebted to Mr. H. Ross Perot and the gifted doctors at the Southwestern Medical Center in Dallas, Dr. Gene Frenkel who made the longest house call in the world, and Dr. A. Harold Urschell. Finally, we cannot express our appreciation adequately to the saintly nurses of Hospice of Northwest Ohio who treated our mother with the tenderest and most humane care.

For us, her children, mother's loss is profound, beyond measure. We know God has blessed our family by affording us the privilege and honor to know and love this heroic woman for half a century. We admire her totally. Our love and respect for her has grown more with each passing day. We shall never know a more loving, unselfish, nor courageous human being. Somehow it is mystical that this service is being held at a time when seasons are converging, as spring dawns in this season of new life. Within the last week, we have experienced freezing rain, bright sunlight with blue skies, winter snowfalls, blustery winds, and spring rains. The geese and birds are returning, and there is a new moon. We believe this is nature's way of welcoming our mother.

My brother and I also must beg our mother's forgiveness. Because, you see, she chose to be a very private person—a woman of deepest humility. She sought no fanfare nor acknowledgment. She would have been quite uncomfortable with the attention being directed her way today. But we couldn't fathom how to avoid this occasion of the celebration of her life.

We would wish for each of you to have in your life the gift of Anastasia—love constantly and freely bestowed, as she has given us for five decades. She has been our life-long partner in all adventures, large and small, and our most ardent supporter—whether it was working with my brother on his latest patented invention or on his race car—literally, she sat behind the wheel revving the engine while he tinkered under the hood. She acted as my chief political confidante, inspiring me always, as well as touching citizens across this district and nation. Her love for her children could not be contained.

Make no mistake about her resolve. She was a rugged individualist. In an age of materialism, she countered the tide. She coveted no bauble. She preferred "making" to "buying." In an age of television, she remained a literary woman of the written word, known for her independent thought and resistance to commercialized brain washing. In an age of mega mergers and faceless bureaucracies, she supported the small family businesses—Bayer's Hardware, Wolfert and Sofo's Markets, Brodbeck's Greenhouse. We can still see her each spring in that greenhouse, negotiating down all the aisles, appreciating the vast display of acres of flowers under glass, and leaving with carloads of petunias and other sundry selections, along with trunkloads of potting soil. In an age of shallow commitments, her word and her life remain as true as the North Star. For us, she remains ageless, a woman for all seasons.

Our mother's life symbolizes triumph over adversity, the story of a woman from the working classes who never yielded. Let us tell you Anastasia's story . . .

Mother was born in Toledo to Polish peasant immigrant parents who had journeyed to America in 1912 before World War I from a tiny village in Burtyn, Ukraine, at the nexus of the Polish and Ukrainian borders. Her father was a forester and her mother a peasant girl of 17 years. They suffered the abuse of making the month-long journey to America in steerage class in the bottom of a ship that left from Rotterdam and disembarked at Ellis Island in New York. They sought to improve their lot by working to earn enough money to buy farmland in their native country where they had been forced off the land as land was collectivized and they could no longer graze their cows. But the Russian Revolution intervened, then World War I, and mother's parents were cut off from their relatives, never able to return home.

Our mother was the second-born of their four children—Anna, Anastasia, Anthony, and Stanley. She was nicknamed "Cherie" in a childhood game they invented in which they renamed one another—Al, Cherie, Fritz, and Skip.

Mother grew up during the Depression utterly poor from a financial standpoint. That searing memory of bitter poverty would remain with her throughout her life. This was a time in America before our social safety net laws were in place. In her early years, the family moved at least eight times—always renters, never owners—from Belmont Avenue, to Avondale, to Vance, to Pulaski, to Lucas, to Montrose, to Blum, to Pinewood. And with those moves, she was forced to change elementary schools and disrupt those tender learning years—from Indiana School, to Pickett, to St. Teresa where she made her Communion and Confirmation, to Hoag School. At age 13, mom was already working to support her family. She would rise at 4:30 A.M., take two buses across town in Toledo to babysit and also clean houses for her teachers, as well as wealthier people in Toledo. She herself later would write: "Being a child of depression, making $5 a week, my father out of work for years, my sister dying, no money at all. No hope at all. My two children know the history."

Though highly gifted academically and an all-A student in the seventh and eighth grades, she was forced to drop out of Libbey High School to work as a waitress to bring home a few dollars a week to help the struggling family that also took in boarders to make extra cash. Her father, always the last hired and the first fired, could not keep steady work so her mother cooked, washed clothes, did ironing—anything—to earn cash, and also labored at Miller's Greenhouse picking tomatoes, then in the kitchen at the Commodore Perry, then at Kuhlmann's Potato Chips, and at Industrial Belt company on Summit—but like her husband always at the bottom of the seniority list. Her treasured and only sister, Anna, one year older than mom, died tragically at age 17 of leakage of the heart, an event that remained deeply poignant to our mother throughout her years. Mom became the oldest surviving child. At age 16, she hired on at Dean's Confectionary across from St. Anthony's school for $5 per week. Many times that was all her family had to live on. At 18, she worked at Liberty Lunch for $8 a week, and then at Broadway Bar-B-Que for $11.75 a week. The minimum wage law was passed at that time, but her boss made her sign her check, then he cashed it, and she was still paid only $8 a week. One day a lady came in looking for people to work at Kresge's downtown, where mom became employed, earning $14.50 a week.

When she was in her early 20s, she landed a job at the Champion Spark Plug Company in Toledo where she had applied at the employment office every day for one year. She never missed a day of work between any of her jobs. Here, her weekly wage rose to $40 a week. She worked the production line at plug tamping where she was paid based on her output and she always did the maximum number each day. It was at Champion that she was elected to the Charter Committee of the Local 12 United Auto Workers Trade Union that was forming. She summarized for her children why she helped form the union—"primarily to assure seniority rights of employment so you couldn't be fired because the supervisor brought family members to replace you. A bidding system was established so any open job was put up on the board so the one with the most seniority got the job if qualified. Discrimination was outlawed so the foreman could no longer put his pets or relatives on the best job. The right to ask for a pay raise was assured through negotiation and the right to strike granted to employees. Leaves for illness were granted so people wouldn't be fired if a doctor's certification was provided. Bathroom privileges were allowed for personal contingencies. Three months leave was allowed for pregnancy. Layoffs would occur according to seniority. And a grievance procedure was established to curb harassment by mean foremen."

Elected union Secretary, Mom gained respect by both company and union members for her knowledge of the bidding system, her ability to handle grievances, and her detailed grasp of the labor contract.

On November 26, 1938, at 9:00 A.M. at St. Teresa's Church, she married our happy-go-lucky, wonderful father, Stephen or "Kappy"—a produce man and truck driver. He came from an even larger family where his mother had 16 children, though many did not survive the illnesses of that period. They lived with mom's family for awhile but then, together in 1945, they bought a small home in Reynolds Corners in Adams Township, totally retrofitted it, landscaped the property, waterproofed the outside walls, handstripped the woodwork. While they were at it, they gave birth to two children, their daughter Marcia Carolyn in 1946, and their son Stephen Jacob in 1952. Mom left her job at Champion when Steve was born.

In 1952, mom and dad opened their own family meat market and grocery called Supreme Market in Rossford, Ohio on Dixie Highway across from the Libbey Glass Plant. Cherie's homemade pies were sold there, along with dad's fresh and smoked Polish sausage, veal loaf, pickled herring, and lots more. But due to her husband's illness, the family was forced to sell the store at decade's end, and dad went to work at Kaiser Jeep to assure the family income and health benefits. He retired from there in 1968. Mom worked at a number of part-time jobs to supplement the family income, with their daughter in college and their son in high school—Daso Bakery, Mareks' Supermarket, cleaning physicians' offices, and even pet-sitting.

She continued working after she was widowed in 1969.

During the 1970s, with her children grown, and after receiving her first Social Security check, Anastasia pursued the life-long dream she had placed on hold while she helped everyone else—completing her high school education and advancing her own formal education. She received her high school certification of graduation from the State of Ohio in 1975, and passed with flying colors. She also enrolled in Russian courses at the University of Toledo, took painting courses at the Toledo Museum of Art, polished her knowledge of the Polish language from books and letter-writing, honing those skills for decades by writing relatives in Poland and the Ukraine. She became the best "Friend of the Library," faithfully checking out 10 to 20 books each month. And the reading list was not light—Halberstam, Updike, McCollough, Grisham, *Elements of Style*, *Raven's Wing*, *The Recycled Citizen*, *The Reckoning*, *Brand Fires on the Ridge*. History. Travel. Adventure. Geography. Fiction. Mysteries. Mom often used the expression "thirst for knowledge." And, she certainly possessed it. She was self-taught in so many facets, cultivated a stellar vocabulary on a daily basis, and was a life-long learner.

She began to travel extensively with her children—throughout the United States, and the world. Her deep interest in geography enlivened at every turn. Niagara Falls, British Columbia, New Orleans, Miami, Montreal, Vermont, Maine, Pennsylvania, Indiana, Chicago, New York, California, Oregon, the Upper and Lower Peninsulas in Michigan, Germany, France, Czechoslovakia, Hungary, Poland, the Ukraine, even when the Iron Curtain made travel difficult . . . Mexico, Toronto . . . Her most memorable trip involved discovering the village of her mother and father, hidden inside the western Ukraine, placing flowers on the graves of her grandmothers, and learning of their fates—one starved to death during Lenin's drive to squelch peasant rebellion in the countryside, and the other shot together with her grandchildren for refusing to divulge the whereabouts of a grandson being sought for conscription into the Russian army. While there, mom discovered a grove of full grown trees at the opening to the village, planted by her mother before she departed for America. While there, she also found her mother's brother, Casimer, the sole surviving son who had been placed in Siberian concentration camps for 20 years by Joseph Stalin. It was an unforgettable journey as the blanks of 63 years of family history were filled in.

Mother is most at home in the outdoors with nature, and in her gardens. She advised "everything in life must have a center, just like the universe, or a flower, or a family." She could grow anything—certainly children. But also animals—dogs, ducks, rabbits, birds, squirrels, crescendos of plants and flowers, roses by the thousands, flowers of all varieties—the usual ones like marigolds and sweet peas. But more often the unusual and rare ones—moon flowers, balloon flowers, lupines, tulips, foxglove, columbine. Her own potatoes, planted lovingly each year, were harvested for a special meal. And her evergreens and spruces, grown from shoots or small seeds, all came to have symbolic value in our yard like the large blue spruce on our front lawn, planted the first year she had both a son and a daughter. If by a loving act of nature, that tree over the years has sprouted two tops.

Always, she was beautiful, so delicate and tiny physically, with the clearest blue eyes my brother and I had ever seen, and flawless skin, rarely wearing makeup. Natural. She wore her hair like no other person we ever met. Distinctive. She wore hats and clothing she crafted herself. She loved to dance, especially polkas in both clockwise and counterclockwise directions. She had a flair, whether it was the way she held a napkin, or planted a garden, or signed her name.

She was always usefully occupied and her project list never ended. She built furniture, designed and sewed clothing, painted oil sketches, landscaped, wrote newsy personal let-

Everything in life must have a center, just like the universe, or a flower, or a family.

ters, baked, did masonry. She enjoyed people, one at a time, and took a personal interest in each person's story. When she finished a conversation, it was likely the person had told her much more about him or herself than they ever knew about mom. The first day she was admitted to the hospital for tests, a nurse came up to her and said she was going to take extra good care of her because when the nurse's husband was a little boy, he was mom's paper boy and mom always invited him in and fed him cookies.

She would refer to people she truly admired as the "salt of the earth." Indeed, that epitomizes her. And she would remind us the "strongest steel goes through the hottest fire." And she has. She always prayed for others' physical, mental, moral, and spiritual strength. But, she possessed them all. She walked toward physical death with full knowledge, her shoulders straight, trying to bolster us, with her eyes fixed on the horizon. She never flinched once. She never complained. She accepted. And, her spirit triumphed. I only wish we could reveal to you the depths of her courage. She taught us how to live, and she showed us how to die.

We are grateful to God for granting us the time to say goodbye. Never have we known a person of such goodness. She would caution us "Never give anything with the idea of getting something in return." She was completely selfless. In knowing her, we came to know the full meaning of the words—love, truth, beauty, unselfishness, humility, wisdom, generosity, grace, refinement, ingenuity, perseverance, serenity, and courage. For those of you who wonder why she didn't confide in you these last several months, please know she was protecting you, not wanting you to worry. She was always thinking of the other person.

If you ever looked into her sparkling eyes, or shook her hand, you knew you met someone of substantial character and abiding virtue. In the heavens, some stars emanate a pure light, so full, constant and strong, they quietly draw the gaze of earthly creatures, large and small, to their wondrous, serene luster. They usher in the night and the day. In their light, sojourners never lose their way, never fall, never tire, and are never alone.

In her memory, our family will establish "The Anastasia Fund" (to be formally incorporated as the Anastasia Swiecicki Rogowska Kaptur Fund) for the adoption, education, and medical care of children from the newly democratizing nations of Eastern and Central Europe, beginning with Burtyn, Ukraine, the ancestral home of her parents. Mother would say, "Goodness never dies." May this fund honor her memory, that of her mother and father, and their mothers and fathers as we move to a 21st century that offers hope in the most forgotten places.

There is no way to say thank you sufficiently, mother. We love you beyond life and time itself. May eternal rest be granted unto you and may perpetual light shine upon you.
     Your profoundly grateful son and daughter,
     Steve and Marcy

September Song[4]

Forrest Church

Minister, All Souls Unitarian Church, New York, NY, 1978– ; born Boise, Idaho, 1948; A.B., Stanford University, 1970; M.Div., 1974, and Ph.D. in early church history, 1978, Harvard University; Montgomery Fellow and visiting professor, Dartmouth College, 1989; author and editor of 16 books, including Father and Son: A Personal Biography of Senator Frank Church of Idaho by His Son *(1985),* The Devil and Dr. Church *(1986),* Entertaining Angels *(1987)* The Seven Deadly Virtues *(1988)* God and Other Famous Liberals: Reclaiming the Politics of America *(1992);* Life Lines: Holding On and Letting Go *(1996); articles on New Testament studies, the history of early Christianity, the history of liberal religion, and contemporary theological topics.*

> *We know that we are going to die and then question what life means.*

Editors' introduction: Dr. Forrest Church gave this address to 600 members of his congregation at All Souls Unitarian Church on September 7, 1997, at Sunday morning services. Contrasting meanings of the lives and deaths of Mother Teresa and Princess Diana, Church explained the nature of public vulnerability and the power of humility. Rarely has he "received a more emotional response" to a sermon.

Forrest Church's speech: How strange that this year's September Song was written by Elton John, "A Candle in the Wind," written in honor of Marilyn Monroe, brilliantly and appropriately revised for the funeral of Lady Diana. And then Mother Teresa died. What song would you rewrite for her funeral? "Imagine"? "All We Need Is Love"? Maybe "Ave Maria"? They wouldn't even have to be rewritten.

I had a sermon for this morning which you obviously are not going to hear. September Song. Endings and beginnings. A nice, non-threatening, impressionistic invitation to the next season of your life. But our September Song has changed and my sermon with it. The subject is the same but the song has changed. The new song was sung yesterday morning before most but not all of us were up. My wife set her alarm for 6:30 and just missed it. I slept through, continuing, even wanting to believe, that nothing all that far out of the ordinary was happening.

She was right. I was wrong. This past week's events finally sneaked up on me, and with Mother Teresa's death I was overtaken. This is no time for business as usual. Certainly

---

4. Delivered in New York City, on September 7, 1997, at 10 a.m. and 11:15 a.m. Reprinted by permission of Forrest Church.

not a time for cynicism. It is a time for us to pay our respects
to two people who, in remarkably different and remarkably
similar ways, changed our lives—not just by being famous,
but by investing fame with meaning, by touching our hearts.

Let me step back for a minute and share my thoughts
about a preacher's job. I'm just beginning my 20th year with
you. This is about my 600th sermon. I draw from a strong
faith tradition, which, if not orthodox, invites me to explore
everything from the scriptures to ancient philosophy and
current events. But the object is always the same. For me,
*religion is our human response to the dual reality of being
alive and having to die.* We are not the animal with tools, or
the animal with advanced language; we are the religious animal. We know that we are going to die and then question
what life means. This week two deaths both cast a shadow
and shone a light on what it means to be alive and then to
die. For several days I tried to avoid the shadow; yesterday I
felt the light.

Let me tell you what I hate about much organized religion.
It obliterates the ragged edges of our lives, imposing in their
place a sterile, dogmatic form that encompasses everyone
and no one at the same time. Let me give you an example.
Last Sunday the royal family worshiped at their local church
in Scotland. These two bereft boys, William and Harry, sat
through a church service in which their mother's name and
death were never mentioned. The preacher delivered a sermon he had written the week before Princess Diana died. It
was filled with sly humor and correct theology. It had nothing to do with anything that really mattered.

Most weeks I can preach to you a sermon I have deter-
mined on a month before. At their best such sermons are
worth pondering. This morning I am simply going to give my
own, unpolished thoughts about what you are pondering,
the deaths and lives of these two women, so very different
save in this: Each was thrust into a caste system—Windsor
and Brahmin—and refused to be governed by it. Instead they
let their humanity shine through by embracing the constitu-
ency of the rejected.

How many of you watched some part of Diana's funeral
yesterday? You and one to two billion others. I believe that
we are one, all of us, mysteriously born and fated to die, but
how often do we even get close to experiencing that. Yesterday we did.

So let me try to make some sense of this, for me as well as
for you. I have to begin with a confession. I didn't want to
preach about Princess Diana this morning. I decided to on
Friday, before Mother Teresa died; but until yesterday I was
still ambivalent. I don't believe in fairy princesses. I didn't
want to concede more to the death of a fashion plate than to
a forgotten young woman in East Harlem, who surely died

this week and left two children and whose names we will never know.

The first thing that touched me was my wife's tears. They fell every morning and evening this week. Let me tell you something. Don't try arguing with tears. They come from someplace deep. They almost always matter.

And then I started to cry. I finally got it. Yesterday morning, the little envelope on Diana's casket that said "Mummy." And then the song. And Prime Minister Tony Blair reading First Corinthians 13 as it has almost never been read before, and then Lord Spencer, who spoke the truth, his love expressed in anger, and I was crying. Again and again.

As Lord Spencer said, Princess Diana was not a saint. Mother Teresa was. Yet, when I heard that Mother Teresa had died, I felt nothing other than respect and appreciation for her life. Let me put this bluntly: I didn't feel my own death. But when Diana was killed in a Paris tunnel I did. Not that I wanted to think about it. I didn't. I fought all week not to. But I did. I felt my death.

Even that's not quite right. I felt death itself. Sudden, untimely, the trap door falls: bang, that's it. Remember John Lennon's last song: "Life is what happens to you when you are busy making other plans." Life, and especially death.

I read all the papers, all the pundits. I even half agreed with most of what I read. But it wasn't until Lord Spencer spoke that I got it. Why did this woman touch so many hearts so deeply? No one had said this before. The reason she touched our hearts so deeply is because she felt unworthy. Isn't that amazing. She touched us because of her openly acknowledged sense of insecurity, because of her lifelong struggle with a feeling of unworthiness.

If you want to know what to do with your own sense of unworthiness, think for a moment about this woman. She touched the untouchables: first children with AIDS, then lepers, finally land-mine victims without limbs. Along the way she paid her price, bulimia, a desperate willingness to give love to anyone who would offer kindness in return. But just think for a moment about this unbelievably beautiful woman who had so little confidence in herself and yet somehow managed to give so much confidence to others.

That picture of her with Mother Teresa in the Bronx taken less than two months ago—we have all seen it. Mother Teresa didn't have—at least she didn't seem to have—a sense of unworthiness. But she embodied humility. Yet even here the two share something deep. As Princess Diana demonstrated time and again, humility is not always born from saintliness. It can also be born from a sense of unworthiness. In some ways that is even more remarkable. A woman has everything anyone could want, everything other than love and self-esteem, which are perhaps the only things that we should really hope for in this life. And so what does she do?

We can identify with Princess Diana . . . because we could see our own tears in her eyes.

She gives her love to others and builds their self-esteem. In a zero-sum game the result would be nothing. In life, it means everything. Empty yourself and be filled. Lose yourself and be found. Give and you shall receive—but more importantly you give. And the world is changed.

How strange it is that those we cannot help but keep remembering almost always die young. How even stranger that the only woman I can think of from the last century who already has anything close to the legendary status Princess Di will soon attain also struggled throughout her life with a sense of unworthiness. And how appropriate that Elton John honored both of them with the same song.

Marilyn Monroe didn't cuddle AIDS babies or fight for the abolishment of land mines. But she possessed exactly the same magic Lady Di did. She was everyone's fantasy but her own. This was captured for both of them in Elton John's original song better than in his beautiful reworking of the lyrics. One line he changed could well have been kept. After he sings "She lived her life like a candle in the wind," instead of "never fading with the sunset when the rain set in" leaving the words, "never knowing who to cling to when the rain set in."

We don't need to be titled, beautiful, or successful. We don't even have to have a sense of worthiness.

What does this have to do with us? Surprisingly, though I fought this all week, almost everything. We admire other people's strength; but, I think, when it comes right down to it, we identify with other people's weaknesses. We can identify with Princess Diana not because she was royal—none of us is—not because she was beautiful—almost none of us is—but because we could see our own tears in her eyes.

When this beautiful person died, the beauty lost had nothing to do with her looks. In a strange way, as so often is the case with physically beautiful people, her looks in fact were as much a personal curse as a boon. Remember, this was a woman who often hated what she saw when she looked into a mirror. But when she looked into the mirror of other people's eyes she recognized their pain. It is this that opened our hearts to hers and made her the people's princess.

A sense of unworthiness is not the same thing as humility. A person who feels unworthy may often simply feel humiliated. This leads more often to self-absorption than to compassion. The distinction is important because many of us feel unworthy, unworthy when we measure ourselves against others, our parents' expectations, people more successful than we in work or love. But, even as humiliated people are abased, humble people somehow manage to abound. That's the difference.

Princess Di's sense of unworthiness translated into something redemptive: a connection with others. Her death is tragic, not because her promise was unfulfilled, but because it *was* fulfilled and might continue to have been. Not her promise of happiness, the fairy tale princess story we were invited to believe in 16 years ago, but the larger promise of love—given, if never, because of her sense of unworthiness, fully received. My guess is, this would not have changed. Yet, Princess Diana more than fulfilled her unwanted mission. She found a way to invest her pain into other people's hope.

Let me try to bring this home. Because of her position, her beauty, her grace, even her public vulnerability, this woman was bigger than life. Mother Teresa was also bigger than life. History only allots a saint or two every generation—public saints, at least. In my book, there are saints everywhere doing Mother Teresa's business. She was different only because of her fame, but rare therefore because fame does everything it can to destroy sainthood.

Yet, though both of these women were larger than life, Diana is the one to whom we can relate. And yesterday morning I finally got it. We relate to her because of her sense of unworthiness. That and her triumph, not over but in spite of it.

Earl Spencer said that her sister didn't need a royal title to "dispense her own form of magic." Neither did Mother Teresa, not even a title from the church. Neither do we. We don't need anything to dispense our own form of magic. We don't need to be titled, beautiful, or successful. We don't even have to have a sense of worthiness. All we have to do is help others: To see our tears in their eyes, to recognize that the same sun sets on each of our horizons, that the mortar of mortality binds us fast to one another, that we are one.

In a strange sense, we witnessed our own funeral yesterday. No, the pomp won't be there, the horses, the crowds; but when we do die the same questions will be wafting in the air. Did we take what God gave us and make the most of it? Did we overcome adversity when hard times came? Did we love our neighbor as ourselves—perhaps especially this. And did we make the world a more loving and interesting place?

Elton John sang to Diana, and he was right: "You were the grace that placed itself where lives were torn apart." Could we be that? Could we be the grace that placed itself where lives were torn apart? I have to think so. We know about lives being torn apart. We have even done a little of the tearing. But so had she. And we are here. And this is the day that *we* are given. A new year is beginning. It is *our* new year.

So let us inaugurate it well. Let us give our hearts to others. Let us do this before, sooner than you might imagine, either we or they are taken from us.

VI. Twenty-first Century Challenges

If Labor Has No Role, Democracy Has No Future[1]

John J. Sweeney

President, AFL–CIO, 1995– ; born Bronx, NY, 1934; graduated with a degree in economics from Iona College, New Rochelle, NY; Local 32B, New York City, 1960– , and president, 1976; Service Employees International Union (SEIU), 1960– , and president, 1980–95; International Ladies' Garment Workers; vice president AFL–CIO and chair, Executive Council Committees on Health Care and Organizing and Field Services; co-editor, UNA-USA Economic Policy Council's Family and Work: Bridging the Gap *(1987); co-author,* Solutions for the New Work Force *(1989); author,* America Needs a Raise: Fighting for Economic Security and Social Justice *(1996).*

Does labor have a role in defining the future?

Editors' introduction: AFL–CIO President John J. Sweeney gave this address at a plenary session sponsored by the World Economic Forum to 1,000 chief executive officers, economists, elected officials, heads of state, and academicians from several nations. President Sweeney was one of five labor leaders from around the world attending the conference. His purpose was to show "that labor plays an important role in the new global economy." As president of a 13 million-member union, Sweeney was pleased with the address because it "let our workers'" voices be heard." C-SPAN carried the speech.

John J. Sweeney's speech: It is a privilege and a pleasure to address the World Economic Forum, and to join the distinguished members of this panel.

Does labor have a role in defining the future? In the United States, ask the opponents of the minimum wage. Or the management of United Parcel Service. Or the proponents of fast track trade accords that ignore labor rights and environmental protections.

Let us be very clear. If labor has no role, democracy has no future. Social justice does not "compromise the efficiency of the model." It is essential to its survival. If this global economy cannot be made to work for working people, it will reap a reaction

---

1. Delivered in Davos, Switzerland, on January 31, 1998, at 10:30 a.m.
Reprinted by permission of John J. Sweeney.

that may make the 20th Century seem tranquil by comparison.

We meet at an historic turning—one that everyone in these meetings must see. The long effort to build the global market has succeeded. Capital and currencies have been de-regulated. Great corporations have built global systems of production, distribution, marketing. Barriers have been dismantled. Technology's miracles are turning our world into one neighborhood.

But the turmoil afflicting the Asian economies sounds a dramatic alarm. The question now is not how to create the global market, but how to put sensible boundaries on the market that already exists. How to make the market work for the majority and not simply for the few. In this new effort, labor and other democratic citizen movements will and must play a central role.

Look around the world. Japan mired in recession, Asia in crisis that China still faces. Russia plagued by a kind of primitive, gangster capitalism, Europe stagnant, Africa largely written off by global investors, Latin America adrift.

The U. S. is hailed as the great "model." Our prosperity is unmatched; the dollar is strong; our budget balanced. Unemployment and inflation are down and profits are up. But, most working people in the United States today labor longer and harder simply to hold their own. One in four children is born to poverty. One in five workers goes without health insurance. The blessings of prosperity have been largely captured by the few. Inequality is at levels so obscene that New York investment houses this year warned executives not to talk about the size of their bonuses.

And now, the Asian nations are forced to export their deflation to the U. S. Our annual trade deficit will soar towards $300 billion. Over one million U. S. workers are projected to lose their jobs. Wages, only now beginning to recover, will once again be depressed. And this is the "model" in the best of times.

The current collapse calls into question not simply Asian practices but the global system itself. As Korean President Kim Dae Jung has said, authoritarian systems in Asia lived a lie. But their crony capitalism was bankrolled by the reckless high rollers of the global casino, including Japanese, European and American banks and investment houses.

The response to the crisis reveals the limits of the current arrangement. Conservatives say let the market solve the problem. But since the Great Depression, no sensible leadership would take that gamble. The IMF is called in to stop the hemorrhaging. It bails out the speculators and enforces austerity on the people. Its prescription reinforces the very affliction it seeks to cure.

Treasury Secretary Robert Rubin has wisely warned about the "moral hazard" of bailing out profligate speculators and banks. But too little has been said about the "immoral hazard" of forcing working people across the world to pay the price—in lay-offs, declining wages and increasing insecurity.

I have just returned from Mexico, which has been presented as a "success" for Asians to follow. There, speculators and bond holders had their losses covered. But some two million workers lost their jobs. The middle class has been crushed. Wages lost over half their value. Environmental poisoning is worse than ever. Political violence is spreading. Crime is spiraling out of control. Few nations can weather this form of success.

This global system broadcasts its stark contrasts—of untold wealth for the few and growing insecurity for the many, of laws that protect property and expose people, of liberated capital and repressed workers. The inequities are indefensible ethically, but they are also unsustainable economically— as U. S. Federal Reserve Chair Alan Greenspan suggests with his warnings about deflation.

I suggest to you that we must usher in a new era of reform. One that seeks not more de-regulation, but greater accountability. Not further unleashing of speculative capital, but channeling of real investment. Not greater license for corporations, but empowerment of workers and citizens.

Labor, environmental, and democratic citizen movements are already struggling to define this new internationalism in practice and in policy. At the AFL-CIO, we are building stronger working relations with unions across the world. We fight to defend labor rights at home and abroad. We are uniting with other citizen movements to struggle for basic environmental, consumer and civil rights. We will demand coordinated efforts to stimulate growth, to regulate currency and capital speculation, to extend labor and democratic rights as part of the response to the Asian collapse.

At the beginning of this century, the industrial revolution created new promise and glaring inequities. It took many decades—and revolutions, wars and a Great Depression—to elaborate the protections that saved that system from itself. Now at the beginning of the 21st century, the global economy poses the same challenge. Let us hope we need not relive the horrors of the past to reach its promise for the future.

Adapting to a Revolution: the Challenges Facing Energy Companies in the 21st Century[2]

Philip J. Carroll

President and chief executive officer, Shell Oil Company, 1993– ; B.S. in physics, Loyola University; M.S. in physics, Tulane University; Shell Oil Company, 1961– , including vice president of public affairs, 1979– , executive vice president of administration, 1988– , and director; director, American Petroleum Institute, the Boise Cascade Corporation, the National Action Council for Minorities in Engineering, and the Texas Medical Center; vice chairman, Business Higher Education Forum; National Petroleum Council; Texas Governor's Business Council; numerous civic and charitable boards.

Editors' introduction: Philip J. Carroll, the president of the Shell Oil Company, gave the keynote address at Energy Week Conference & Exhibition in General Assembly Hall "B," the George R. Brown Convention Center, to about 800 attendees and exhibitors from around the world. The conference was sponsored by the American Petroleum Institute and the American Society of Mechanical Engineers [ASME] International. Carroll's purpose was to "outline challenges to energy companies now being faced and how to adapt to the revolution."

Philip J. Carroll's speech: I have been invited here today to talk to you about one man's view of energy companies as we near the close of the 20th century and begin looking forward to the 21st. It's somewhat awkward standing before an energy audience at the end of the 20th century. I feel a bit like a Tyrannosaurus Rex in a Gary Larson cartoon speaking before the Society of Late Cretaceous Dinosaurs on "How to Enjoy the Cooler Weather"—he had the idea right, but didn't fully understand the implications of what was going on in his environment.

While there are no meteors crashing down from the sky, we all know that we are nonetheless in the midst of a change in our environment—a true revolution. This particular revolution is the "information revolution" and I want to talk to you about how it will change our markets, our organizations, and most importantly, how it will impact you individually.

---

2. Delivered in Houston, Texas, on January 28, 1997, at 8:45 a.m.
Reprinted by permission of Philip J. Carroll.

A revolution is a brief period of time where the whole nature of a system makes a radical transformation from the way things "are" to the way things "will be." A revolution usually begins when existing institutions fail to meet the present needs. When coupled with a vision of the way things "ought to be" from forces outside the establishment, a revolution results in great turmoil as the opposing sides struggle to define the future.

I believe that a dominant theme of this revolution will be to place less value on physical assets and much more value on human. This will mean that our organizational structures, and the people within them, will have to adapt rapidly to changing and increasingly competitive markets.

Background

Allow me to go back in history a bit to try to set the stage. Humankind spent thousands of years making the first revolutionary transition from hunting to farming. This time scale was so long, that its study is relegated mostly to the field of archeology. Life during the agrarian age was simple, but quite hard. People toiled physically day in and day out, just to provide for the basic human needs of food and clothing. Change continued during this age as organizations moved from large feudal systems to single family farms. With each change came new responsibilities, but also new freedoms and opportunities. In spite of the drawbacks and tough conditions, the human welfare was nonetheless improved as civilization continued to grow.

The next revolution, the industrial revolution, was a phenomenon principally of the last century. It began at the dawn of the 19th century with the introduction of simple machines in the British textile mills, and the perfection of the steam engine in the British coal industry—both of which substantially reduced production costs. Although commerce itself had been around for thousands of years, these new industrial capabilities caused the birth of new industrial enterprises. The changes had a profound effect on society as people began to move away from the farms and into the factories. Although this revolution was also fraught with turmoil, once again the overall physical condition of humanity improved.

The essence of the industrial age was the physical transformation and transportation of goods and services. It was characterized by big physical "machines" that changed raw materials into physical products. There was no missing this revolution—it changed the skyline of civilization around the planet and it changed it rapidly. The energy industry was central to this age because energy itself was at the very heart of the revolution—it was the common requirement for running the machines that changed and moved things.

When coupled with a vision of the way things "ought to be" from forces outside the establishment, a revolution results in great turmoil as the opposing sides struggle to define the future.

New Markets

Now, the experts tell us we are in the midst of the "information revolution." It is a bit harder to see on the city skylines, but it is no less real. The industrial revolution was about applying physical leverage—a multiplier for the power of human muscle. The information revolution is all about intellectual leverage—a multiplier for the power of the human mind.

It is easy to see how the information technology industry itself will be central to this revolution. However, the information revolution will also profoundly affect the energy industry, just like the industrial revolution changed the way we farm.

The demand for food did not go away at the end of the agrarian age—the means of production and delivery simply changed. The industrial age dramatically lowered the costs of food production. First farm machinery, and then new chemicals increased crop yields on both a manpower and acreage basis. We also saw a whole new service sector develop in the form of highways and supermarkets for the transportation and delivery of food products. You could still get your green beans before and after the revolution, but now you could buy them fresh, frozen, or in a can.

Likewise, the basic need for energy will not dissipate in this revolution. However, energy products and services will change form as this current revolution has profound effects on the drivers of both supply and demand.

On the supply side, information technology will dramatically reduce the costs of finding and extracting conventional fossil fuels. Three-D seismic, horizontal drilling, and deep water structure design are all examples where information technology has been a multiplier for the human mind. Information technology will also reduce the costs of transforming these raw materials into various conventional products such as gasoline and electricity. Furthermore, information technology could become *the* critical cost reduction enabler which finally makes renewable energy resources such as solar, wind, and biomass economically viable.

The very same forces will also cause fundamental changes to the demand side of the energy industry as well. We will see new demands emerge in both industrial and residential consumer markets. These demands will be driven by new work processes and lifestyles which are themselves influenced by the changes in information technologies.

For all the debate about electric versus gasoline cars, how many of us truly understand the ramifications of consumers who can choose between driving to the theater, or bringing their next entertainment experience home with the click of a mouse? Even if motor transportation demand shifts away from gasoline and into electricity, will consumers choose to purchase it at a quick-charging station, or will they plug in at home? How will they prefer to pay for it?

One way or another, the marketplace will continue to demand energy. The question is simply one of form. Products will become replaceable with services. The information revolution means that the "value add" no longer has to be a physical product—it can be information. Or the "service" that accompanies the "product."

I enjoyed a recent example from my colleague Robert Shapiro of Monsanto. He offers that the chemical products division of our industry could move away from producing chemical sprays for crop protection. In its place, we should be able to add value by inserting information directly into the plant to serve the same purpose. Thus, genetic engineering, or rearranging the information in a plant, becomes a competitive "service" to chemical "products."

Even the traditional "services" we have provided will change. Although the industrial revolution brought us a broad diversity of service choices, when compared to the information revolution, the industry was characterized by relative sameness. The age was defined by mass replication of a particular product or service. You wanted gasoline in your car, there was only one means to get it—drive to a corner filling station. You could fill up at my pump or someone else's, but for all practical purposes, the delivery system was the same.

In the future, some consumers will choose to purchase their energy in one form delivered in one particular way. At the same time, others may choose both a different product and a different delivery service. This diversity of demand will only increase the opportunities for a wide variety of businesses to enter and thrive in the marketplace.

As in the case of the genetically engineered plant, it also means that our competition will be harder to define. The "fully-integrated major" model which was well suited for the industrial age is already breaking apart. "Independents" are a major force in the upstream sector once dominated by majors. Likewise, they are a growing force in the downstream sector as well.

We also see changes in the traditional roles of the "operating" and "service" sectors as "service companies" begin to participate in investment risks for a share of the rewards. The change will continue as "operating companies" begin to offer services to the broader industry. Shell's newest independent subsidiary, Shell Services Company, is today offering a broad array of information technology and business processing solutions to the entire energy industry.

Structures

As the old adage goes—"form follows function." If the processes driving supply and demand in the marketplace change, then it stands to reason that the structural forms around which we organize ourselves are also subject to change. Organizations of the industrial age were modeled after machines they operated. We built clearly defined hierarchies with assigned responsibilities to carry out specific tasks in specific ways. This was well suited to machinery which, once constructed, would continue to produce the desired output in a very predictable way.

Allow me to present a new model for information age organizations through the use of a metaphor. Our conventional description of chemical compounds consists of the elements of which they are made. In the energy industry, our personal favorite compounds—hydrocarbons—are made of hydrogen and carbon atoms. Yet, they are more than just random mixtures of carbon and hydrogen. Their value is not contained in the physical *particles* of which they are made, it lies in the bonds that hold them together. Break the bonds or recombine them in different ways, and you get valuable substances which can be converted into either energy or products. Someone is willing to pay good money for these mixtures, not because of their raw carbon and hydrogen content, but rather because of the special nature of the bonds which hold them together.

A "bond" is truly "information" in its purest form. It is a rule by which two "things" are connected to create value. A system of bonds between many things may then be called a "network." A molecular "network" actually contains very little physical substance. That which appears to be a *thing*—is little more than a bit of substance connected by bonds in a very special way. The relationships, or networks, contain all the value. The information revolution can thus be thought of as focusing on the relationships between things, rather than the things themselves—for that is where the "information" lies.

A study of "things" of the highest form, living creatures, yields two additional observations. First, the bonds in "living things" contain a great deal more information—DNA is a lot more complicated than polyester. Secondly, living things change—they are capable of adapting to changes in their environment. A *living* tree puts out new leaves when the weather warms up in the spring. A *dead* log simply decays on the forest floor.

I therefore propose that if the energy industry wishes to thrive—not decay—it must change and adapt. Specifically, I believe that we must alter our model whereby value is primarily extracted by finding or owning a physical asset. We

> *The information revolution can .. . be thought of as focusing on the relationships between things, rather than the things themselves.*

must modify it to become a model where one can also add value by establishing relationships with an asset's owner which leverage one's human talent. The information age in our industry will increasingly be characterized by a shift away from the physical—and towards a focus on human assets. It's no longer just the things—refineries, chemical plants, or oil fields—but also the skills applied to them that creates value. How we build the bonds, relationships, and networks between organizations in order to add value to an asset—regardless of present ownership—will be the key to information age economic success.

The simplest forms of such new relationships would be alliances. Alliances can take the form of any partnership between suppliers, customers, and even competitors. An alliance can form any time there is an opportunity to survive or thrive which is enhanced by being together rather than remaining apart. A good alliance will be one which causes market information to flow more efficiently and effectively so that the organization may adapt.

We must make the choice to adapt or die.

As you all know, Shell has a keen interest in alliances. We are already moving beyond the early stage of customer/supplier alliances and beginning to explore competitor alliances in both our upstream and downstream businesses. Our first E&P venture with Amoco in the Permian Basin should be closing very shortly now. We are developing a similar relationship with Mobil in California, and are working diligently on a new downstream alliance with Texaco covering the whole United States. These alliances are our first efforts towards creating flexible and adaptable business structures positioned to maximize value in the information age.

People

Just as the industrial revolution changed the lives of people everywhere, so will the information revolution affect our lives as well. As the working class moved from the farms to the factories, they had to learn new behaviors and skills. Despite the similarity of human tasks involved with operating a plow and a machine, this transition was very painful. Early 19th century Britain had to deal with the Luddites—a group of people so concerned about the replacement of human labor by machines that they resorted to sabotage.

The Luddites did not succeed in stopping the last revolution, and none of us will be able to resist this one. We must make the choice to adapt or die.

First, each of us will need a more diverse set of business and technical skills than we presently employ. The skills needed at any given time will change rapidly depending on market opportunities. Second, we will need the ability to both attract and release talent dependent on the changes.

Third, each of us must also realize that we must individually grow to meet the ever changing market demands. The capacity and willingness to learn will likely be the most important characteristics of successful people in the information age.

Finally, the behaviors suitable to these new organizations will be fundamentally different than in large industrial "machines." Incenting and compensating people for efficient repetition of prespecified tasks is not necessarily a winning proposition. Results-oriented variable compensation and portable benefits are almost certain to be part of our future.

You may take some comfort in knowing that all of these revolutions have been scary to the people experiencing them. Nonetheless, they have all improved society in the end. Their common impact on people has been an increased role of choice, freedom, and responsibility. No longer will it be "the machine" which determines your future for you. You will have to make choices about where you think your talents will be the most valued. You will then have a greater role in educating yourself in order to aspire to these new opportunities. You alone will be responsible for the outcome. You will all have the freedom to choose your own destiny. Good choices will yield great rewards.

You will have to make choices about where you think your talents will be the most valued.

Conclusion

Soon, this dinosaur standing before you today will be gone. But many of you will remain behind. You will make many choices that will determine not only your own future, but that of the people and the organizations around you. I don't claim to have a crystal ball about what that future looks like, but I do believe that if you seize control of it, the opportunities for greatness are abundant.

No matter what the precise outcome, I expect to find that successful organizations and people of the future will be the ones who best adapted to this time of great change. The age ahead will be characterized by a declining focus on physical assets, and an increased emphasis on diverse human skills. The need for energy in the information age will not dissipate, but it will change form.

The road ahead is certainly fraught with peril, yet ripe with opportunity. If we remain rigid and resist, like the Luddites, the only place they will find us in the future is the history books. For those who choose to learn and grow, the future looks very bright from where I stand.

Thank you for having me here today, enjoy the revolution, and good luck with your future.

Women Mean Business[3]

Sheila W. Wellington

*President, Catalyst, the nation's premier national nonprofit
research and advisory organization on women's private sector
leadership, 1993– ; Phi Beta Kappa graduate, Wellesley College; master's degree in public health and in urban studies,
Yale University; director, two major mental health facilities: a
model federal/university program, and a large state facility
for the chronically mentally ill poor; secretary and vice president, Yale University; trustee of the Nuveen Select Portfolios;
director, Business Council of New York State, Institute for
Women's Policy Research, and Tri-State United Way.*

Editors' introduction: Sheila W. Wellington gave the keynote
address at a Catalyst Annual Awards Dinner in the Grand
Ballroom of the Waldorf Astoria to over 1,300 CEOs of major
corporations, human resource professionals, and individual
women from corporations and professional firms. The 11th
Catalyst Award went to the Allstate Corporation and to Avon
Mexico, for their company-wide initiatives to advance
women into top leadership roles. This was the first time the
Catalyst Award was given to an international business initiative. In her speech, Wellington called for a renewed commitment to women's advancement.

Sheila W. Wellington's speech: Harry Pearce . . . Mike Cook
. . . Catalyst affiliates . . . friends old and new. Welcome to
our 22nd Catalyst Awards dinner.

As you all know, Catalyst is the force working for women's
advancement in corporate and professional America. For
those of you less familiar with Catalyst, we tackle the topic
on multiple fronts. First, there's our research to dispel the
myths about women's capabilities and commitment . . . and
to investigate what works to advance women. Then, Catalyst
provides the help organizations need to make change for
women. Third, we place women on corporate boards. And
annually, we offer the Catalyst Award to companies that
have proved what can be done.

For over 20 years, some of the companies present tonight
have helped women move to new levels of achievement and
respect. Some of us are here right now because those companies had that kind of confidence, and we will never forget
that. We are at the Catalyst dinner tonight to remind our-

---

3. Delivered in New York City, on March 25, 1997, in the evening.
Reprinted with the permission of Sheila W. Wellington.

selves how far we've come, and to claim the future for women—alongside men—in business.

One thing that American business cannot do—and that most of you in this room do not do—is ignore reality. And the reality is that women mean business. Women comprise 46 percent of the workforce and make nearly three-quarters of all purchasing decisions. Women earn over half of BA degrees and a third of MBAs. Half of new professionals are women. Half of those climbing the corporate ladder are women. And the reality is that business must capitalize on the talent it invests in. Simple math shows that business loses money when half of those hired don't have an open shot at the top.

This past year, more and more corporate and professional leaders have told me of their commitment to women's advancement. You're implementing initiatives, you're calling on Catalyst for advice and help, and you're ensuring that more women reach senior ranks.

But recently, as I scan the scene in business, in government, and in academia, I notice just a trace of "been there, done that," as if the goal were won. It's the "There's already a woman on the board," or "We have a woman SVP; we're diverse," or "We've all had diversity training, so that problem's solved."

This pops up in the media as well. A January editorial in the *Wall Street Journal* entitled "Women's Figures" stated, and I quote, "The problems for women in the workplace are fading." The editorial argues (incorrectly) that few women have the requisites for senior corporate positions—namely the MBA and 25 years' experience. "Women have not been in the pipeline long enough" and time will cure this, alleges the editorial.

However, that's not what Catalyst has learned from the women who've "been there, done that." Our 1996 survey of over 1,200 senior executive women—the vast majority within two reports of the CEO—shows a third had MBAs and most had 25 or more years of experience. So it isn't degrees or time that have kept these women from the highest jobs. These women report that their advancement was hindered by barriers in the work environment—specifically stereotyping and exclusion from informal networks. Subtle assumptions that meant missed opportunities.

These women, themselves very near the top, know that time alone isn't the answer. They know the pipeline will never sluice them to the corner office. The women in our study can't and won't say this openly. But that's what they tell Catalyst when confidentiality is guaranteed.

Yes, a number of women have reached positions of real authority. These "firsts" serve as role models, as heroes for striving executive women. But though these few heiresses-apparent are encouraging, primogeniture prevails. In many organizations, broken glass is replaced posthaste. We need more deferred maintenance in the glass ceiling department.

This is why Catalyst counts. It's been our challenge this year to provide accurate numbers—benchmarks, baselines, and headcounts—of women on corporate boards, top earners, corporate officers, and senior managers. Here are a few of them:

- Women make up 10 percent of corporate officers, but hold only 2.4 percent of top titles.
- 47 of 2,500 top earners in Fortune 500 companies are women.
- Women hold 10 percent of board seats, but 97 percent of Fortune 100 companies have at least one woman on the board.

We've got lots more numbers, but I will spare you their delights this evening.

Still, all this counting is critical for business. Before Catalyst released the first *Census of Women Corporate Officers* last fall, no one had measured women's progress through the pipeline. Business had no baseline data against which to track women's progress. In America, we measure what we value . . . and we value what we measure. A fundamental reality of American business is that corporate leaders, numbers-driven, make things happen. So Catalyst gives "just the facts, ma'am." And sir.

In America, we measure what we value . . . and we value what we measure.

Another important Catalyst finding is that most obstacles to women's advancement are unintentional. They result from unexamined assumptions about women's career interests. They result from policies and practices that have existed unquestioned over time. But they can be overcome—with real commitment to change. They must be overcome, if the vital resource in which you invest is not to be wasted.

In 1920, Virginia Woolf quoted a Thomas Hardy heroine who says, "I have the feelings of a woman, but I have only the language of men." Woolf points out that women writers at the turn of the century (and earlier) wrote in existing genres and styles—forms created by another gender that didn't always work for them. Before there is achievement, she said, "women must try the accepted forms to discard the unfit, to create others which are more fitting."

Woolf could be talking about businesswomen in the 90s. Today's women have tried on the existing styles and forms of corporate and professional America. Women have learned the rules and excelled at their jobs. They've worn the corporate coat cut for another gender—but it does not always fit those "women's figures."

Actually, the corporate coat doesn't fit anyone the way it once did. The workforce today differs enormously from two decades ago . . . and not just in shape and color. Forty-five percent of today's workers are members of dual-career couples. In Catalyst's work inside corporations and firms, we hear men and women alike expressing a basic concern: how can I have time to raise my family *and* raise my living standard? The needs of the workforce have changed because society has changed. Nimble organizations—though founded in the forms of former times—are changing to meet this new demography. They are cleaning their closets of outmoded operating practices.

So I ask all our great corporations and firms, can you not only create, but also *sustain* an environment for women's achievement? Is your investment in women paying off? More and more women are leaving professional firms and corporations, but for the most part, not to go home. Women are leaving to work where their aspirations can be realized. Smart women will not work where their endeavors go unrecognized and unrewarded.

Women will find a workplace—or they will found one—where there is no intrinsic exclusion.

Women will find a workplace—or they will found one—where there is no intrinsic exclusion. The talent you want will find or found a workplace where opportunities are color blind and gender blind. They will find or found a workplace where there is an environment and expectation of achievement for women and men alike. That workplace should be your workplace.

Now is not the time for complacency. Companies must renew and reinforce their efforts to bring down the barriers . . . and Catalyst can help.

It is true that American women enjoy the most rewarding job market on the planet. But the fact is this: the most open, free, and mobile society in the history of the world has yet to capitalize fully on the talents of women. And yes, this is a loss. But it's also an opportunity. I believe that the audience in this room knows this. And you know that if you grow complacent with today's gains, you will miss tomorrow's talent.

Let me ask you, as I close, to look beyond the workplace obstacles of today to the workplace of tomorrow. Beyond the efforts of women in your company or your firm to the potential of women in all companies and firms. Beyond the glass ceiling to the day of equity in American commerce. When that day finally comes, as it will, those of you who have led the effort can take satisfaction in knowing you served the national interest, ensuring that an under-utilized, priceless resource—women's brainpower—has reached the market mainstream.

Because women mean business. Thank you.

Cleaner Air and Economic Progress[4]

Carol M. Browner

Administrator, U.S. Environmental Protection Agency, 1993– ; born Miami, FL, 1955; B.A., University of Florida, 1977; law degree, University of Florida, 1979; general counsel, Florida House of Representatives Committee on Government Operations, 1980–81; associate director of Citizen Action, a grassroots consumer group in Washington, D.C., 1983; worked in office of Florida Senator Lawton Chiles, 1986–88; counsel for U.S. Senate Committee on Energy and Natural Resources, 1989; legislative director for Tennessee Senator Al Gore Jr., 1989–91; Secretary of the Department of Environmental Regulation, Florida, 1991–93.

Editors' introduction: Although major industry groups and some governors criticized her staunch stand for toughening environmental standards, repeatedly Administrator Carol M. Browner, an "unrepentant pragmatist," refused to back away. In a speech to the Center for National Policy, Administrator Browner insisted that "action on air pollution is what American wants." Reducing pollution, she, explained, would be good for both public health and the economy.

Carol M. Browner's speech: Thank you, Mo, for that introduction. I am delighted to be back at the Center for National Policy, which does a truly fabulous job of providing a framework for discussing and advancing the vital issues of the day. The Center has proven to be leader in the public policy arena, and I am grateful for the opportunity to join you once again.

Those of you who live here in the Washington area know that it has been an especially brutal week for the air we breathe.

Every day since Sunday, we have been under an "ozone red alert."

What does that mean? Well, for one, it means that, from my office, the view across the Potomac River and into the Virginia suburbs has been shrouded in a milky-white haze.

But for most people, a spoiled view is the least of their worries.

Pediatricians are warning parents to keep their kids indoors. Elderly people and those with heart or respiratory

---

4. Delivered in Washington, D.C., on July 17, 1997. Reprinted by permission of Carol M. Browner.

ailments have been cautioned that the outdoor air can make them very sick—even kill them—if they are not careful. Healthy people are urged not to jog or engage in other strenuous outdoor activities.

And if your kids are among the 5 million American children who have asthma—the nation's number one chronic childhood illness—then this can be the kind of week that nightmares are made of.

The fact is that, despite all the progress we've made on the environment over the past quarter-century, air pollution remains a major public health issue in this country.

And there is little doubt as to where Americans stand. They want clean air. They want the public health to come first in setting clean air standards. They want their children protected.

They want EPA to do its job—which is ensuring that the air they breathe is safe and healthy. They want government to be honest about when the air is unhealthy—and what it is doing to them.

And they have confidence that government, industry, citizens and communities will rise to the occasion, work together, meet the challenges, and reduce pollution of the air they breathe.

Action on air pollution is what America wants. And today I am proud to say that *action*—bold, decisive *action*—is what we have taken.

Last month, the President announced new, updated and more protective public health standards for two common air pollutants—ozone, otherwise known as smog, and particulate matter, otherwise known as soot.

Yesterday, I signed those standards into effect.

And today, I'm here to tell you about how those standards make sense—not only for public health and the environment—but for the nation' s economic future as well.

How do I know they make sense? Just look at the record of the past 25 years. Look at the experience of this administration on environmental and public health protection.

As we have moved forward on environmental and public health protection, the economy has moved forward. as well.

Across the nation—in city after city—the air, the land, and the water is better, cleaner, and healthier than it once was. Why? Because of a bi-partisan commitment to address the serious pollution issues we faced. The Clean Air Act, with its central focus on public health protection, is a shining example of this commitment. It has worked for America. And these updated air quality standards build on that progress.

Today, unfortunately, some are questioning our commitment to a public health standard for air pollution. They say it conflicts with our economic goals.

But that's not what history tells us. What the President has said, on many occasions, has proven to be true—environ-

[Americans] want the public health to come first in setting clean air standards.

mental protection and economic progress *do* go hand-in-hand. We do *not* have to choose between our health and our jobs. In fact, the two are inextricably linked. A healthy economy helps us achieve a healthier environment. And a healthy environment helps to build a stronger economy.

Three years ago, when I last appeared here before the Center for National Policy, I spelled out the President's formula for success: Set tough, effective standards for protecting the environment and public health, and then work closely with all who are affected by those standards—businesses, communities, citizens, state and local government—toward meeting these standards in reasonable, flexible and common sense ways.

I want you all to know that the air quality standards we issued yesterday are fully consistent with that philosophy.

For one, these standards amount to the most significant step we've taken in a generation to protect the American people—and especially our children—from the health hazards of air pollution.

Together, they will protect 125 million Americans, including 35 million children, from the adverse health effects of breathing polluted air.

They will prevent approximately 15,000 premature deaths, about 350,000 cases of aggravated asthma and nearly a million cases of significantly decreased lung function in children.

These standards are based on evidence from more than 250 scientific studies—all of it published, peer-reviewed, checked and double-checked, as required by law, by an independent review panel.

The evidence leads to an inescapable conclusion. Smog and soot in the air are causing adverse health effects in Americans—and especially in the elderly, people with respiratory problems, and in children—at levels that, until yesterday, were considered acceptable under government standards.

Clearly, we had to respond to this evidence with these tough, more protective standards. The independent scientific panel agreed. The Clean Air Act required us to act. And that is precisely what we did.

Now we proceed to the next step—and the next challenge: Finding ways to meet these new standards, and ensure that the air in our communities is safe and healthy to breathe, by working together toward the goals we have set.

Even though, under the Clean Air Act, EPA is prevented from considering the costs of public health standards to businesses and communities, costs did play a role in developing our plan for *implementing* the standards.

We have gone the extra mile. For the first time ever, accompanying new air quality standards is an implementation

Costs did play a role in developing our plan for implementing the standards.

package that will ensure that these public health protections will be achieved in flexible, common sense and cost-effective ways—providing for both cleaner air and the nation's economic progress.

The central focus of that package is cooperation—people working together for a better future. Everyone has a role to play in seeing that these standards are met—citizens, industry, government, the scientific community. Indeed, EPA's implementation plan taps right into the very spirit of innovation and ingenuity that is the foundation of America's leadership in the world.

The plan includes a number of major initiatives designed to enable businesses and communities to meet the standards—and provide clean air for the American people—while our communities continue to thrive.

Will this challenge us? Of course. Will meeting these standards require some large industrial sources to reduce their pollution of the public's air? Absolutely.

But by focusing on those large sources—particularly large power plants that contribute most significantly to regional, "transported" pollution, we can go a long way toward meeting these new standards in our cities.

This implementation package relies on an emissions trading plan for major utilities—one that was developed collectively by some 37 states. This plan will greatly help solve the problem of "transported" ozone pollution—the kind that originates in one area, yet causes downwind areas to have "ozone red alert days."

While much of our air pollution problems here on the East Coast are caused by local sources, a large measure of the bad air that has plagued us over the past few days actually originated some 200 to 300 miles away. In other areas, ozone may be transported by winds more than 500 miles.

That is why addressing this transported ozone pollution with a *regional* plan—rather than city by city—is so sensible.

As this plan is allowed to take effect, and regional pollution levels fall, we believe that many areas that might not today meet tougher public health standards will be able to do so without taking an addition anti-pollution measures. If fact, we have even developed a "transitional" category for these areas.

Our philosophy is: Let's give the regional plan time to work. The air in many areas will get cleaner. And local officials will find that they can achieve the new standards with much less difficulty than some have predicted.

Our implementation package is also based on EPA's determination to continue on the path to clean air by respecting agreements already reached by businesses and communities, and not disrupting the progress that is currently being made.

And, for those communities that still can't meet the new standards, we're going to make sure they have ample time to

Ozone may be transported by winds more than 500 miles.

reduce pollution and bring themselves into compliance. We're talking no new local pollution controls until the year 2004 for ozone, and the year 2005 for particulate matter. We're talking another three years—until 2007 and 2008, respectively—to determine who is in compliance, and who is not.

We believe this extended timetable—developed in light of the concerns expressed by those who will be affected most by these standards—will facilitate a more cooperative atmosphere in which EPA can work with all who are affected by these new standards to ensure that they are able to comply.

And because we believe so strongly that businesses will be able to provide these health protections to the American people in an affordable way, we are making this guarantee to them: If you cannot identify cost-effective pollution reductions, you may instead pay money into a Clean Air Investment Fund. States will then be able to use this fund to purchase pollution reductions from cheaper sources. This will cap the costs to industry and serve as an insurance policy against unpredictable future costs. And, through this creative implementation approach, these funds can be invested in innovative, pollution-reducing technologies.

Some may ask—if the process is going to take such a long time, then why set tougher standards now? Why not wait? Why do it at all?

The answer is simple. As with many important, complex, difficult problems, you have to begin your long journey to a solution with a first step. And the President's bold decision on these standards is that first step—a first step toward giving future generations of Americans clean air to breathe.

Our approach will give us time for technology to continue its onward march—and give us new and more cost-effective ways to reduce pollution.

That is what the framers of the Clean Air Act envisioned more than a quarter-century ago—setting tough standards for air pollution, encouraging cooperation between governments and businesses on compliance measures, and thereby tapping into America's vast reserves of innovation and ingenuity to meet those standards in a way that grows our economy.

As many of you know, some members of Congress have indicated that they will thoroughly review what this administration has done to fulfill the mandate of the Clean Air Act— and to ensure that the air in our communities is safe and healthy to breathe.

I welcome that review. And I believe that if members of Congress look at what we did—fairly, thoroughly and responsibly—then they will see that the President made the right call. They will determine, as he did, that the public's interest—and the public's right to breathe clean air—must prevail over the special interests.

Why set tougher standards now? Why not wait? Why do it at all?

Don't let anyone tell you that we cannot meet the twin goals of clean air and a strong economy.

We've done it before. We can do it again.

And, when we do, future generations of Americans will remember us fondly for enabling them to breathe easier.

Cumulative Speaker Index: 1990-1998

A cumulative speaker index to the volumes of *Representative American Speeches* for the years 1937-1938 through 1959-1960 appears in the 1959-1960 volume; for the years 1960-1961 through 1969-1970, see the 1969-1970 volume; for the years 1970-1971 through 1979-1980, see the 1979-1980 volume; and for the years 1980-1981 through 1989-1990, see the 1989-1990 volume.

Index

Aaron, Henry (Hank) 6
ABC (TV network)
    Food Lion supermarket case and 44
Adams, Henry 5
Adams, John 58
    quoted on Jefferson 10
    Thomas Jefferson and 12
Adarand case 79
affirmative action 36, 100
    at the University of Michigan 38
    Proposition 209 79
Afghanistan 118
agrarian age 177
air pollution 188
    ozone and soot 188
air quality standards 188–191
Alabama
    fair housing activities in 78
Albright, Madeleine
    "NATO Expansion" 135
American Civil War
    firing on Fort Sumter 6
    issue of human freedom in 8
    questions about 7
    Robert Penn Warren on 10
    Walt Whitman and 7
American culture
    call for redefinition 38
    diversity of 99
American English
    Yiddish and 14
American history
    baseball and 5
    biography and 9
    family memory and community rec-
      ollection 4
    historical documentary 7
    political narrative 4
    struggle for human freedom 8

Anastasia Fund (Anastasia Swiecicki
    Rogowska Kaptur Fund) 166
Angola 119
Arendt, Hannah
    quoted 19
Armey, Dick
    Educational Opportunity Scholar-
      ships 93
Arnold, Matthew
    quoted 19
Asian economies
    problems 174
Associated Press (AP) 146
Atlanta Journal-Constitution
    Richard Jewell and 44
atomic bomb 125
Austin, James 59
Axworthy, Lloyd 121

Banning Landmines 117
Baseball
    as American game 13
    Ebbets Field 2
    Yogi Berra 3
baseball
    Jackie Robinson and 5
Beauregard, Pierre Gustave Toutant 6
Berra, Lawrence Peter (Yogi) 3
    quotes by 3
Biggie Smalls 34
biography
    importance of, literature and 21
Black, Hugo L. 60
blacks
    earnings vs. white earnings 99
    employment (1998) 99
    fair lending and fair housing activi-
      ties for 77
    racism in America and 36